YOU
DON'T
NEED TO
FORGIVE

Trauma Recovery on *Your Own* Terms

YOU DON'T NEED TO FORGIVE

Amanda Ann Gregory, LCPC

BROADLEAF BOOKS
MINNEAPOLIS

YOU DON'T NEED TO FORGIVE
Trauma Recovery on Your Own Terms

29   28   27   26   25   24   1   2   3   4   5   6   7   8   9

Library of Congress Cataloging-in-Publication Data

Names: Gregory, Amanda Ann, author.
Title: You don't need to forgive : trauma recovery on your own terms /
    Amanda Ann Gregory, LCPC.
Description: Minneapolis : Broadleaf Books, [2025] | Includes
    bibliographical references. |
Identifiers: LCCN 2024020543 (print) | LCCN 2024020544 (ebook) | ISBN
    9798889831150 (hardback) | ISBN 9798889831167 (ebook)
Subjects: LCSH: Forgiveness--Psychological aspects. | Psychic trauma--Treatment.
Classification: LCC BF637.F67 G744 2025 (print) | LCC BF637.F67 (ebook) |
    DDC 155.9/2--dc23/eng/20240809
LC record available at https://lccn.loc.gov/2024020543
LC ebook record available at https://lccn.loc.gov/2024020544

Cover image: © 2024 Shutterstock; adhesive bandage cross/2109683348 by
Mindscape studio
Cover design: Studio Gearbox

Print ISBN: 979-8-8898-3115-0
eBook ISBN: 979-8-8898-3116-7

Printed in China.

For my clients,
Your courage and persistence to not only survive,
but also thrive, inspires me.
I cannot adequately express how proud I am of all of you.

In memory of my grandmother Dorothy,
Your dream was to write a book, but you never did.
I wrote one for you.

Author's Note

The stories of the trauma survivors in this book are true. Still, to ensure anonymity, I have changed all names and identifying details. In addition, in several instances, the survivors described are composite stories created from the experiences of multiple survivors. These steps were taken to protect client confidentiality in accordance with both ethical and legal guidelines. Conversations are depicted as recalled or, in the case of interviews, audio-recorded.

The information contained in this book is for informative and self-help purposes only. Although I am a trauma therapist, I am not your therapist. Therefore, this book is not meant as a substitute for medical or mental health treatment. You should consult with your doctor, therapist, or counselor in all matters related to your specific treatment.

Read this book at your own pace. At times, you may find the content challenging or triggering. Your feelings of safety take priority. When you feel overwhelmed or experience any trauma responses, take a break. Take all the time you need. This book will be here if and when you are ready to continue.

Contents

Introduction

DO I NEED TO FORGIVE?

As a trauma psychotherapist and a survivor of childhood physical and emotional neglect, I ask my therapists questions that other clients don't, as it's impossible to turn off the therapist's part of my brain. I asked questions of my clinicians such as "What's my official diagnosis, and what's my unofficial diagnosis?," "What's that intervention called?," and "Do you have two sets of notes, and if so, what do you write about me in the 'other' set of notes?" My therapists answered all my questions except for one that stopped them dead in their tracks: "Do I need to forgive my parents in order to make additional progress in my recovery?" I asked. "Will not forgiving make me feel stuck?"

"What do you think?" asked my talk therapist, which is the typical response of a therapist who's trained never to give advice.

"Let's see what happens when you focus on that," replied my EMDR therapist as she turned on the bilateral stimulation tappers, which vibrated back and forth in my hands.

"I'm not sure. Did you try taking the ten milligram dose? Notice any changes?" deflected my psychiatrist.

"When you think of forgiving your parents, what do you notice in your body?" asked my somatic therapist.

"The hell if I know. What do you think?" asked my sassy psychologist.

I didn't receive a straight answer, but I needed one. I had not forgiven my parents. This didn't matter so much concerning my father, as he'd been dead for years, and I'd never felt attached to him. However, my mother was still living, and I was attached to her as a young child. Her incapabilities as a parent had had a significant negative impact on me, and even after I've undergone years of therapy, they still do—and always will. I knew I didn't—and couldn't—forgive her. Yet, I had made so much progress in my recovery. How was this possible? Was I in denial? Was I missing out on an experience that would propel me forward? Was forgiveness the missing piece?

I went to my colleagues for answers. When one asks clinicians questions as a peer rather than as a client, they tend to be more direct. I asked them, "Do you believe trauma survivors need to forgive their offenders to progress in their recovery?"

"Yes, if they can forgive, they should. It would improve their lives and strengthen their relationships," said a marriage and family therapist.

"I can't say for sure. I've had clients who forgave and those who didn't, and I honestly haven't noticed a difference in treatment outcomes," said a trauma therapist.

"Absolutely. Forgiveness is the key to healing. You cannot truly heal without forgiveness. I encourage all my clients to forgive," said a Christian counselor.

"I think it all depends on what the client needs. I've had many clients who didn't forgive, and they made great progress in therapy," said a psychologist.

"Everyone needs to forgive. Holding grudges isn't good for mental or physical health," said a child therapist.

"If forgiveness were a proven cure-all we'd recommend it to every patient. As you know, nothing in psychology is all-or-nothing," said a psychiatrist.

There was no consensus among my colleagues. How could that be? How could we not know? As a trauma survivor and as a trauma therapist, how could *I* not know? Did I need to forgive my mother to continue progressing in my recovery? Did my clients need to forgive their offenders?

I spent the next three years researching forgiveness from the perspectives of psychology, sociology, philosophy, and religion as it applies to trauma survivors in recovery. I interviewed mental health clinicians, scholars, religious leaders, social advocates, and forgiveness therapy practitioners. I listened as my trauma survivor clients shared their own perceptions, experiences, and struggles with forgiveness. As a result, I formulated the thesis that forgiveness should be considered an elective option—not a requirement—in trauma recovery.

A TRAUMATIZED TRAUMA THERAPIST

At thirty-one years old, I discovered that I was incapable of love.

When people left me, I didn't miss them; when they touched me, I couldn't feel them; when they died, I couldn't grieve. I neither loved them nor sought to be loved by them. I had no attachments, not to myself or anyone else.

I was a successful trauma therapist by day and a dissociated, detached woman by night. This would still be my life today if that biker hadn't died in front of me. As I watched him dying, I felt nothing. No anger, fear, confusion, or sadness—*nothing*. I walked away feeling numb, and it was then that I realized that something was seriously wrong with me.

I was on a motorcycle trip with my husband in Arkansas. The narrow winding roads through the timber forests made for a treacherous journey. We couldn't see the road beyond each deep curve, which made the ride exciting. We parked on the shoulder of a remote highway to take a break when another biker stopped to check in on us. Bikers, like many social outcasts, are often not what they seem. They appear tough and rugged in their leather jackets and vests but are often kind and generous. They wave with one arm stretched downward at a forty-five-degree angle when you pass them on the road; it's their way of saying "I see you," "you're not alone," and "ride safe." Bikers often worry about other bikers, as they know how dangerous the road can be.

"You two all right?" yelled the gray-bearded biker over his motor. He looked like someone's cool grandfather.

"Yeah, just taking a break," I yelled back.

He smiled. "Okay. Be safe, kids." He then continued along the highway and disappeared behind the next curve. A couple of minutes later, we followed him.

"NO!" my husband screamed as he slowed his bike. Our cool biker grandfather was lying face down in the middle of the highway. An injured deer crawled in the grass nearby, desperately trying to escape back into the forest. We parked horizontally in front of the biker to protect him from ongoing traffic, and my husband called 911. The ambulance was forty minutes away. We didn't speak. There was no point in asking whether he would be okay; the brain matter leaking from his helmet answered that question clearly enough. There would be no rescue or recovery. I stood over him, and I spoke the only words that might make any difference.

"We're here. We're right here. You're not alone."

These phrases of comfort were delivered mechanically and without feeling, like one who recites a prayer without faith. As I waited for him to die, I remembered my father's death. He had died suddenly from heart failure six years ago. I had sat staring at my father's body, which was found eleven hours after he died in the living room of my childhood home. I'd desperately tried to cry, but couldn't. I didn't cry when I told my brothers that he was gone. I didn't cry at his funeral. I didn't cry at all. I'd felt no shock, anger, or grief—*nothing*. I experienced the same emotional void as I listened to this biker take his last gargled breaths.

We stayed with the biker until the ambulance arrived. The state trooper assured us that no matter what we could've done, he would not have survived, as his skull was crushed upon impact. His obituary reported that he was indeed a grandfather of three. In the days following his death, I tried to cry, but once again no tears would come. This sensation of emotional nothingness, of utter numbness, was familiar and comfortable, but I knew it was wrong. Was I a sociopath? A monster? I did know one thing: I couldn't continue to live this way. In any case, this was surely my rock bottom.

Two months later, I abruptly left my emotionally and financially abusive husband. He came home one day, and I was gone, never to return. The one good thing about not being able to attach to others is that it's easier to end abusive relationships. You don't have to struggle to break the cycle of leaving and reconciling. Leaving is easy when you don't love your husband; it's even easier when you don't seek or feel the need to be loved by anyone. I quit my job at a residential treatment facility where I worked with teenage trauma survivors. This position consumed every part of my life and contributed to my self-neglect. I took a less intensive position at a community mental health center, which gave me the time and space I needed to begin my recovery.

To start, I completed multiple evaluations with mental health clinicians to find out what was wrong with me. I prepared myself to hear words or phrases such as *sociopath, narcissist,* or *antisocial personality disorder*. Yet, these words were never mentioned. Instead, my clinicians used phrases such as *complex trauma, developmental trauma, emotional and physical neglect, dissociation, generalized anxiety,* and *avoidant attachment*. Like many childhood trauma survivors, I didn't know I was a survivor. You'd think that a masters of arts degree in counseling and five years working as a trauma therapist would have given me some indication that I was a trauma survivor, but that was not the case. Fancy degrees and clinical licenses provide little internal insight. Being incapable of love—or, as my clinicians called it, being *insecurely attached*—was normal for me; it was all I'd ever known.

FIRST, MY PARENTS DISAPPEARED

I'm not sure when my father disappeared. I have few memories of him, although we lived in the same home for my entire childhood. I could see him, but he wasn't there. He went to work, sat in the kitchen alone eating his meals, and retreated to the den or the porch to read the newspaper. He avoided his three children. Everyone viewed him as a kind, gentle, shy man, but trauma survivors know that those who are publicly perceived as friendly and charismatic are often the most vicious offenders.

My father had an affair and fathered a child when I was six. He was covertly paying a considerable amount of monthly child support, which I later learned was partially blackmail money intended to keep the mother and her family silent. No one in my family would discover the affair, the child, or where the money went until after he died. This revelation explained why our lower-middle-class lifestyle was quickly reduced to invisible poverty. At times, food was scarce, and as a child, I was responsible for fielding calls from bill collectors. We didn't qualify for food stamps or free school lunches because my parents' joint income was too high, and the blackmail payments were not documented. My father was financially abusive, as he controlled all the family's money and never explained to my mother where it went. He also began controlling, manipulating, and isolating my mother. I believe that my father—whom I suspect suffered from undiagnosed and untreated depression and avoidant attachment—was destroyed by the strain of keeping his secret. He isolated himself for the remainder of his life. He lived in front of newspapers and TV screens, rarely speaking. He didn't cook, clean, or care for his basic hygiene needs. He officially retreated into a hell of his own creation. That might have been tolerable since I never truly felt I had a father. Yet it became intolerable when he took my mother with him.

I was nine years old when my mother disappeared. This happened gradually due to an accumulation of adverse experiences, including a drastic and unexplained change in her financial security, working long hours, enduring spousal abuse, and the birth of her third child. I suspect she also suffered from undiagnosed and untreated depression and childhood complex trauma, which prevented her from coping, seeking help, and advocating for herself. The gardener who planted tulips in our front yard, the artist who sewed home-made Halloween costumes, and the loving mother who called her children by the pet names of Pretty Ditters, Mr. K., and Lambikins slowly slipped away. She stopped cooking and cleaning, and when she wasn't working long hours to pay for a child she didn't know existed, she locked herself in her bedroom. My father and extended family members told me that my mother was delicate and needed support.

"You need to be nice to your mother. She needs you," said my grandmother.

"Promise me that you will look out for your mom," my aunt implored.

"You need to behave so your mother doesn't get too stressed," my uncle insisted.

"Don't upset your mother; you'll kill her," my father warned.

"Your mother matters; you don't," said my nine-year-old internal voice as it interpreted these messages during such a vital stage of development.

"Your mother matters; you don't" became my motto. By the time I was eleven years old, most of my decisions were motivated by how they would impact my mother. *If I get a B in math, would that upset mom? Will she get stressed if I tell her I feel sick and need to go to the doctor? Will she die if I misbehave?* There was no consideration for what I wanted or needed. I was consistently told to leave my mother alone, and I—the "good daughter"—did what I was told. I stopped knocking on her closed bedroom door, stopped telling her about my day, and left her alone. All I could do was watch as she slowly, steadily, and silently disappeared.

My childhood home became a physical manifestation of my disappearing family. My house was infested with colonies of cockroaches and spiders whose bites left welts. The floors were caked in dirt, the carpets were drenched in cat urine, and it was always cold because the windows leaked. I was isolated in that home and learned to create my own joy. I used kitchen knives to scrape the black grime from the floors, and I'd peer at the clean tan wood underneath in amazement. I fed the spiders who lived in the corners of my bedroom walls with ants and rollie pollies that I'd captured in the backyard. My favorite game was the "cockroach hunt." My brother and I would creep into the kitchen at night and turn on all the lights at once. Colonies of cockroaches would then scurry away, and we'd see how many we could squash with our bare feet before they disappeared into the cracks in the walls and the rotted holes in the floor. We'd push and shove each other to sabotage the other's success, yet we could never keep track of our kills, which caused heated late-night arguments. This is one of my happiest childhood memories.

From my point of view, my childhood was not unusual. The children who lived in clean houses with parents who were present, caring, and attentive were strange to me. Why did their parents want to know where their ten-year-old daughter, my friend, was at all times? Why did they cook her meals? How did they know her teacher's name, her grades, and what she liked to do? Why did her parents talk to me? Why were they asking me about school and things that I liked? I assumed these girls were rich, as I attributed my living conditions and my parents' disappearance to poverty. In fact, not having money was the excuse my parents used when others questioned their lifestyle. Yet, many children live in poverty and don't experience emotional or physical neglect. The truth is that I was a victim of physical and emotional childhood neglect, and that neglect had become my way of life.

THEN, I DISAPPEARED

When you're a child and your parents disappear, you have no choice but to join them. How does a child know they exist if their parents cannot see them? They don't. How does a child acknowledge their value if their parents do not show them their value? They can't. Without others, a child doesn't truly exist.

Children need safe, healthy, capable adults to be their attachment figures. These adults serve as the foundation upon which children build other relationships. Imagine that you are building a house upon a foundation that is not stable. Perhaps the concrete foundation was not laid properly and, as a result, there are large cracks in it. You can build a house on this foundation, but it will need constant repairs and might collapse. This is what happens when you're a child without an attachment figure. You are constantly trying to build your house on a shaky foundation. To survive, I learned to disappear just like my parents. The clinical word for disappearing is *dissociation*, which means that you feel disconnected from yourself, others, and the world.

At thirteen years old, I had limited emotional capabilities, as I couldn't feel intense emotions. My brain and body could only tolerate mild-to-moderate short-term emotions. This meant that I rarely felt furious, fearful, or sad. Yet, I also didn't feel much comfort, joy, or love. Dissociation is an automatic and unintentional survival response that impacts thoughts, emotions, and physical sensations. When I didn't have enough food to eat, my body shut down, so I didn't feel the hunger pangs. When I didn't have warm clothes, my body went numb, so I didn't feel the sting of the cold. When I was ill, I didn't feel much pain at all. Dissociation helped to protect me, but it also left me feeling as if I did not physically or emotionally exist in the world; it made it difficult for me to know when I was seriously ill or injured, and it prevented me from connecting with others. When people physically touched me, I rarely felt it. I went through the motions of life mechanically, as if I were not fully alive, but not yet dead. I was neither truly present nor wholly absent; I was a ghost.

"Don't you love your parents?" a high school classmate once asked me when they noticed I never mentioned my family.

"Of course I do. All kids love their parents," I responded.

But I didn't. As a teenager, I'd developed full-blown avoidant attachment. It's challenging to explain attachment wounds to those who have not experienced them. This is why I don't try to explain it. Instead, I show people a video clip of Dr. Edward Tronick's "Still Face Experiment," which explores the impact of childhood emotional neglect. The video shows a mother playing with her toddler daughter. They smile and laugh together until, suddenly, the mother stops engaging with her daughter and sits silently, motionlessly, with a blank stare on her face. The baby immediately knows that something is not right. Her mother has disappeared. The baby instinctively tries everything she can to get her mother to reengage. She smiles, points, reaches for her mother, screeches, and eventually cries with her arms and legs flailing at her sides. She has lost control of her body. Then, she looks away from her mother and disconnects. Perhaps she is trying to disappear, to follow her mother into whatever other world she entered. After two painful minutes, the mother reengages, and her daughter quickly smiles and reaches for her as they promptly repair the break in their connection.[1] This cycle of connection–break–repair happens in all healthy relationships. However, when there's no reengagement or repair, a child is left to figure out how to meet their emotional needs independently. I was that toddler, but my parents never reengaged, and all I could do was disappear. Some trauma survivors have nightmares of their offenders harming them or of the terrible events they experienced. My nightmares are of my parents' still faces and vacant eyes and of that constant reminder: your mother matters; you don't.

After watching the biker grandfather die, leaving my husband, and starting a job suitable for recovery, I began intense trauma therapy. I participated in EMDR (eye movement desensitization and reprocessing), attachment therapy, somatic experiencing, internal family systems therapy, and animal-assisted therapy; I engaged in support groups, took psychiatric medication, and embraced my realization that I was not a sociopath or a monster but a trauma survivor. After five years, I'd made significant progress. I began to feel like I existed in the world and had value. I learned how to experience emotions and physical sensations. I rekindled my relationship with my older brother, began to build authentic friendships, and married a safe, loving partner. As a clinician, I continued my work with trauma survivors with renewed vitality, empathy, passion, and insight. I earned a reputation in Chicago as one of the top referrals for clients with severe complex trauma. Yet, there was one glaring obstacle in my recovery progress: forgiveness.

During therapy, I ceased all contact with my mother without any plans to reconcile. I did this for two reasons: First, she hadn't changed much, and I didn't see any evidence that she was capable of participating in the adult mother-daughter relationship that I needed. Second, I didn't feel safe. She and my extended family were stuck in an intergenerational trauma dynamic, and I was determined to break the cycle. If I were to be in her life, I would be expected to act as her caregiver until her death, with no consideration given to how this would impact me. I knew that I needed estrangement. But did I need to forgive her to make more progress in my recovery?

CAN FORGIVENESS BE HARMFUL?

Before we consider that question, we need to start by recognizing that when forgiveness is forced, pressured, encouraged, or recommended by those in positions of perceived authority (mental health clinicians, religious leaders, authors, politicians, social media influencers, family, and friends, etc.), it can cause harm. Indeed, forgiveness can be one of the most significant obstacles in trauma recovery. Many believe that you will progress in therapy only if you forgive your offenders. Though usually well-intentioned, such a prescription can unintentionally cause harm when it fails to meet, or suppresses, your actual needs. Imposing forgiveness can sabotage trauma recovery by overriding or compromising your feelings of safety, by reinforcing damaging gender roles, by reinforcing societal inequalities, by hindering or attempting to repress your need to feel, express, and process negative feelings such as anger and rage, and by promoting shame and self-blame. Unfortunately, some people even intentionally use forgiveness as a weapon to harm, silence, or police you—or to in fact center and prioritize the interests of your offenders rather than those of survivors themselves—under the guise of moral virtue.

WHAT IS ELECTIVE FORGIVENESS?

How can we avoid harming trauma survivors with forgiveness? We can offer forgiveness not as a recovery requirement but as an *elective*. When a student attends college in America, they have several optional courses they must complete, called electives. A few of my college electives were creative writing, feminist literature, and badminton. I did not need to take a feminist literature class to earn a degree in psychology, but I found it to be a helpful addition to my academic course of study. Many students wouldn't find a feminist literature course helpful and are free to choose a different elective.

What happens when we consider forgiveness as an elective? You may choose to forgive, you may choose not to, and you may not initially choose to forgive yet find that you unintentionally experience organic forgiveness. You may forgive on your own terms in your own time, while others may experience various levels of forgiveness (which may fluctuate over time). You might choose to withhold, resist, or forgo forgiveness. You might not be capable of authentic forgiveness no matter how hard you try and therefore cannot make a choice. Elective forgiveness can meet you where you are at in each moment regarding your capabilities, as it creates an environment where forgiveness is no longer an obligatory component of trauma recovery. When I permitted myself to consider forgiveness as an elective, I experienced forgiveness for some of my offenders and not for others, and I continued to progress in my recovery.

Forgiveness should never be forced, pressured, encouraged, or recommended for trauma survivors in recovery. Elective forgiveness can take the experience of forgiveness off the recovery table unless you need it to be on your table or it organically appears. In contrast, forgiveness should never be discouraged, shunned, or sabotaged in recovery when it does not negatively impact your safety. Forgiveness should be viewed as an elective component of trauma recovery. You should have the agency to explore, discover, embrace, ignore, oppose, or withhold forgiveness throughout your recovery. This neutral approach to forgiveness can be helpful to you and anyone involved in their recovery journeys, such as mental health clinicians, family, friends, life coaches, religious leaders, and community members.

In case I haven't been clear enough already: I'm not antiforgiveness. My thesis is not that forgiveness is *always* wrong or clinically counterproductive; indeed, many trauma survivors benefit from forgiving their offenders. My position, rather, is that forgiveness is not universally necessary for trauma recovery and that not only are suppositions to the contrary poorly supported by actual empirical research, but they are also problematic for both ethical and clinical reasons. To question forgiveness feels like an act of all-out rebellion.

As philosopher Jeffrie Murphy would say, I am "bucking a trendy and almost messianic sentimental movement that sees forgiveness as a nearly universal panacea for all mental, moral, and spiritual ills."[2]

This book will begin by defining trauma and forgiveness, and then we will proceed to explore the benefits and limitations of forgiveness in trauma recovery and common obstacles you may experience regarding forgiveness, such as safety concerns, shame, stigmatized anger, religious beliefs, and equality status. I will then share strategies for embracing elective forgiveness, and the book will end by providing alternative recovery methods that do not require forgiveness.

If you are a trauma survivor, you may choose to forgive or not to forgive, or you might not be able to forgive at all. I hope that your journey is based on your specific recovery needs. If you are a mental health clinician, you'll need to determine how you perceive forgiveness in trauma recovery. I hope your clinician integration is based on the specific needs of your clients and not your own. If you are a family member, friend, or loved one of a trauma survivor, you will have to decide whether you will accept the survivor's choice to incorporate or exclude forgiveness as part of their recovery journey or their inability to forgive. I hope you know that whatever your loved one chooses may be precisely what they need, and that an unwillingness to embrace their journey may have deleterious effects on their recovery.

Forgiveness is not a panacea, nor are any of the practical skills I share in this book. I encourage you to use the insights and skills that work for you, and to abandon the rest.

CHAPTER ONE

Trauma

What It Is and What It Is Not

What is trauma? There is no simple answer to this question. Over the past several decades, there has been greater awareness and discussion in mainstream audiences of the prevalence of trauma and of how it impacts individuals, generations of families, communities, and societies. Unfortunately, this heightened awareness has caused *trauma* to become a buzzword that is often used loosely and incorrectly. Likewise, other important and technical psychological concepts—such as narcissism, gaslighting, and codependency—have gained popular cultural currency, yet often at the expense of clinical or diagnostic accuracy. Though popular discourse on trauma has helped expose and destigmatize many of the serious mental health struggles we face both individually and collectively, it has also distorted or oversimplified the meaning of *trauma*, thus generating confusion and hindering education, effective treatment, and preventive action. Psychiatrist Bessel van der Kolk wrote, "After trauma the world becomes sharply divided between those who know and those who don't."[1] If you are a trauma survivor, you may feel that the misuse of the word "trauma" invalidates, minimizes, or even dramatizes your experiences, creating a chasm between yourself and those who are not survivors. As physician and trauma expert Gabor Maté writes, "The word [*trauma*] has taken on a number of colloquial valences that confuse and dilute its meaning. A clear and comprehensive reckoning is warranted."[2]

"Getting stuck on that train last week was traumatizing," reported Drew, my therapy client.

"Really? What was it like?" I asked.

"It was hot and uncomfortable. I was pissed. We all just sat there for twenty minutes. I was late for a meeting. Now, I'm traumatized," he replied.

"Take a moment and remember being stuck on the train. When you think about it now, how do you feel?"

"Well, I would have preferred it not to have happened. I really don't feel much of anything now, maybe a little angry because I was late and I'm usually on time."

Drew was not truly traumatized, as the stressful event had occurred just one week prior to our session, and he was already reporting evidence of healthy emotional processing. He was less angry and never felt unsafe during or after the event. He expressed a realization that the event was disturbing because he was late, yet he did not experience any shame or take on the identity of being a late person. He also expressed a clear cognitive and emotional awareness that the event didn't have much of an overall impact on his life. Despite these experiences, Drew continued to use the word "trauma," which has become a buzzword used to describe anything shocking, distressing, or even slightly uncomfortable or disruptive.

According to the Substance Abuse and Mental Health Services Administration (SAMHSA), "Individual trauma results from an event, series of events, or set of circumstances that is experienced by an individual as physically or emotionally harmful or threatening and that has lasting adverse effects on the individual's functioning and physical, social, emotional, or spiritual well-being."[3] The long-lasting effects of trauma are profound and often include *dysregulation,* which is an inability to manage your physiological or psychological responses. For example, if you cannot cool down your body when you're overheated, you are experiencing physical dysregulation. If you experience rage and cannot calm your anger when exposed to minor inconveniences (such as getting stuck on a train), you are experiencing emotional dysregulation. There is a vast difference between being distressed and being *dysregulated.* Distress is usually a temporary experience; your mind and body eventually return to a state of emotional and physical equilibrium once the stressful event has passed. This return to equilibrium may occur immediately after the event, or it may occur days, weeks, or even a month later. Dysregulation caused by trauma, however, is more prolonged, as it lasts months, years, or a lifetime, long after the stressful event has passed. Trauma-induced dysregulation impacts many aspects of one's life, such as one's sense of safety and self-worth, emotional stability and physical health, and ability to engage in and maintain healthy relationships.

Before I expand upon what trauma is (and what it isn't), a word of caution: one should always be hesitant about correcting those who misuse the term. Psychiatrist Peter A. Levine wrote, "Trauma is perhaps the most avoided, ignored, belittled, denied, misunderstood, and untreated cause of human suffering."[4] When you attempt to educate others, you might unintentionally contribute to our society's tendency to minimize, stigmatize, or disown trauma. Policing how people represent or express their physical and psychological experiences often isn't helpful, and it is important that we foster a culture in which people feel at liberty to name and express their lived experiences without inhibition, self-censorship, or fear of judgment. In correcting others' use of the term, you might inadvertently reinforce certain norms that shame, silence, or even gaslight survivors. It's important for people to feel empowered to articulate their experiences as they perceive them.

So, if you feel someone is misusing the word *trauma* and wish to provide them with education, ask yourself: *What is my intent?* and *Would this correction be helpful or beneficial to them?* Clinicians provide psychoeducation regarding the clinical use of the word *trauma* in order to help their clients better understand their symptoms, diagnosis, and treatment recommendations. Researchers might provide education because they need an operational definition of the term in order to conduct their research. Trauma survivors may need to educate others on the meaning of the term to help foster understanding, decrease stigma, and maintain a community of fellow survivors. Many factors may determine whether the situation, context, or relationship are appropriate for educating someone who misuses the term. One thing is clear, however: people often misuse the word for good reasons.

"I feel better about it now, but getting stuck on that train was traumatizing," Drew insisted.

Drew was clearly not traumatized, nor was he intentionally misrepresenting his experience. He was trying to communicate that the event caused him significant distress. I have noticed that when people misuse the term *trauma*, they often need to be seen, heard, understood, and accepted. Once I met these needs for Drew, he no longer felt the need to use the term *trauma* to describe his distressing experience.

Why has *trauma* become a buzzword in the first place? Many people feel unseen, unheard, misunderstood, invalidated, or shamed when articulating their emotional struggles. *Trauma* is a powerful word that can quickly convey the severity of an experience to those who may not otherwise understand it or take it seriously. It might not be enough to say "I'm struggling," "I'm not OK," or "I'm distressed." Phrases such as "I'm traumatized," "I have trauma," or "my trauma was triggered" have a greater chance of being heard. The word *trauma* carries a force that's difficult to ignore. However, an unfortunate effect of its widespread use and broadened meaning is the diminishment or undermining of its force. If everything or anything might be traumatic, then nothing is.

Can we legitimize impactful physical and psychological experiences yet also have a reasonably clear and generally applicable clinical definition of *trauma*? Yes, we can. "Tightening the definition of trauma doesn't take anything away from terrible personal experiences, the horrors of history, or the difficulty of being alive within our current social structures," writes journalist Lexi Pandell. "It doesn't limit our capacity for empathy or undercut the need to recover from tragedy, crises, or challenges. It doesn't ignore the truth of violence and existential horror—though it recognizes that there can be consequences without necessarily being trauma."[5] Every person's destabilizing experiences deserve acknowledgment, respect, and attentive consideration, even if they do not fit the clinical definition of trauma. For the purposes of this book, we need to define *trauma* because trauma survivors have specific needs that must be taken into account in considering forgiveness from a clinical perspective—that is, in considering the question of whether it is right or desirable for a person to extend or withhold forgiveness. Let us, then, proceed to examine carefully what trauma is (and what it isn't), how clinicians and survivors alike define it, and what distinct features any adequate or useful definition of it must capture.

TRAUMA IS NOT AN EVENT

Trauma comes from an ancient Greek word—τραύμα (*traûma*)—that means "wound" or "physical injury." If you break your leg, you have experienced trauma in this sense of the term. Medical professionals thus use this word to describe physical injuries; for instance, they might say "the patient has suffered trauma" or "the patient was referred to the intensive care unit due to trauma." However, over time, the word evolved to describe psychological injuries as well.

The American Psychological Association (APA) defines trauma as "any disturbing experience that results in significant fear, helplessness, dissociation, confusion, or other disruptive feelings intense enough to have a long-lasting negative effect on a person's attitudes, behavior, and other aspects of functioning. Traumatic events include those caused by human behavior (e.g., rape, war, industrial accidents) as well as by nature (e.g., earthquakes) and often challenge an individual's view of the world as a just, safe, and predictable place."[6] This definition focuses not only on the traumatizing events but also on the psychological wounds caused by those events.

One of the biggest mistakes people make when using the word *trauma* is focusing solely on an event. The statement "my father's sudden death from a heart attack was traumatic" seems to focus only on the event of the sudden and unexpected loss of a parent. However, trauma consists not simply in the event but in the persistent psychological and physiological wounds that result from such an event. Moreover, events that inflict trauma on some people may not do so on others. Many people have experienced the sudden, unexpected death of a parent yet never developed trauma. Thus, psychiatrist Peter A. Levine writes, "Certainly, all traumatic events are stressful, but all stressful events are not traumatic."[7] Since not all sudden and unexpected parental deaths are traumatic, we cannot state that if someone has experienced the death of a parent, they will automatically experience trauma. For these reasons, even though certain events or circumstances may typically be traumatizing, trauma cannot be *equated* with any particular event or set of circumstances.

Events that can cause trauma are highly diverse, which makes it impossible to assess trauma by simply attending to the occurrence of a specific event. The concepts of "big-T" and "little-t" traumas are often used to conceptualize this broad range of diversity. Big-T traumas are single, usually extraordinary events that appear to be obvious sources of trauma, such as exposure to war, rape, and natural disasters. Little-t traumas refer to an accumulation of events or acts, or an adverse set of circumstances, in which one can experience the same event or act (e.g., physical abuse), a combination of multiple events or acts (e.g., physical abuse, emotional abuse, financial abuse, and sexual abuse), or the same set of adverse circumstances (e.g., racism, poverty) over a period of time. Often, little-t traumas occur during childhood, negatively impacting a survivor's physical and psychological development. In such cases, they consist in either the occurrence of adverse events and circumstances or in the absence of developmentally vital and healthy ones, such as lacking or being denied emotional support and nurturing as a child during crucial stages of cognitive and psychosocial development. "Childhood trauma comes as a result of any violation of trust and safety, which includes a full spectrum of events that can cause it," writes psychotherapist Kaytlyn Gillis. "It is less about what happened and more about what you took from it—how it changed or affected you."[8]

Little-t traumas can include any disruptions to a child's access to a safe, capable, and secure attachment figure, such as an attachment figure's death, physical or mental illness, trauma responses, or substance abuse; they may also involve a radical change in familial circumstances, such as divorce, separation, estrangement, military deployment, imprisonment, or adoption. Little-t traumas may involve or result from a wide variety of harmful experiences, such as physical neglect, emotional neglect, abandonment, emotional or verbal abuse, physical abuse, sexual abuse, substance abuse and addiction, medical illnesses and accidents, community or school violence (including bullying), witnessing domestic violence, subjection to poverty or economic precarity (e.g., homelessness), and subjection to discrimination. The Adverse Childhood Experiences (ACEs) scale is one tool used to determine whether one has experienced little-t traumas. It's a measurement consisting of questions that assess experiences such as those just listed.[9] This is a helpful tool for clinicians and survivors alike because survivors of little-t traumas often have no idea that they have experienced trauma.

Even though I had a master's degree in counseling psychology for six years and had worked solely with trauma survivors for five years, I had no clue that I myself was a trauma survivor. How was this possible? It's simple: it was my "normal." My type of trauma (little-t) did not result from a singular, unusual event or situation but developed gradually from a consistent, everyday set of adverse and abusive circumstances—circumstances that, given their consistency and predictability, I experienced as "normal" or as "just the way things are." Big-T survivors might remember a time before the traumatic event when they were different, but not all little-t survivors remember a time before their events occurred. It is crucial to recognize that trauma need not index a radical deviation from normal, everyday life; for many people, it is embedded in everyday life itself, and is thus far less visible—and far more insidious—as a result. A chaotic or dissociated physical and psychological condition can feel normal, safe, and even *comfortable*. Attempting to explain to a little-t survivor what it's like to live without trauma is like trying to explain to a person born blind what it's like to see. You can try to do it, but it isn't easy, as their lived experience differs significantly from your own. Moreover, survivors of little-t trauma might consider what did or did not happen to them as "not that bad." Indeed, the term *little-t* inadvertently implies that these traumas are less important than the big-T traumas, when in fact the former are often just as severe as—and in some cases even more severe than—the latter. Most of my therapy clients are survivors of little-t traumas, and they did not begin to seek trauma treatment until they were middle-aged or older. Concerning the categorization of traumatic events, trauma expert Gabor Maté warns us not to be inflexible. He writes, "Even as we make the distinction between big-*T* and small-*t* traumas, given the continuum and broad spectrum of human experience, let's keep in mind that in real life the lines are fluid, are not easily drawn, and should not be rigidly maintained."[10] Whether one's trauma is big-T or little-t, the vast diversity of experiences that can cause trauma make it impossible to define or assess trauma based on one event or accumulation of events.

The medical field does not complicate things when they use the word *trauma* to describe physical injuries. Imagine surviving a bear attack with multiple open wounds on your legs. A doctor would use the word *trauma* to describe your injuries. Now, imagine that you have survived an attack from an angry housecat with multiple open wounds on your legs. The doctor would also label your injuries as *trauma*. Thus, medical professionals describe physical injuries as *traumas* regardless of their particular cause. Doctors do not assess physical injuries by solely relying on the event that caused them. If your injuries from a cat attack were more significant than those from a bear attack, your doctor would likely be more concerned about the former, which would impact the type of treatment they recommend. However, both types of injuries are nevertheless considered physical traumas.

In the field of psychology, things get more complicated. Despite what the APA's clear definition of trauma may suggest, mental health researchers and practitioners are often not always on the same page when it comes to defining it. As psychiatrist Bruce D. Perry writes, "The dilemma of defining trauma is not completely solved, and that leads to continued confusing use of the term."[11] In my experience, mental health clinicians often assess and describe trauma with an overemphasis on events, which in turn confuses trauma survivors.

We might be able to make reasonable inferences concerning the likelihood of a person suffering from trauma if they have experienced or been subjected to certain events or acts (such as war, a natural disaster, a mass shooting, or rape). Yet trauma is a phenomenon that is highly variable across individuals, and therefore one has to bracket generalizations and be sensitively attentive to the individual and their particular reactions in any given case. SAMHSA reported that trauma comprises of "three E's": the *event*, the *experience* of the event, and the *effects* of the event on the person who experienced it.[12] To assess and conceptualize trauma, we must give the experiences and the effects (the wounds) as much attention as we do the event itself.

TRAUMA IS NOT A DIAGNOSIS

To date, no diagnosis exists that can be used to define trauma, including post-traumatic stress disorder (PTSD). PTSD is not synonymous with trauma, nor is it a universally reliable or accurate basis for diagnosing trauma or for determining whether one has experienced trauma. PTSD is a psychiatric disorder assigned to trauma survivors who meet specific criteria outlined by the *Diagnostic and Statistical Manual of Mental Disorders, Fifth Edition Text Revision* (DSM-5-TR). However, many survivors do not meet all of the necessary diagnostic criteria for PTSD. Thus, though everyone who suffers from PTSD suffers from trauma, not everyone who suffers from trauma suffers from PTSD.

The DSM-5-TR is a flawed and limited tool for diagnosing trauma. First, the DSM is outdated and slow to catch up with research and treatment. The American Psychiatric Association revises the DSM every five to seven years when they delete, add, or update diagnoses based on new research. However, even after this period of time, not all research is integrated or considered. Currently, several trauma diagnoses—such as developmental trauma and complex PTSD—are being researched, assessed, and treated, yet they are not recognized in the DSM-5-TR.[13] Moreover, the DSM is unavoidably influenced by the politics and cultural prejudices of its time, and thus has since its inception wrongly pathologized many psychological traits, conditions, and phenomena (and in some cases even included diagnoses for "disorders," like female hysteria, which were never truly real at all but were entirely constructs used to marginalize and subjugate certain kinds of people). Homosexuality, for example, was considered a mental health disorder and was included in the DSM-II until 1974, when it was finally removed. However, many clinicians stopped diagnosing and treating homosexuality before this revision occurred. Thus it's common for clinicians to stop diagnosing and treating outdated "disorders" before they are removed from the DSM and to begin treatment for new disorders before they are added. The DSM-5-TR is not a sterile diagnosis tool that exists in a vacuum.

What do clinicians do when they encounter a trauma survivor who needs treatment but does not meet the criteria for a diagnosis of PTSD? They play the well-known but little-talked-about "diagnosis game"; it's not a fun game, as no one enjoys playing it, but it's required if you wish to provide services in the broken American healthcare payor system. In the United States, if you do not have a diagnosis from the DSM-5-TR, your payor (private insurance, state or federal insurance, Medicare, or Medicaid) will not pay for mental health treatment. And when there is no funding, there is usually no treatment. Mental health clinicians claim that they don't play this game are working with clients who can afford to pay their out-of-pocket fees, which can range from $90 to $350 per fifty-minute session. Clinicians navigate this game by finding a co-occurring diagnosis that a client meets the criteria for and documenting it so that they can receive the funding they need for treatment. Child-aged trauma survivors often receive diagnoses of oppositional defiant disorder, adjustment disorder, reactive attachment disorder, and attention deficit hyperactivity disorder (ADHD). Adult-aged survivors often receive diagnoses of substance use disorders, personality disorders (including the highly stigmatized borderline personality disorder), dissociative disorders, bipolar disorder, adjustment disorder, generalized anxiety, and major depression. As a result, a survivor who does not meet the criteria for PTSD might find themselves diagnosed with another disorder that does not mention trauma at all. In addition, those who meet the criteria for PTSD may find themselves with not only a diagnosis of PTSD but also a long train of additional diagnoses in its wake. It's not uncommon that I come across clients who've been diagnosed with more than six different psychiatric disorders, often by multiple healthcare providers.

This diagnosis game might be necessary, but it can increase the unfortunate likelihood of survivors experiencing stigmatization. The more psychiatric diagnoses one has, the greater the chance one will be stigmatized by others, including employers and loved ones. Indeed, one may even stigmatize *oneself*, given how easily social stigmas come to be internalized. Moreover, multiple co-occurring diagnoses can confuse survivors and their treatment providers. One clear diagnosis of PTSD can lead to a treatment plan that focuses on trauma, but multiple diagnoses may create an overcomplicated treatment plan that does not include trauma or that may excessively focus on symptoms rather than address the underlying cause (i.e., trauma).

"I've tried everything," cried the father of my new client, a sixteen-year-old girl. "When she gets better in one area, she gets worse in another. I don't know how to help her."

His daughter, Gem, was diagnosed with oppositional defiant disorder, generalized anxiety disorder, a substance use disorder, and ADHD. She participated in individual and family therapy with a colleague of mine for two years, and in that time her therapist addressed each symptom in order of priority. First, they addressed Gem's alcohol use, and months later she was sober. Then, they addressed Gem's refusal to attend school, and months later her school attendance improved. Her therapy appeared to be a success. Yet with every positive behavioral change, a new symptom would emerge. When Gem attended school consistently, she also began having sex with adult men. When she became sober, she started self-harming. Then, her therapist took a closer look at Gem's family history and discovered that, at the age of nine, she had helped her father care for her dying mother for a year before her mother died in the home. The therapist attempted to explore these experiences with Gem, but she was resistant. The term *resistant* is unfortunately often used by clinicians to refer to behaviors or reactions that reflect and stem from trauma survivors' feelings of unsafety and their efforts to protect themselves accordingly. When Gem was asked to speak about her mother, she either could not think or speak about her (which is referred to as a *freeze response* or *dissociative response*) or she expressed rage (a *fight response*). Her therapist referred Gem to me for trauma therapy, and I discovered that Gem had not only experienced small-t traumas connected to acting as a caretaker for her mother and to losing her mother, but she also had a persistent fear of her father dying and had emotionally detached from him as a defense mechanism. Gem was now dealing with the impacts of trauma on her own. I reassessed and revised Gem's diagnoses and created a trauma-focused treatment plan. After a year, her negative behaviors had significantly decreased, and she was able to reestablish her attachment to her father.

Though Gem technically met the criteria for the diagnoses of oppositional defiant disorder, generalized anxiety disorder, substance use disorder, and ADHD, such diagnoses were insufficient in helping her providers to recommend trauma-focused treatment; such diagnoses addressed the symptoms of an underlying cause without addressing that underlying cause itself. Her experience is not unique, as many trauma survivors receive recommendations for treatment modalities that do not address trauma simply because they do not qualify for a diagnosis of PTSD. This is why many seasoned clinicians do not rely solely on diagnoses in treatment planning, as they are aware that diagnoses are often utilized for funding purposes as opposed to identifying treatment needs.

"Look, you're in the field, so I won't bullshit you. Diagnoses are crap; they exist so that insurance companies can sleep at night, if they sleep at all," said my psychologist as she informed me of my diagnosis of generalized anxiety disorder. "You've got anxiety; that's true. But you've got to address your childhood trauma that created and is maintaining this anxiety. Focusing solely on the anxiety would be like putting a Band-Aid on an open infected wound. It might help a bit, but it won't last. You deserve better."

That statement stuck with me: *you deserve better.* It completely contradicted what I was raised to believe (*your mother matters; you don't*). That was the beginning of my five-year trauma recovery journey, and whenever I started treatment with a new clinician, I made sure to advocate for myself and demand that I receive trauma-focused therapy. I do not consider myself an anxious person; instead, I consider myself a trauma survivor. Trauma is my core, and anxiety is my symptom.

HOW TRAUMA SURVIVORS DEFINE TRAUMA

Books such as this often focus on how researchers and clinicians define trauma. However, it's important to consider how trauma survivors themselves conceptualize trauma. Holocaust survivor and psychologist Viktor Frankl defined trauma as *normal adaptive responses*, as opposed to *pathology*, as he wrote, "An abnormal reaction to an abnormal situation is normal behavior."[14]

I asked a diverse group of survivors, represented by their initials to protect their anonymity, to articulate their own definitions of trauma, and here are their insights:

"Trauma is distress at a cellular level." —NP

"It's when your mind goes into a permanent hiccup stage; your hippocampus gets hiccups." —KG

"Trauma is my body, mind, and heart's response to a situation that I experienced as unnatural, unpredictable, and unsafe." —KN

"It's when you didn't have control, and now you cannot give up control because it doesn't feel safe to do so." —EM

"It's the feeling that my body is my enemy, not my ally." —SP

"Trauma is fighting daily to survive, even after you've been safe for decades." —AB

"It's about my faith in humanity, each other—and how it's lost—and the damage in every system of my mind, body, and brain—from that rupture. When the inconceivable happens, one's whole worldview, including ourselves in it, must change." —LH

"Having trauma is like being a part of a secret club that you didn't sign up for and would quit at any moment if you could." —AA

"Trauma is unintegrated pain." —CN

"It's when your rational mind tries to let go of the past, but your heart, body, and soul don't know how." —VB

"Trauma is the inability to love myself and others. I know that I'm worthy, deserving, and lovable, but I just can't feel it." —HT

"It's a feedback loop of pain that no one can see." —CR

"It's why I'm triggered when my toddler hits me, throws things, spills things, or does normal kid things. Trauma has been the biggest hurdle in my ability to be a parent." —CC

"Trauma is an adaptation. It's a response. It's not only about what happened to you but also how it changed you." —KC

"Trauma isn't about getting hurt. It's about what we didn't have access to when we got hurt. We needed support, love, guidance, and safe spaces to heal. It's the lack of these things that causes trauma." —EJ

"Trauma is dysregulation, not a disorder. No one is disordered." —CF

WHAT IS TRAUMA?

Trauma is exactly what the original Greek word τραύμα means: a wound. This kind of wound is at once physiological and psychological. A state of prolonged dysregulation creates invisible wounds that can impact every part of your body and remain locked in your body for a lifetime. Over the past decade, many studies have demonstrated the significant impact that trauma can have on the body. Researchers have taken brain scans that clearly show how trauma impacts the physical structures of the brain, clear evidence that psychological trauma creates lasting changes in the physical body. The mind–body connection is fundamental and powerful, as everything that impacts your mind impacts your body, and much of what impacts your body impacts your mind. We have ample evidence that psychological trauma can cause, compound, or elevate one's risk of developing many medical diseases, such as cardiovascular disease, arthritis, asthma, chronic pain, diabetes, and gastrointestinal disorders. You cannot define trauma as solely a psychological concept; it's inextricably connected to the body.

Trauma is also a complex web of deceptions about our self-worth and life circumstances. It tells us that we are not good enough, that we are unlovable, unworthy, incapable, unsafe, bad, weak, and so on; it infects us with negative core, all-or-nothing beliefs about ourselves that aren't true or rationally justified. Such a web may have been initially spun by one or many spiders, but we unknowingly and unintentionally take over the job of spinning this web ourselves. As though it is not enough that we are often gaslighted by myriad social forces and institutions, trauma typically leads us to gaslight *ourselves*. When we spin this web of deceptions about ourselves, we call it low self-worth, low self-esteem, impostor syndrome, or any other number of cognitive distortions. This web becomes so thick, strong, adhesive, and ingrained—so tightly and thoroughly wound around and through our being—that we struggle to break free of it long after the spider(s) that first trapped us in its tangle and taught us how to spin are long gone.

Trauma is inherited. Studies have shown that trauma can impact the DNA of offspring for generations.[15] Your trauma web may have been spun long before you were born. It's not uncommon for survivors to become curious about their family history in order to identify the source of their pain. Some survivors discover that they experience historical trauma, which includes slavery, colonization, oppression, genocide, and war. Survivors who are a part of marginalized populations find that their historic trauma extends far beyond three generations. If your ancestors were abducted from Africa in 1700 and their descendants were slaves in the New World for the next 150 years, and then their American descendants experienced consistent oppression, which continues to this day, that's centuries of familial trauma. Your web will likely look very different from the web of a member of a privileged group.

Trauma is a thief. It steals our childhoods, years of our adult lives, or even our entire lifetimes. It takes away our ability to feel connected to others, to feel like we belong in the world, and to receive and extend love. It prevents us from growing and thriving. It steals our relationships, work, physical health, families, communities, spirituality, hobbies, passions, and identity. And to add insult to injury, trauma then demands that we grieve these losses in order to heal from them, which can feel overwhelming. Survivors report that this grieving process is one of the most challenging aspects of trauma recovery. Anger can feel safe and empowering, yet grief can feel vulnerable and unrelenting. If I could, I'd choose my rage over my grief any day of the week.

Trauma inhibits our ability to assess our own safety. It tells us that we are not safe even when we are. Trauma says the world is dangerous even when, in the present moment, it is not. Trauma screams that people, or at least certain kinds of people (men, women, authority figures, romantic partners, etc.), are out to harm us even when we have good evidence to the contrary. Trauma informs us that we cannot take up space in the world or exist freely. Trauma makes us feel like we are still children, young adults, or victims—even after we have grown up or learned how to protect and take care of ourselves.

Yet, for all its deceptions and complications, trauma is also wisdom. Ask a trauma survivor this question: What can you do that you believe those who haven't had your experiences cannot? You may be surprised at their response. My clients have answered: "I feel like I have more empathy and compassion for people than others do," "I can see people, really see them, when others cannot," "I can survive anything. Bring on the zombie apocalypse; I'll be fine," "I'm a talented writer, and I owe some of that to what I went through," and "I live every day with gratitude. How many people can say that?" Trauma can provide valuable lessons that we can use to benefit ourselves, our loved ones, our communities, and our society. This perception of trauma is not meant to romanticize it but to acknowledge and appropriately appreciate the reality of *post-traumatic growth*. Richard Tedeschi and Lawrence Calhoun coined the term *post-traumatic growth*, defining it as "the positive psychological change that is experienced as a result of the struggle with highly challenging life circumstances." They identified several areas of growth, including a greater appreciation of life, a strengthening of close relationships, an increased capacity for compassion and altruism, the identification of new possibilities or a renewed sense of purpose in life, a greater awareness and utilization of personal strengths, enhanced spiritual development, and creative growth.[16] Psychotherapist Resmaa Menakem wrote, "Trauma is not a flaw or a weakness. It is a highly effective tool of safety and survival."[17] Survivors in recovery often fear that recovery will deprive them of the wisdom they have gained. Fortunately, I've never seen this happen. We can recover from trauma and continue to take advantage of its wisdom.

Trauma cannot be cured. It will not magically disappear one day, as it always leaves a permanent mark on us. We will never truly be able to forget it. We cannot start over from a blank slate, as trauma marks a rupture in time—a break in the ordinary continuity of life—that cannot be effaced or reversed. Once trauma happens, it irrevocably frames our personal identity and history: there is only ever time "before trauma" and "after trauma," and we can never truly retreat to a time before trauma. Psychiatrist Judith Herman reminds us that the goal of trauma recovery is "integration, not exorcism."[18] Trauma can be integrated and transformed, and thus our life in the wake of trauma need not be reduced to it. That web in which trauma ensnares us can be loosened, untangled, and healthily interwoven into the larger fabric of who we are. We can protect ourselves and our loved ones by welcoming our former nemesis—the spider—into the fold. We can even help others befriend their own spiders.

And we can do all of this with *or without* forgiveness.

CHAPTER TWO

Forgiveness

What It Is and What It Is Not

Early in my research on forgiveness, I asked my clinical colleagues:

"What is your definition of forgiveness?"

"Forgiveness allows the opportunity for safety and trust to be reestablished in a relationship," said a marriage and family therapist. "It is the capability and willingness of one to reconnect with the other once a break has occurred in the relationship. I encourage all my clients to forgive." This seems to me more like a definition of *reconciliation* than a definition of *forgiveness*. And I know survivors who have forgiven yet decided not to reconnect or reconcile with their offender. Also, some offenders are incapable of safety and trust, and therefore it is not in the survivor's best interest to repair the break in the relationship. Thus, though reconciliation may, in some cases, be a natural outcome of forgiveness, it is not the same as forgiveness.

"Forgiveness is a virtue that follows the teachings of Jesus Christ," reported a Christian counselor. "Jesus taught us that if you forgive the transgressions of others, then God will forgive you. Everyone should embrace forgiveness." This definition is unhelpful to most people who do not identify as Christians. Though forgiveness may be a Christian or biblical virtue, is it exclusively or necessarily a religious concept? If it is, why should *everyone* embrace it? And if a survivor is not a Christian, need they convert to Christianity to practice forgiveness and, moreover, recover from trauma? This definition of forgiveness is inaccessible to many survivors.

"Forgiveness is a choice to let go of resentment," said a psychologist. "Forgiveness is good for the forgiver, the forgiven, and the community. It's a gift that benefits everyone." This definition is unclear. Have I really forgiven if I choose not to feel resentful? I might feel other negative emotions (such as fear, rage, and betrayal), and I may enact vengeance upon my offender. So, have I forgiven as long as I do not feel resentful? Forgiveness is commonly defined in ways that are problematically unclear or vague, and this leaves survivors confused about what is being asked of them when they are encouraged to forgive.

My colleagues could not adequately define forgiveness and were either unaware of or unwilling to admit their lack of knowledge. I do not fault my colleagues. There is no single, universally agreed upon definition of forgiveness, and its meaning—including its normative characteristics—remains a subject of academic debate (both within and outside of psychology). Most forgiveness advocates struggle to provide a clear definition of forgiveness or any practical justification for advocating it; rather, they recommend forgiveness without thoughtfully considering it—even without understanding its meaning.

Psychologist Mono Gustafson Affinito reflects on this struggle to define forgiveness, writing that "philosophers, theologians, psychologists, psychiatrists, counselors, self-help advisors, and authors have failed to define their terms with sufficient precision to meet the needs of counselors."[1] The clinical research on forgiveness is still in its infancy, and we have yet to establish a single, clear clinical or operational definition of forgiveness that would inform such research. How can I expect clinicians to either ethically recommend or avoid recommending forgiveness to trauma survivors when they do not have a clear clinical definition of it? I cannot. Unfortunately, many clinicians have recommended forgiveness without considering a definition, and thus, they did not know what they were recommending. The lack of an adequate, cohesive understanding of the concept of forgiveness has compromised its clinical applications and harmed survivors.

Before I explore the complexities of forgiveness in trauma recovery, I must first try to define the term as clearly as possible; in order to do so, I will attempt to identify the characteristics—both positive and negative—that most agree are integral to its meaning. This is the necessary first step toward developing a working definition of forgiveness that will be helpful for you and your clinicians alike.

FORGIVENESS IS NOT . . .

Clinical researchers and scholars may not agree on what forgiveness is, yet they tend to agree on what forgiveness is *not*. A review of the literature states that forgiveness is not any of the following:

Impersonal

Forgiveness is either interpersonal—occurring between two or more people—or intrapersonal (self-forgiveness)—occurring within oneself. We cannot forgive events or objects, as inanimate things are incapable of moral intentionality and action and, therefore, cannot accept moral credit or accountability. I can forgive someone who pushes me into a concrete wall. However, I cannot forgive the concrete wall. I can forgive myself for not seeking shelter during a tornado, but I cannot forgive the tornado.

Forgetting

Forgiveness requires memory, as one must have some awareness of the harm that they are forgiving and a right to retain that memory going forward. The cliché phrase *forgive and forget* causes confusion, as this implies that one who forgives will have no memory or should have no memory of the harm. This expectation is unrealistic and dangerous, as people rely on past experiences to promote their safety and well-being. I can forgive a friend who lied to me, and if they lied again, I would be aware of a pattern of behavior that would influence my choices in that relationship going forward. *Forgive, but don't forget* is a more realistic phrase that implies that one can forgive without erasing the memory of the harm.

Rationalizing

Forgiveness is not a psychological defense mechanism like *rationalizing*, which is when a person has arrived at a belief and seeks evidence to support their belief and discounts evidence that disproves it. "In rationalization, the 'evidence' comes after the belief has already been determined," writes philosopher T. Edward Damer. "The rationalizer is simply using premises that make his or her questionable position or action appear to be rationally respectable."[2] For example, my former client believed the priest who repeatedly raped her son was "a good man." She had this belief for years before she learned of the sexual assaults. When rationalizing, she sought and accepted evidence that supported her belief that the priest was still a "good man" despite his actions. She celebrated the priest's contributions to the community and his respected position in the church and minimized his actions as a rapist. She had not forgiven the priest. She had rationalized his actions. The goal of rationalizing is often to avoid experiencing emotional pain. This mother attempted to avoid feeling rage, profound sadness, and guilt, which she needed to experience in order to recover.

Excusing

Forgiveness requires one or more responsible agents, the offender(s). The offender can be someone who directly or indirectly caused or contributed to the harm of a survivor. Offenders who indirectly cause trauma can be bystanders who fail to act or family members who create or sustain family dynamics that enable offenders. Offenders can be living or deceased. Survivors can include those who are directly or indirectly harmed. *Excusing* occurs when one minimizes, dismisses, or altogether negates an offender's responsibility or blameworthiness for an offense they have committed by attributing their offense to factors or circumstances outside the scope of their knowledge or control. Certain psychosocial characteristics and circumstances (such as the age of an offender or a disability) may make an offender incapable of understanding and acting according to moral norms or of being appropriately responsive to moral considerations. They are therefore not responsible for their harmful conduct. An offense is excused because there is no responsible agent, and there is no one to forgive.

Forgiveness can masquerade as excusing an offense when the offender is a responsible agent. The mother, who rationalized the actions of the priest who raped her son, also attempted to excuse his actions while claiming to have forgiven him. She stated that since the priest was required to abstain from sex by the Catholic Church, he was unable to control his sexual impulses. She stated, "If he had been able to marry, he would never have hurt my son. I forgive him because he couldn't stop himself." Since she was convinced that the priest was not a responsible agent for his actions, there was a need for her to forgive him. The prosecutor and the public did not agree with these excuses, and the priest was charged and is serving time in prison.

Justifying

Forgiveness requires that a wrong be committed. There are circumstances when an offender's actions may be justified: though such actions may involve inflicting some kind of harm, they are not considered wrong. Murphy writes, "To regard conduct as justified (as in lawful self-defense, for example) is to claim that the conduct, though normally wrongful, was—in the given circumstance and all things considered—the right thing to do."[3] You cannot forgive when an offense has not occurred because the offense is justifiable.

Forgiveness can be disguised as justifying. For example, Andrew Lester, a white man in Kansas City, shot Ralph Yarl, a Black teenager, after Yarl knocked on his door, arriving at the wrong address to pick up his siblings. The two did not speak before Lester shot Yarl twice through a locked glass door. Lester claimed self-defense. If Lester's neighbors stated that they forgave him because they believed he shot the boy in self-defense, they would be justifying his actions, not forgiving him. If an act is justified, no wrong has been committed, so there is nothing to forgive. The neighbors would not need to forgive Lester if they truly believed that his actions were justifiable. As it turns out, one neighbor did not justify or forgive his actions, as she reported, "This is somebody's child. I had to clean blood off of my door, off of my railing. That was someone's child's blood. I'm a mom. . . . This is not OK."[4]

Condoning

Forgiveness requires acknowledgment that an offense was wrong and should not continue. *Condoning* is when a person fails to acknowledge an offense, denies that an offense has been committed, or allows (whether actively or passively) an offense to continue to be committed. Thus, to condone an offense is, in fact, to be complicit in it. If one believes that genetic family members should be allowed to abuse one another—or if one is incapable of acknowledging that such abuse is happening in the first place—one will not see any need to forgive family members who abuse oneself or others in one's family. Survivors have condoned offenses for years while believing that they were forgiving.

"I thought I had forgiven my parents, but I did not realize the damage they caused," said trauma survivor Leroy, whose parents emotionally abused him throughout his childhood. "I thought they could do anything to me because they were my parents. Once I realized how wrong they were and how much they hurt me, I discovered that I had not forgiven them." When a survivor begins to consider or struggle with forgiveness, it is often a sign that they do not or no longer condone the offense.

Denial

Forgiveness requires an honest reckoning with the truth—that is, a clear awareness and explicit acknowledgment of an offense that has been perpetrated against oneself or others. When we engage in denial, we know the truth but nonetheless refuse or cannot admit it. Thus, denial is a defense mechanism and a form of self-deception. Almost every survivor has experienced denial during their recovery, as denial is a healthy and expected part of the grieving process.

"I was in denial for years," said survivor Aaron. "I knew my husband was gambling our money away. I knew he was controlling and abusive, but I could not fully believe it. I simply wasn't ready to." Forgiveness therapy practitioner Robert D. Enright writes: "Forgiveness stands on the truth that what happened to me *was* unfair, it *is* unfair, and it will *always* be unfair, but I will have a new response to it."[5] Survivors cannot forgive while they are in denial about the harm they have suffered. They can extend forgiveness to an offender only if they are able to acknowledge and accept that an offense has actually been committed in the first place.

Pardoning

Forgiveness does not imply that there are (or ought to be) no consequences for the offender(s). Survivors can forgive while also advocating for or demanding consequences for the offender. A *pardon* is when the offender is relieved of some or all consequences. The parents of a murdered child can decide to forgive their child's murderer and still expect the murderer to experience legal consequences. In civil court, a car accident survivor can forgive the distracted driver who hit them yet sue the driver for monetary damages. You can forgive without pardoning, and offenders can be pardoned without forgiveness.

A Trauma Response

Genuine forgiveness requires safety. Survivors often mistake a trauma response for forgiveness. A *trauma response*—such as fawning or people-pleasing—occurs in order to promote survivors' safety or help them cope with overwhelming thoughts, emotions, and physical sensations. Fawning is when you comply with your offender(s) in order to keep yourself safe. While fawning, you may verbalize forgiveness to your offender in order to protect yourself or cope, but this is not authentic forgiveness.

"I used to tell my husband that I forgave him," says survivor Aaron. "I did this so he wouldn't get angry and start a fight that would last for hours. He'd scream, curse, make threats, and punch holes in our walls. He wouldn't let me leave or go to sleep until I forgave him. I had to forgive him to make it stop." Aaron verbalized forgiveness in order to keep himself safe. Forgiveness is not *appeasement*. You may confuse forgiveness with your efforts to promote your safety by preventing further abuse, rejection, abandonment, or judgment. Authentic forgiveness is not a survival technique. Genuine forgiveness can only proceed *from* a condition of safety; it cannot be motivated by a desire for safety or by an experienced lack of safety.

Premature

Forgiveness in the wake of trauma requires time. Forgiving an offender can take months, years, or a lifetime. *Premature forgiveness*—also called *cheap forgiveness*—is when we forgive without going through the emotional processes necessary in order to forgive authentically. "Cheap forgiveness is a quick and easy pardon with no processing of emotion and no coming to terms with the injury," writes psychologist Janis Abrahms Spring. "When you forgive cheaply, you seek to preserve the relationship at any cost, including your own integrity and safety."[6] Premature forgiveness does not repair relationships, nor does it alleviate trauma responses.

"Once I realized how much they hurt me, I thought that if I quickly forgave my parents, I wouldn't feel angry or depressed," says Leroy. "It didn't work. I felt the same. Years later, I realized that I hadn't really forgiven them at all." Premature forgiveness is rarely sustainable; those overwhelming trauma responses and those breaks in the relationship either persist or return. Offenses that cause or contribute to trauma usually involve a journey of emotional processing that isn't quick, easy, or simple.

Reconciliation

Forgiveness is often confused with reconciliation, and many assume that those who forgive will automatically reconcile with their offender(s). *Reconciliation* occurs when two or more people restore a relationship after harm has occurred in that relationship. This restoration can be loving, friendly, amicable, polite, or civil—treating someone as you would a stranger. You may come to forgive and reconcile with your offender, and you may also forgive without reconciliation. Forgiveness and reconciliation are often linked, yet forgiveness does not automatically lead to reconciliation.

"I've forgiven him," said Aaron, two years after he divorced his emotionally and financially abusive husband. "I don't feel any animosity toward him, and I want him to be happy. I really do. I just don't want or need him in my life." Aaron's friends and family encouraged him to remain in contact with his ex-husband, who experienced severe depression after the divorce. They said, "If you've forgiven him, you should be able to talk to him" and "If you care about him, you will help him." Yet, whenever Aaron resumed contact, his ex-husband would eventually demand money. When Aaron refused, he was met with anger and continued emotional abuse. Eventually, Aaron severed all ties and informed his family and friends that although he had forgiven his ex-husband, there would be no reconciliation.

Unfortunately, many people attempt to force, pressure, or encourage survivors to forgive, believing this will automatically lead to reconciliation. The misconception that those who forgive will automatically reconcile with their offender(s) may cause you to avoid forgiveness, as you might fear that if you extend forgiveness to your offender(s), you will be required to reconcile with them. Some survivors who forgive their offender(s) reconcile, and others do not.

Acceptance

Oprah Winfrey defines forgiveness as "giving up the hope that the past could be any different."[7] This is a definition of acceptance, not forgiveness. *Acceptance* is when we acknowledge the reality of a situation, state, or process without trying to revise or resist it. Acceptance is not agreement. One can accept the death of a loved one and not agree that they needed to die or should have died. Acceptance, like reconciliation, is often linked to forgiveness, as those who forgive experience acceptance. Yet, those who experience acceptance do not automatically experience forgiveness.

"Forgiveness is a form of acceptance, but not all forms of acceptance constitute forgiveness," writes forgiveness researchers Robert D. Enright and Richard P. Fitzgibbons. "If a client accepts what happened but does not accept the offender as a human being worthy of respect, he or she is not forgiving. Some people make peace with the past but not with the people of the past."[8] You can experience acceptance without forgiving your offender(s).

"Dad was hitting her, so she was hitting me," said Quinn, referring to her sister, who'd physically abused her in childhood. "I get it. We were both victims. I know I can't change what happened to her and to me. I also know that I don't love her or even like her. I don't see her as an actual person. But that doesn't matter so much because I finally feel like I've moved on." Quinn did not experience forgiveness, she experienced *acceptance*, which is one of the most powerful transformations that can occur in trauma recovery. Although acceptance is not forgiveness, it shouldn't be overlooked, as many survivors consider it one of the most essential experiences in recovery.

DEFINING FORGIVENESS

Because there is no consensus in the field of psychology on how forgiveness ought to be defined, I have collected a variety of definitions from research studies, academic texts, and treatment theories in order to identify the most commonly asserted and disputed aspects of forgiveness.

A Decision

Academics and psychologists often define forgiveness as a decision or willful act, or at least as a certain kind of willingness or disposition to orient and comport oneself in relation to others. Legal scholar Martha Minow writes that forgiveness is "a conscious, deliberate *decision* to forgo rightful grounds for grievance against those who have committed a wrong or harm."[9] Forgiveness researcher Everett L. Worthington Jr. writes that "a *decision* to forgive is primarily a *decision* to try to act differently toward the offender and, not seeking payback, treating the person as a valuable and valued person."[10] Forgiveness researcher Robert D. Enright and philosopher Joanna North define forgiveness as "a *willingness* to abandon one's right to resentment, negative judgment, and indifferent behavior toward one who unjustly injured us."[11] These definitions include some aspect of a decision or willingness that is required before one is able to experience forgiveness.

How important is the decision to forgive? Many clinicians, including myself, have observed clients who initially approached forgiveness in a cognitive manner by stating that they forgave their offender or are deciding to forgive, and then later, they reported experiencing authentic forgiveness. This is not uncommon. Many survivors decide to forgive despite not having experienced the emotions or attitudes associated with forgiveness. Indeed, many people report having forgiven someone without being aware of the fact that, at least on a subconscious level, they had not truly, authentically forgiven that person at the time they decided to do so, and only belatedly—often months, years, or even decades later—experienced authentic forgiveness. As psychologists Robert D. Enright and Thomas W. Baskin write, "The *choice* to forgive is described as both a decision, with immediate opportunity, and as the opening of doors to a journey that encompasses an entire forgiving *process*."[12]

Does one have to engage in a conscious decision to forgive before one is able to experience the process of forgiving? Some say yes, as the decision and willingness to forgive is a prerequisite to engaging in the process of forgiveness. This decision initiates the process and can even obstruct it if the choice is not made to forgive. "Forgiving is intentional," writes Worthington. "Because forgiving is intentional, the spontaneous dissipation of resentment and ill will over time that is occasioned by injury does not constitute forgiveness."[13] However, I've witnessed trauma survivors—who had been adamantly against forgiveness—achieve emotional forgiveness without making a conscious decision. On the other hand, many survivors report that they decided to forgive or felt a willingness to forgive yet were unable to do so. Some say that these situations occur because forgiveness depends upon an emotional experience and is not the sole result of a single decision or act of will.

Consider the emotional experience of love. Is love a choice? I suppose some people say love is a choice, as we can choose to perform actions that are expressive of love, and we can choose to act in ways that are necessary to sustain loving relationships, but the love itself that one experiences for others—especially romantic love—seems to be something passive. Hence, when we talk about falling in love, we are stating that love is an emotional experience that happens to us. Love is largely a response to qualities in others we esteem, and responsiveness is a form of passivity—it's not based solely upon a decision.

What if forgiveness is an emotional experience that can be supported by a conscious decision to forgive or a level of subconscious receptiveness to the experience of forgiving? A survivor who decides to forgive or who verbalizes forgiveness without having yet genuinely forgiven or without having yet experienced the psychological processes associated with achieving authentic forgiveness may simply be receptive to the possibility of achieving authentic forgiveness in the future. Let's return to the concept of falling in love. Love isn't an emotion that one can decide to feel or will into being. However, it seems necessary for one to adopt certain attitudes—that one open oneself up in specific ways—in order for love to come to fruition. I must have an appropriate level of receptiveness to allow myself to love another and to allow that person to love me. Also, there's still a certain amount of work, or time and effort, that I have to put into our budding relationship for such love ever to develop. It seems that one has to adopt a particular existential orientation toward the possibility of love and that one has to decide to act and comport oneself in specific ways in order for love to develop. Perhaps something similar can be said about forgiveness; whether we can forgive may not entirely be up to us, but there is a certain amount of work we need to do in order to make forgiveness possible or in order to undergo the sorts of experiences and processes necessary for forgiveness to be possible.

In trauma recovery, there are many recommendations that clinicians provide survivors with to encourage them to be open to whatever safe experiences they need in order to recover. I have witnessed many trauma survivors who, having initially chosen not to forgive, were later shocked to discover during their recovery process that they had indeed forgiven their offender(s). They were unaware that they had developed any type of receptiveness to forgiveness. This implies that forgiveness isn't entirely something chosen, or at least does not require a conscious choice, but instead requires a level of receptiveness to the experience. Therefore, instead of requiring you to make a decision to forgive, perhaps clinicians can instead suggest a level of receptiveness to the experience if that is what you need.

A Process

Forgiveness is defined not only in terms of the forgiver's choice or willingness to forgive but also in terms of the process of experiencing forgiveness itself. On this account, forgiveness is less something one does and is more something one undergoes. "Forgiveness is not an act but a process," writes psychologist Frank D. Fincham. "Rather, the decision to forgive starts a difficult process that involves conquering negative feelings and acting with goodwill toward someone who has done us harm."[14] Fincham focuses on the importance of the experience of forgiveness as opposed to solely making a decision to forgive. Worthington distinguishes between decisional and emotional forgiveness: "Decisional forgiveness is a decision about one's intention to behave differently toward the offender, stating agreement to try to treat the offender as a valuable and valued person (and to forgo vengeance). Emotional forgiveness is the emotional replacement of negative unforgiving emotions with positive other-oriented emotions of empathy, sympathy, compassion, or love for the transgressor."[15] You might decide to forgive without experiencing emotional forgiveness. Yet, the concept of decisional forgiveness without the presence of emotional forgiveness is not considered to be genuine forgiveness. Almost every forgiveness researcher and scholar will state that there is some aspect of a change in one's emotional experience when one experiences forgiveness. Therefore, one could argue that emotional forgiveness is a required component of forgiveness, as few researchers and scholars would debate this requirement, and emotional forgiveness is achieved only by engaging in the process of forgiving.

Psychologist Sharon Lamb calls forgiveness "the porn of movies" because the film industry's depictions of forgiveness are typically just as inaccurate as the pornography industry's depictions of sex.[16] Films do not have the time or the audience's attention to show what forgiveness from a survivor's perspective actually looks like. Forgiveness is not one event that occurs at the end of a movie when a soundtrack plays and everyone cries. It is a long, tedious, back-and-forth, and at times boring experience, often fraught with internal turmoil and ambivalence. "Forgiveness is a process," writes child abuse survivor and author Nancy Richards. "We forgive a piece at a time as we go on with our lives. After we think we have finished, more pain often arises from the same circumstance, and we must work through the next layer. Each time, we become that much more liberated."[17] You may never know when you have achieved forgiveness, as the process may not have a definitive, perfect ending, a moment of complete closure.

Forgiveness, like trauma recovery, is not a linear journey. It does not progress from one stage to the next in a perfectly sequential manner. It is not an organized to-do list that can be completed one task or item at a time in a strictly defined order. It cannot be illustrated by drawing a line that consistently travels upward. Instead, trauma recovery looks like messy lines with jagged edges, which are long and winding and travel upward, downward, and to the side. It's not uncommon for survivors to feel like they are regressing, relapsing, or stagnant during their recovery. Even small dips after huge gains can feel like complete failures.

Elizabeth Kübler-Ross's stages of grief (denial, anger, bargaining, depression, and acceptance) are recognized in the field of psychology as a complicated process.[18] The stages bleed and fold back into and give way to one another, with several sometimes occurring all at once, dynamically cresting and receding in waves, and it probably can never be said that someone has ever "fully" "achieved" grieving, but that grieving is a lifelong process, that closure when it comes to a profound loss is never perfectly attainable. Some survivors say this reality of grieving feels like "one step forward, two steps back," and the process of forgiveness is no different. Relapses, regressions, or taking "two steps back" are natural and healthy components of the process of forgiveness.

Forgiveness exists on a continuum.[19] Imagine a line in which purely positive emotions, thoughts, and behaviors (e.g., loving the offender, sacrificing oneself for the offender, etc.) lie on one side and purely negative emotions, thoughts, and behaviors (e.g., hating the offender, actively harming them, etc.) lie on the other side. Between these binary concepts is a wide range of emotional experiences and patterns of thought and behavior along which you can move back and forth. Movement in both directions along a continuum is a healthy response in trauma recovery. This movement can be fast, fleeting, or slow, with less movement occurring over time.

"There are moments of forgiveness," says survivor Leroy. "There are moments when I'm okay, and I can see why my parents hurt me, and I know it had nothing to do with me. Then, there are moments when I am angry at them and everything they took from me." Leroy doesn't lie still on one end of the continuum or the other. His process involves fluctuations, vacillations, and interchanges in patterns of thinking, behavior, and emotional experiences. The concept of experiencing forgiveness along a continuum normalizes healthy emotional processing. All emotions are expected to change, to undergo alterations and alternations over time, and this is a sign of healthy emotional processing.

Conditional versus Unconditional

Is forgiveness based on the offender's participation? Does the offender need to acknowledge and accept responsibility for their actions (or inactions), experience remorse, provide an apology, and make amends in order to be forgiven? Some would say yes. Survivors cannot be solely responsible for forgiving, as the offender must contribute to this process. As Spring writes: "Genuine forgiveness must be earned. It comes with a price that the offender must be willing to pay."[20] Conditional forgiveness, also called transactional forgiveness, occurs when the offender engages in the process by providing the survivor with what they need in order to forgive them. The needs of survivors vary greatly. Some might need their offender to admit their wrongdoings to their family, friends, community, or to the public. Others may need an apology and/or the offender to express consistent behavioral changes before forgiveness is considered. Conditional forgiveness can be earned by offenders and might be a good option for some—but not necessarily for all—survivors. Conditional forgiveness places responsibility on the offender, which can empower you, but it can also place the offender in a position of power, as they are now largely in control of the forgiveness process. Conditional forgiveness allows the offender to decide whether you will experience forgiveness and any of its benefits. Some offenders are motivated by forgiveness and will work hard to provide you with what you need. Others couldn't care less and might enjoy the power that conditional forgiveness gives them. Conditional forgiveness may be considered if you plan to continue to engage in a relationship with your offender(s).

In contrast, unconditional forgiveness does not require any involvement from the offender. "Forgiving is unconditional," writes Worthington. "Conditions that influence forgiveness (e.g., transgressor's confession, apology) are not necessary conditions for it to occur even though they may facilitate forgiveness."[21] The power to forgive or not lies with the survivor alone. Unconditional forgiveness occurs without needing the offender to apologize, express remorse, take accountability, or attempt to make any amends or behavioral changes; indeed, it does not even require the offender's desire to receive forgiveness at all. On this account, forgiveness cannot be *earned* by the offender; it can only be *granted* by the survivor. Unconditional forgiveness does not mean that the offender "gets away with it" and has permission to continue abusing the survivor because, as we've seen, forgiveness is not reconciliation, excusing, denying, justifying, or pardoning. Unconditional forgiveness may not benefit the offender in any way. Some offenders are never told that they have been forgiven, as unconditional forgiveness is focused on the survivor's needs, not the offender's. Unconditional forgiveness is the only option for survivors whose offenders are deceased or unsafe or unreceptive to engaging in the forgiveness process. Some survivors have experienced retraumatization when they have involved their offender(s) in their recovery for the purposes of achieving conditional forgiveness.

Many people will say that your ability to forgive or not forgive should not be dictated by your offender(s), as this requirement provides the offender(s) with the same power and control they had while offending. You may need your offender(s) to acknowledge their actions, accept accountability, express remorse, apologize, or provide evidence of behavioral changes in order for them to engage in relationship repair or reconciliation, but these should not be requirements for forgiveness. Unconditional forgiveness is focused on your needs alone. Offenders might benefit from a survivor's forgiveness, but that is not the object of unconditional forgiveness, which does not rely upon the participation or engagement of the offender. The power of unconditional forgiveness lies with the survivor, and it cannot be earned by the offender. Remember, forgiveness is not reconciliation, which may require the offender's participation.

Unconditional forgiveness can be obtainable even when you cannot involve your offender(s) in your recovery. Your offenders might be unsafe, unwilling, unreachable, or deceased. If forgiveness is conditionally based upon the offender(s), are survivors out of luck? No, for they too can experience forgiveness, and many such survivors—especially those whose offenders are deceased—report forgiving their offenders without their offenders participating in their recovery or even knowing that they have been forgiven. Offenders who are willing and safe to engage in and contribute to recovery might nevertheless not be able to meet the needs of survivors. You might need an apology or expression of remorse. However, genuine apologies from offenders who have caused or contributed to trauma are often not forthcoming, as offenders might not be ready, willing, or capable of offering sincere apologies. Psychiatrist and complex trauma researcher Judith Herman writes, "No matter how passionately survivors may wish for an apology, they must be fully prepared for disappointment since they are more likely to meet with denial, excuses, or blame than with acknowledgment and repentance."[22] You may not benefit from a single-event apology but may need multiple apologies and constant reassurance from your offender. Offenders must be able and willing to provide multiple experiences (which are emotionally and physically taxing for them) over a period of time in order to benefit your recovery, and these actions may still not support the process of forgiveness. Many offenders do not have the willingness, emotional safety, or capacity to satisfy these needs. Unconditional forgiveness does not preclude the involvement of the offender(s) in the forgiveness process; it simply does not rely upon their involvement in order to occur.

A Change in Disposition toward the Offender

Most conceptualizations of forgiveness focus on a change in the forgiver's emotional, cognitive, and behavioral constitution. These changes often refer to a reduction in negative emotions of anger, resentment, fear, and the desire for vengeance. Robert D. Enright and Richard P. Fitzgibbons, the cocreators of forgiveness therapy, define forgiveness partly as occurring when "people, upon rationally determining that they have been unfairly treated, forgive when they willfully abandon resentment and related responses (to which they have a right)."[23] This definition stipulates a reduction in antagonistic or retributive emotions, thoughts, and actions. Enright and Fitzgibbons clarify this definition: "When abandoning resentment, a person is likely to show fewer (a) negative emotions ranging on a continuum from annoyance (on the 'lighter' side of negative emotions) to hatred (on the 'heavier' side of negative emotions); (b) negative thoughts ranging from judging the person as inadequate (on one end) to evil incarnate (on the other); and (c) negative behaviors ranging from ignoring or being 'cool' to serious revenge-seeking."[24] Thus, a reduction of negative thoughts, emotions, and actions are a necessary part of forgiveness, and there are few who will dispute this claim.

Scholars and researchers commonly define forgiveness not only in terms of a reduction in negative emotions, thoughts, and behavioral dispositions toward the offender(s) but also an increase in positive emotions, thoughts, and behavioral dispositions toward their offender(s). "Forgiveness involves negative and positive dimensions," writes Worthington. "Forgiveness is not achieved simply by relinquishing a negative motivational state vis-à-vis the harm-doer. Overcoming the resentment, anger, retaliatory impulses, and so on of unforgiveness reflects only one of two dimensions of forgiveness."[25] Enright and Fitzgibbons also provide a two-dimensional definition of forgiveness as endeavoring "to respond to the wrongdoer based on the moral principle of beneficence, which may include compassion, unconditional worth, generosity, and moral love (to which the wrongdoer, by nature of the hurtful act or acts, has no right)."[26] Enright and Fitzgibbons clarify their focus on the positive dimension of forgiveness as they explain, "When exercising beneficence, a person is likely to show more (a) positive emotions such as slightly liking the person (on the lighter side) to selfless love (on the other end of this spectrum)—there are a number of moral emotions that could be part of forgiveness: compassion, caring, and concern, for example; (b) positive thoughts from wishing the person well to considerations of unconditional worth (not because of the other's immoral actions but because he or she is a person and all people are worthy of respect); and (c) positive behaviors from making eye contact or smiling to taking an active interest in the other's welfare."[27]

Enright and Fitzgibbons' definition of forgiveness requires a forgiver or survivor to experience, at the very least, the emotional state of "slightly liking" their offender, thoughts of "wishing the person well," and positive actions such as "smiling" at them. You might be able to meet this expectation of forgiveness, while others may not. You may experience a diminishment in negative emotions, thoughts, and dispositions but no increase in positive emotions, thoughts, or dispositions. In this case, you have not forgiven. Philosopher Norvin Richards writes that "advocates of forgiveness therapy might reply that for some patients, it could be said that unless they have come to feel positively toward the wrongdoer, they have not completely abandoned all their negative feelings towards him."[28] Forgiveness may be an ideal that can be very difficult, if not impossible, for some survivors to experience.

Other psychologists would argue that forgiveness does *not* require a drastic increase in positive emotions, thoughts, and dispositions toward the offender(s). Psychologist and forgiveness researcher Suzanne Freedman believes there are two aspects of forgiveness: "1) a decrease in negative thoughts, feelings, and behaviors and 2) perhaps an increase in more positive thoughts, feelings, and behaviors." According to Freedman, the increase in positive emotions, thoughts, and behavioral dispositions toward the offender occurs, but it does not need to be extreme. I asked Freedman whether she believes that a forgiver must love their offender in order for it to count as forgiveness. She responded, "No, that may never happen. You don't need to love them in order to forgive them. Perhaps you notice a slight increase in positive thoughts or emotions, or maybe you are simply more able to see them as a human being."[29]

Many survivors have been encouraged to experience compassion, generosity, and love toward their offender(s). Some survivors have tried and succeeded, while others have failed and felt guilt or shame as a result, and many have felt unseen, unheard, and manipulated by those who encouraged them to experience positive emotions, thoughts, and dispositions toward their offender(s). Spring writes, "It is commonly assumed that when you forgive, your negative feelings are completely replaced by positive ones. The problem with this expectation is that it is so categorical, that it puts forgiveness out of reach and leaves you with no alternative but to not forgive at all."[30] This unobtainable goal is an obstacle for trauma survivors who are told that forgiveness is required in order to recover from trauma.

This concept of forgiveness directly challenges the notion that the survivors who forgive cannot experience any negative emotions, thoughts, or dispositions toward their offender at any time. On this account, forgiveness is not an all-or-nothing phenomenon but is instead on a continuum that allows various thoughts and emotions—positive as well as negative—to come and go, to surge up and subside to varying degrees and for varying lengths of time.

A WORKING DEFINITION

So, what is forgiveness? Since there is no single, universally agreed upon definition of forgiveness in the field of psychology, we must use a working definition. It is admittedly difficult to build on an exhaustive definition. However, based on research studies, academic analysis, and treatment theories, we can piece together the most commonly asserted aspects of forgiveness.

Forgiveness is a decision to open oneself to, or cultivate a certain level of receptiveness to, an emotional process that results in a reduction in negative emotions, thoughts, and behavioral dispositions toward the offender(s) and an increase in positive thoughts, emotions, and behavioral dispositions toward the offender(s), all of which lie on a continuum. Forgiveness is typically an unconditional gesture, which can involve conditions when necessary.

This definition could be helpful to you and your clinicians as you navigate the process of trauma recovery.

FORGIVENESS IS (OR OUGHT TO BE) ELECTIVE IN RECOVERY

Forgiveness is not a requirement to recover from trauma; it's *elective.* You can experience forgiveness, the opposite of forgiveness, or something in between—you may experience emotions and thoughts along a continuum in constant fluctuation—while progressing in your recovery. The notion that forgiveness is required in order to recover from trauma is the opinion of some clinicians, researchers, and scholars, but there is no good evidence to support this claim and thus, it is unsurprising that we often find that such a claim rests upon ulterior moral or ideological motivations, rather than a genuine attentiveness to the needs of survivors and to the actual complexities of recovery. This is why forgiveness should never be forced, pressured, or encouraged for trauma survivors in recovery. Observing the elective nature of forgiveness means taking the experience of forgiveness off the table, unless you need it to be there or unless it should present itself due to a subconscious increase in receptiveness. When clinicians and survivors no longer view forgiveness as a compulsory goal but rather as an experiential process that may or may not occur along a continuum, they open themselves up to many possibilities for successful recovery.

As we will further see, forgiveness that is not considered elective is simply not trauma-informed or trauma-sensitive. Safety is a necessary element of trauma recovery. Attempting to force or pressure a survivor to forgive their offender(s) threatens their safety and restricts their agency. You should be allowed to explore, discover, embrace, ignore, oppose, or withhold forgiveness throughout your recovery. In contrast, forgiveness should never be discouraged, shunned, or sabotaged for survivors in recovery so long as it does not negatively impact their safety.

What about those forgiveness advocates who cite research studies to support their view that forgiveness is required to recover from trauma? Or those who promote forgiveness therapy as a recovery method for trauma survivors? They may not know or openly disclose the limitations of forgiveness research and forgiveness therapy. If you are going to decide if forgiveness has a place in your recovery, you need to be aware of not only the benefits of forgiveness but also its limitations.

CHAPTER THREE

The Limitations of Forgiveness Research and Forgiveness Therapy

"Please, don't ask me to forgive him," implored thirty-two-year-old Marcus.

"Deal," I (his new therapist) responded without hesitation. "We're officially taking forgiveness off the table."

"Really?" he responded, sounding confused. "But the research says that you have to forgive to feel better."

"Which research?" I asked.

"I don't know. All of it?"

"If I understand correctly, your goal is to address your trauma. We don't have to focus on forgiving anyone to do that," I clarified.

"What?" he muttered as he anxiously glanced around the room. Then he hunched over, hid his head in his lap, and cried with relief.

Marcus experienced emotional and verbal abuse from ages six to twelve. His father often screamed at him, called him derogatory names, or completely ignored him for weeks. At age fourteen, Marcus began instigating physical fights at school and was suspended. His school recommended that he participate in therapy. During his first therapy session, he disclosed the abuse, and his therapist encouraged him to let go of his anger by forgiving his father. "You need to forgive him if you want to feel and act better. It's what the research says," his therapist informed him. Marcus's therapist neglected to explore his readiness and willingness to forgive his father, having uncritically assumed that forgiveness would help rectify his behavior, even citing general research. It seems this therapist was attempting to correct a problem behavior quickly by recommending forgiveness without considering the possible negative consequences of this intervention. Many clinicians all too readily assume that their clients will be fine if they cease engaging in certain destructive or maladaptive behaviors. In short, they are placing a Band-Aid over an infected wound. This is a fallacy of treating a symptom rather than the underlying cause that gives rise to it, and—in cases of trauma—it is one that reflects a failure to adopt an appropriately trauma-informed clinical perspective. Clinicians have forced, pressured, and recommended forgiveness in order to treat behaviors and symptoms, not trauma. If some action (or inaction) is a trauma response, then suppressing it will only cause it to reemerge in a new guise—that is, as a different problem behavior—provided that the underlying trauma has not been addressed, and then this new problem behavior will have to be quelled (which will yet again yield a new problem behavior provided that the trauma of which it is a symptom has not be treated), and so on, transforming into a never-ending game of therapy Whac-A-Mole.

A few months after starting therapy at age fourteen, Marcus participated in his first and only family therapy session with his father. Under the watchful eye of his therapist and mother, his father gave a one-minute apology for six years of emotional abuse, after which Marcus sheepishly replied, "I forgive you." After the session, Marcus was no longer allowed to express anger. Whenever he appeared angry, the adults in his life would say "You have no reason to be so angry," "Didn't you forgive your father?," and "It's time to move on." As a result, Marcus stopped expressing anger as well as many other emotions. He stopped assaulting his peers, kept his head down, completed his schoolwork, and emotionally distanced himself from others. He was discharged from therapy, as his problem behavior had been resolved. He appeared to be a well-behaved and emotionally regulated therapy success story.

However, upon leaving home at age eighteen, Marcus abruptly ended all communication with his father. As an adult, he had few close relationships and would experience severe anxiety whenever anyone got too close. He subconsciously sabotaged his relationships by instigating arguments, making unfounded accusations, and reducing contact. He suffered from chronic pain in his shoulders and arms—which multiple doctors reported had no medical cause—and a weak immune system. His primary care doctor referred him to therapy, having suspected that his physical symptoms were rooted in childhood trauma. Marcus then participated in trauma therapy for four years. In that time, he slowly began to feel safer in relationships. He started by adopting a dog and then made a few new friends. He navigated the frustrating world of online dating, met someone, and eventually married. At the end of therapy,

Marcus had established a robust support system, which he called his "chosen family." Then, near the end of therapy, Marcus *truly* forgave his father.

Forgiveness was not the focus of Marcus's trauma treatment; rather, it occurred organically. This came as a surprise for Marcus, though now he embraced and was capable of experiencing forgiveness, which he had not been able to do earlier in his life. "It's not forgiveness that's not helpful. It's being forced to forgive," says forgiveness researcher Suzanne Freedman. "It's all about the context."[1] Marcus was moved to forgive his father only when he was no longer forced, pressured, or prescribed to do so. Nonetheless, he decided not to reestablish contact with his father, whom he hadn't spoken to in fourteen years. Instead, he focused on his chosen family: the people he believed could provide him with safe and trusting relationships. Marcus's example stands as a reminder that forgiveness and reconciliation are not the same.

FORGIVENESS AND HEALTH

Some research has shown a positive relationship between forgiveness and mental health. Loren L. Toussaint and his colleagues found that forgiveness was associated with decreased stress, which was accompanied by a reduction in adverse mental health symptoms over a five-week period. They reported that participants who forgave appeared to experience a change in their perception of their stress, which in turn ameliorated other mental health symptoms.[2] Therefore, forgiveness may help you think and feel differently about your stress, which in turn can help improve your mental health. Katelyn N. G. Long and her colleagues described a positive relationship between forgiveness and psychological well-being. They found that participants who stated a higher level of forgiveness were likelier to report higher levels of positive affect and improved social integration.[3] These two studies indicate a positive relationship between forgiveness and mental health.

"It's not like the abuse never happened," reflected Marcus on his experience of forgiving his father. "It's just that I feel differently about it all. I'm not angry or afraid. I'm still hurt, but not as much. I feel more content. Honestly, even though I don't want anything to do with him, I wish him well."

Marcus reported an overall improvement in his emotional well-being as he experienced a reduction in feelings of anger, and he believed that the improvement in his emotional health was due to his ability to forgive his father.

Research has also found a positive relationship between forgiveness and physical health. Yu-Rim Lee and Robert D. Enright conducted a meta-analysis study that compared 136 physical variables and conditions (such as cholesterol, hypertension, fibromyalgia, lupus, and sleep quality) in order to identify any relationship between those physical variables and conditions and the extent to which participants forgave those who treated them unjustly. They found a positive relationship that indicates that the more you forgive, the more likely you are to report better overall physical health.[4] Martina A. Waltman and her colleagues sought to explore the impact of forgiveness on coronary artery disease (CAD). They found that forgiveness interventions reduced anger-induced myocardial ischemia in patients with CAD.[5] Loren L. Toussaint and his colleagues reviewed fifty-five research studies and found that 73 percent of these studies showed that forgiveness had some positive relationship to health.[6] As a result of these findings, researchers have strongly encouraged conducting further studies to explore the potential physical health benefits of forgiveness.

"Do you realize how long it's been since you've been sick?" I asked Marcus.

"It's been a while," he responded, smiling.

"It's been over three months. You haven't had a cold, the flu, or any type of illness. Also, you haven't had much pain in your arms or shoulders."

"I know. It's so strange. I've lived with that for so long, and now it's gone. I guess this is what it's like to feel healthy."

At the end of therapy, Marcus reported a significant reduction in anger, anxiety, illness, and chronic pain, and an increase in feelings of safety and empowerment and, ultimately, the ability to experience attachment and joy. Did Marcus's forgiveness positively impact his health? Or was it the trauma therapy, not forgiveness, that did it? Or perhaps it was both? Since Marcus was not a participant in a research study, we will never know to what degree either experience positively impacted his health. However, even research studies aren't always able to provide such information with precision, and often, their findings can be misunderstood by the general public.

LIMITATIONS IN SAMPLING

When researchers or writers present their results to a general audience, they typically do so in the form of a brief synopsis in an article, blog, or social media post, as they must present their research in a manner that is accessible to a wide, nonspecialist or nonacademic readership. I utilized the same method in presenting the five studies I just mentioned above. When doing so, writers often exclude detailed information that could change a reader's perception of the study's results. One piece of information that writers often exclude is the nature of the sample from which the study's results have been derived—that is, details concerning the people who were actually studied.

Imagine reading an article with the following headline: *Research Shows That Psychotherapists Are Fifty Times More Likely to Develop Post-Traumatic Stress Disorder.* If I read this headline, I'd feel quite concerned about my colleagues (and myself). Yet, if I look at the study itself rather than the article on it, I might find additional information that would calm my nerves. I may discover that the researchers studied twenty-five psychotherapists who were all Hispanic women from the same small town in which multiple racially motivated hate crimes had occurred in the past five years. In addition, all participants in the study were recruited from trauma support groups. Does this study indicate that psychotherapists are fifty times more likely to develop PTSD? No. The study used a small and significantly biased sample. A better headline would be: *Research Shows That Hispanic Cis Women Psychotherapists Who Live in a Community Experiencing Racial Violence Are Fifty Times More Likely to Develop PTSD.* This headline is far more accurate, whereas the original headline was grossly misleading and dishonest. These women live in a community in which they are not safe, are providing therapy to traumatized community members, and are also aware of the impact of trauma upon themselves by participating in a trauma survivor support group. This group of women is clearly not representative of all or most psychotherapists.

Location Bias

Multiple forgiveness studies involve participants who live in the Midwest of the United States because the study's researchers are often affiliated with colleges and universities often located in the Midwest. Can we generalize Midwest residents to the rest of the population in the United States? No, we cannot, as there are significant cultural differences across different geographical regions in the United States. Those who, like myself, were born and raised in the Midwest know that there are general cultural differences between midwesterners and, say, southerners, people from the West Coast, and people from the East Coast. Midwestern people tend to be friendly and willing to go out of their way to help others, even strangers. Is it possible that midwestern people are more culturally susceptible to forgiving? Perhaps. Are they most likely to report positive impacts as a result of forgiving? They may be. Therefore, the location in which this study was conducted can cause sampling limitations, which should be considered when interpreting the study's results.

Self-selection Bias

Multiple forgiveness studies utilize a convenience sample: researchers subjectively select participants at random, which often relies on location and accessibility. In contrast, a simple random sample occurs when researchers select participants from a larger group, and each participant has the same chance of being selected. For example, every college student is given a number, and those numbers are drawn in a lottery, and those whose numbers were drawn participate in the study. A simple random sample is more likely to represent a population than a convenience sample, which is prone to self-selection bias, where participants in a study select themselves instead of being randomly chosen to participate. Imagine that members of the International Forgiveness Institute forwarded a study's advertisements to their members in order to encourage their participation. This would likely bias the sample in support of forgiveness, and the researchers may never know.

Demographic Bias

Multiple forgiveness studies include samples that lack diversity and do not represent the general population. For example, some studies include mostly or only white female participants. Are women more likely to benefit from forgiveness than men? Are women perhaps more socialized to forgive than men, or is forgiveness perhaps a culturally gendered or "feminized" value? We have to consider these questions before we consider applying these studies to a general population. In addition, few forgiveness studies include a sample of trauma survivors, as most studies do not include survivors. Forgiving an offense that did not induce trauma can be a significantly different experience compared to forgiving an offense that did. Before you consider referring to a research study to dictate your recovery, you should ask if the sample of participants is a good representation of a general population or a population that includes you.

How Can You Discover Sampling Limitations?

The next time you read about a research study that you feel applies to you, ask yourself these questions:

- How many participants were studied?
- How did the researchers find them (fliers on college campuses, advertisements online, doctor referrals, students of the professor conducting the study, etc.)?
- What are the sample's demographics (sex, gender, age, race, ethnicity, nationality, religion, education, class, employment, ability, geographic location, etc.)?
- Does this sample consist of participants who are comparable to me?

You can find this information by accessing the study's report from the journal in which it was published, or you can request a copy from the researchers themselves. You can also access studies on websites such as JSTOR, ResearchGate, Academia.edu, the National Library of Medicine, APA PsycNet, and university libraries. When reading the report, look for the section titled "Method," and then look for subsections titled either "Participants" or "Sample," as these will include details about the study's participants. You can also read the sections titled "Discussion" or "Limitations of the study," which may report sample limitations.

CORRELATION DOES NOT IMPLY CAUSATION

Yu-Rim Lee and Robert D. Enright conducted a meta-analysis study that concluded that the more people forgave, the generally physically healthier they reported to be. Of all the studies mentioned thus far, this has the largest and most diverse sample size, and the findings were consistent regardless of age, gender, race, education level, or employment status.[7] A writer might refer to this study in an article and use the sensationalistic headline FORGIVE OR DIE!, thinking that this study proves that forgiveness improves physical health. Yet, this study (like many studies) doesn't necessarily demonstrate that.

Most research studies report either a correlation or a lack of correlation between two phenomena; that is, a statistical relationship between the incidence of one variable and another. A positive correlation occurs when an increase in one variable leads to an increase in another. In contrast, a negative correlation occurs when one variable increases while the other decreases, and vice versa. For example, a study may indicate that the taller you are, the more you will weigh—a positive correlation—while another study may show that the more physical movement you engage in, the less you weigh—a negative correlation. Also, a study may indicate that no correlational relationship exists at all.

Yu-Rim Lee and Robert D. Enright reported a positive correlation between forgiveness and improved physical health (i.e., the more inclined a person is to forgive others, the better their overall physical health tends to be).[8] One might interpret this to mean that forgiveness improves one's physical health. However, the study in question does not prove that. Correlations are never alone sufficient to prove a causal connection between variables. That is, just because variable A is, say, positively correlated with variable B, it does not logically follow that A causes B. To use just one often-cited example, there's a positive correlation between sales of ice cream and drownings (that is, as sales of ice cream increase, so too do occurrences of drownings). However, it is clearly absurd to suppose this shows that ice cream causes people to drown. In this case, the positive correlation between the two variables is explained by an underlying cause for both of them, namely that ice cream sales and drownings both increase during hot summer months, when people are more likely to both consume ice cream and go swimming. Thus, the study in question does not show that forgiving *will* improve physical health or that forgiveness *causes* an improvement in physical health. The dramatic headline "Forgive or Die!" implies causation, though the study in question only, at best, demonstrates a correlation. Unfortunately, many popularized accounts of scientific studies either conflate correlation with causation or elide the distinction between them altogether. So, an accurate headline would be "Study Finds a Positive Correlation Between Forgiving and Physical Health." However, this headline is less likely to get as much attention as its more dramatic yet misleading alternative, "Forgive of Die!"

A correlation is one piece of a complex puzzle, and it's rarely the piece that solves the puzzle. What type of relationship does forgiveness have with physical health? There are many explanations for this relationship. Here are a few:

- Forgiving improves physical health.
- Healthier people are more able to forgive than those who are less healthy.
- Healthier people are more likely to benefit from forgiveness than those who are less healthy.
- People in physical recovery are more able to forgive than those who are not recovering.
- Healthier people who have not experienced trauma are more able to forgive than unhealthy people who have experienced trauma.
- Healthier people who forgive have certain positive personality traits (agreeableness, compassion, etc.), and it is these personality traits— not forgiveness itself—that tend to improve physical well-being.
- Healthier people tend to be wealthier or more privileged, and wealthier or more privileged people are less likely to belong to oppressed or marginalized populations, which means they are generally less susceptible to the sorts of stressors or to the negative emotions and dispositions that would disincline them toward forgiveness, as well as less likely to suffer from the kinds of wrongs or injustices that are the most difficult to forgive.

Which of these relationships are accurate, and which are not? We don't know. Yu-Rim Lee and Robert D. Enright write, "Because the results are correlational, more forgiveness interventions may be needed to examine the causal effect of the relation between forgiveness of others and PH (physical health)."[9]

Researchers would love to conduct studies that show causation, but the process is not easy. Loren L. Toussaint and his colleagues reviewed fifty-five research studies. They found that 73 percent of these studies showed that forgiveness had some positive relationship to health. However, the researchers were fully aware of the limitations of correlational data, writing that "to be more useful, correlational studies need to employ large, representative samples and implement longitudinal or prospective designs that follow participants over extended periods of time."[10] These types of studies are costly and time-consuming. Universities, researchers, and funding organizations must make a significant commitment of time and money, which is why such studies are not often conducted.

How Can You Discover If a Study Reports Correlation and/or Causation?

Correlation and causation can occur together, but not always. Causation implies correlation. However, the opposite is not true. Here's a helpful phrase to remember when you read any research study: *correlation does not imply causation*. Good researchers are fully aware of the limitations of their studies, whose results tend to indicate correlation rather than causation; thus, they will often qualify their findings by saying "further research is needed" in order to remind readers that these findings are not the final piece of this complex puzzle.

To find out whether a study reports a correlational or causal relationship, look at the sections titled *Results* or *Discussion* near the end of the report. Studies that indicate correlations will use phrases such as *statistically significant*, *relationship*, and *correlation*. Studies that indicate causation usually identify their study as a *randomized experiment* or *randomized control trial (RCT)*, or will use the term *causation*. Also, the sections titled *Discussion* or *Limitations of the study* will often remind the reader about whether the study reports correlation or causation.

The limitations of sampling and correlational data typically impact research on the relationship between forgiveness and health. Moreover, they also impact research concerning the practice and effectiveness of forgiveness therapy.

FORGIVENESS IN THERAPY VS. FORGIVENESS THERAPY

Forgiveness can be a part of many psychotherapy modalities. When forgiveness is a part of therapy, you, the client, ideally should be permitted to discuss, pursue, reject, or experience forgiveness as it meets your needs; you can explore your thoughts, feelings, and needs regarding forgiveness, and few restrictions are placed upon this exploration. You are not pressured, forced, prescribed, or encouraged to forgive. Instead, it's *you* who identifies what you need in regard to forgiveness. Forgiveness is thus viewed as an *elective* rather than a compulsory aspect of treatment. However, some clinicians practice *forgiveness therapy* (not merely forgiveness *in* therapy), which is a psychotherapeutic modality that considers forgiveness to be a necessary part of recovery.

Forgiveness therapy is a specific type of psychotherapy whose goal is for the client to achieve forgiveness. Thus, it is a modality in which forgiveness is actively encouraged and promoted. Prominent forgiveness researchers Robert D. Enright and Richard P. Fitzgibbons define forgiveness therapy as "a way for both client and therapist to examine those situations in which the client was or is treated unfairly for the express purpose of helping the person to understand the offender, to learn to slowly let go of anger with the person and, over time, to make a moral response of goodness toward the offender or offenders."[11] There is no concept of elective forgiveness in forgiveness therapy since forgiveness therapy conceptualizes forgiveness as *necessary* for recovery. Forgiveness therapy encompasses multiple treatment models, but two of them stand out because they are the most established and supported by research: Everett Worthington Jr.'s REACH model of forgiveness and Robert D. Enright's process model of forgiveness.

FORGIVENESS THERAPY:
WORTHINGTON'S REACH FORGIVENESS MODEL

Everett Worthington Jr. developed the REACH model of forgiveness as a self-help tool for use in clinical and nonclinical environments. It's a five-step sequential model, which goes as follows:

1. **R**ecall the hurt.
2. **E**mpathize with the one who hurt you.
3. Give an **A**ltruistic gift of forgiveness.
4. **C**ommit to the forgiveness you experienced.
5. **H**old on to forgiveness.

You are asked to choose one specific hurt that you would like to forgive and to focus on it as you progress through each step. The REACH forgiveness model might benefit you if you need an easily accessible, brief, and cost-effective approach to forgiveness therapy. This model is highly flexible, as you can use it either in therapy or on your own. The free REACH workbook can be found at evworthington-forgiveness.com.[12] This model can be successful for some, but not everyone, and especially not trauma survivors.

There are significant limitations to the REACH forgiveness model for trauma survivors. The model is a skills-based approach that provides fewer opportunities for emotional processing. *Emotional processing* can be thought of as an umbrella term referring to multiple mechanisms and processes that allow the person to move from emotional disturbance to resolution.[13] Emotional processing is a vital ingredient in trauma recovery, as without it, you must attempt to think your way out of your trauma, which is rarely successful. REACH Forgiveness can help you learn the skills necessary to forgive, but you may require extensive emotional processing before these skills can be effective. Trauma means being stuck in certain physical, emotional, and cognitive responses, not simply lacking skills. Perhaps it's possible to practice forgiveness skills on minor offenses and then work up to forgiving offenses that caused trauma. Yet, in my experience, the bulk of trauma therapy consists of emotional processing, which requires you to fully experience emotions such as rage, fear, and grief. This process can take months or years, yet REACH, as reported by Worthington, takes only six hours.[14]

Worthington's REACH Forgiveness was not created to aid in trauma recovery. The model is brief, simple, mainly skills-focused, and does not appear to meet the needs of survivors. Researcher Nathaniel G. Wade and his colleagues reported that REACH Forgiveness has not been tested as a long-term recovery method for those who've experienced severe offenses, and it is severe offenses, not minor ones, that tend to be associated with trauma.[15] In fact, I couldn't find any studies that measured the effectiveness of REACH Forgiveness with trauma survivors. Therefore, research is needed to determine whether this model can benefit those who have experienced trauma. REACH clearly states that it is not a replacement for intensive recovery and that it is only intended to be used as a supplemental resource; it also does not purport to be a successful intervention for trauma survivors.

FORGIVENESS THERAPY: ENRIGHT'S PROCESS MODEL OF FORGIVENESS

Robert D. Enright developed a comprehensive four-phase process model of forgiveness, which clinicians can use to provide forgiveness therapy by referring to his and Richard P. Fitzgibbons's book *Helping Clients Forgive*.

This model claims that if participants complete all four of its phases, they are more likely to forgive. The four phases are sequential and have no time limit. The phases are titled *Uncovering, Decision, Work,* and *Deepening.* Enright's process model embraces forgiveness not as a set of skills but as a *process* whose phases participants may repeat whenever needed.[16] Unlike REACH, this model provides some opportunities for emotional processing, which is necessary for survivors who seek to forgive. However, I do not recommend this model for trauma survivors because it has significant limitations in trauma recovery and limited supportive research.

Enright's process model of forgiveness wasn't created to facilitate the intensive unrestricted emotional processing that is needed for the purposes of trauma recovery. As a participant, you are able to engage in emotional processing only in the uncovering phase and are encouraged to focus on the emotions of anger, shame, and guilt. There is no mention of the other complex and overwhelming core emotions that survivors commonly experience in recovery, such as fear and grief. "It is particularly troubling that the 'uncovering' phase with which the process begins does not appear to attend especially closely to identifying what is troubling the patient so deeply about what happened to her, and that later sessions also seem to ignore it," writes philosopher Norvin Richards as he critiques this model.[17] This limitation in the uncovering phase restricts emotional processing, and this restriction can cause you to miss out on vital opportunities that you need in order to recover.

Enright's process model of forgiveness is the only forgiveness therapy model I've found that has been studied with a sampling of trauma survivors. However, the samples used in these studies are very small and have significant demographic biases. One study included only six white female participants who lived in the Midwest.[18] Another study included twenty women, 90 percent of whom reported they were European Americans, which could indicate that they identified as white.[19] And yet another study included only eleven white women, a majority of whom were Protestant.[20] In addition, all of these studies are susceptible to self-selection bias. If you are a white Protestant woman survivor who lives in the Midwest and wants to participate in a study in which you'll be encouraged to forgive your offender, you might want to look at these studies. If not, you may want to look elsewhere. No clinically useful or scientifically significant inference concerning the efficacy of a type of therapeutic intervention for the general population of trauma survivors may be drawn from any of these samples. Simply put, these studies might include trauma survivors, but they do not adequately represent trauma survivors.

Enright's process model of forgiveness is a process-based intervention with opportunities for restricted emotional processing. It is not an appropriate trauma recovery method because we have no evidence that suggests that it's effective with a general population of trauma survivors. Enright and Fitzgibbons admit that this model has limitations with trauma survivors, writing that "a harsh reality may be that some patients were betrayed so deeply that they may never be able to fully absorb their pain. This response to forgiveness is found frequently in those who were abandoned by loved ones."[21] This model is not effective for survivors because the goal of the model is forgiveness, not trauma recovery, and we have no evidence that forgiving supports trauma recovery. However, if you ask forgiveness therapy practitioners, they will dispute this and will cite research studies that supposedly support the effectiveness of forgiveness therapy. Yet, these studies have significant limitations.

LIMITATIONS IN FORGIVENESS THERAPY RESEARCH

Forgiveness therapy has not been proven as an effective treatment for trauma survivors. If you are attempting to decide whether forgiveness therapy is an appropriate treatment for you or your clients, you should be aware of the common limitations of research into forgiveness therapy. To start, studies rarely use the same definition of *forgiveness*. You can read six research studies that report a positive relationship between forgiveness and mental health, only to find that every one of these studies defines *forgiveness* differently. These differences range from subtle to drastic. For example, some studies state that a participant who experiences no resentment toward their offender(s) has experienced forgiveness, while others state that participants have forgiven only when they report having positive emotions associated with their offender(s). When studies use different conceptualizations of forgiveness, they measure different experiences, and it's challenging to know which studies test actual forgiveness and which simply test their own definition of forgiveness.

Another limitation is that studies rarely compare forgiveness therapy to established treatment modalities. Instead, they provide the same treatment to two groups with a time-lapsed completion and compare those results, or they provide generalized alternative treatments such as psychoeducation, a process group, or learning forgiveness or coping skills. Nathaniel G. Wade and his colleagues write that "only a few psychotherapeutic treatments have been tested against explicit forgiveness interventions, so it is currently impossible to draw definitive conclusions about the superior efficacy of explicit forgiveness interventions."[22] I'd love to see a study with trauma survivors as participants that compares forgiveness therapy to established evidence-based trauma treatment modalities, such as Eye Movement Desensitization and Reprocessing (EMDR), Cognitive Processing Therapy (CPT), or Prolonged Exposure (PE). Such comparisons would help us determine whether forgiveness therapy is beneficial to trauma survivors (and whether it is meaningfully more beneficial than these well-established treatments).

Follow the money is a phrase that became popular after the 1976 film *All the President's Men*, in which it was used to explain that political corruption can be discovered by looking at money transfers occurring between two or more parties. When you follow the money in forgiveness therapy research, you will find that many studies were funded by the John Templeton Foundation and the Templeton World Charity Foundation. These organizations have their roots in Christianity, provide funding to studies that explore the intersection of science and religion, and created the Campaign for Forgiveness Research in order to raise money to fund research that promotes forgiveness. The Templeton organizations appear to want to prove that forgiveness is beneficial, and they fund research studies that align with their goals. Psychologist Sharon Lamb noted the probable biases that would shape research funded by such organizations, writing that the Templeton Foundation sought to "challenge social scientists to design research that will prove the usefulness of forgiveness, a challenge that is reminiscent of drug companies who do research on the effectiveness of their own products. We are most likely to trust the findings of independent scientists, not those paid by the drug companies, to show us which drugs are safe and effective."[23] I'm not implying that the Temple Foundation is corrupt. I'm noting that they are not an objective funding source, as they seek to show that forgiveness therapy is beneficial and, in general, have a vested interest in promoting the value of forgiveness, not the opposite. Therefore, they are more likely to fund studies that align with their goals and moral convictions instead of funding studies that may challenge them. If those who research forgiveness therapy are being funded by organizations that have an antecedent ideological interest in demonstrating the effectiveness of forgiveness, those researchers are more likely to serve the organizations that are paying them, not science. When studies that seek to promote forgiveness therapy receive funding, and those who seek to test its actual effectiveness or challenge its effectiveness do not receive funding, this impacts the data that is available to clinicians and trauma survivors.

MORE RESEARCH IS NEEDED

Forgiveness is often viewed like penicillin, namely as a universal cure. Yet, even penicillin has its limitations. Some patients are allergic to penicillin, and there is a growing number of bacterial infections that have become resistant to it. Is penicillin beneficial for some patients in certain medical circumstances? Yes. Is penicillin beneficial for all patients in all medical circumstances? No. This is also true when considering forgiveness therapy. Some research studies indicate a positive relationship between forgiveness and mental and physical health, yet these studies have a number of significant limitations. Researchers commonly say (and commonly state in their reports) that "more research is needed," and indeed, this phrase can sum up this entire chapter. We need more research with large, diverse, random samples of survivors (not solely those based on small and homogeneous populations and participant self-reports), those that use the same conceptualization of forgiveness, and those that compare forgiveness therapy to well-established evidence-based trauma treatment models. As of now, these studies do not exist. Yet, we need them before we conclude that forgiveness should be a goal of trauma recovery. Even then, it likely shouldn't be the *only* goal of recovery.

CHAPTER FOUR

Safety Precedes Forgiveness

"Without safety, you have nothing," said Landon Kirk, my first supervisor and clinical director at a facility specializing in treating developmental trauma. "Your client *must* feel safe. No interventions come close to the experience of feeling safe. If you do nothing else, help your clients to feel safe."

Safety is the top priority in every therapeutic interaction, and establishing and maintaining safety is the clinician's responsibility. However, not all clinicians embrace this responsibility. Some adopt the attitude that they shouldn't have to work harder than you, who they believe are largely responsible for your own safety. While this approach works well in some types of mental health treatment, it is inadequate for treating trauma. When it comes to trauma, feeling unsafe isn't merely a symptom; it's the core issue. Without safety, trauma psychotherapists have no foundation to stand upon. They must establish and maintain safety in therapeutic relationships and spaces throughout recovery.

Most living organisms prioritize their safety; it is a built-in mechanism to ensure their survival. Human brains are wired to seek survival and the survival of offspring, and whenever a person's survival is threatened, their focus quickly shifts from living happily to simply living. Imagine that you're getting ready to go to work one winter morning. The temperature is below freezing and a patch of ice has formed on your driveway, right in front of your car. It's the same patch of ice that was there the day before and the day before that, and usually you take care when walking across it, but today your thoughts are elsewhere. Yesterday, you got a hint from your boss that a promotion is coming your way, and you wonder if this could be the day that your career takes a leap forward. Distracted by the possibility of advancement, you don't watch where you're going and slip on the ice. You fall and hit your head on the pavement, and the injury could very well be fatal. Your brain then automatically switches focus from thriving (getting a promotion) to survival (avoiding death), and your body responds accordingly. Surviving is the priority, and thriving is now secondary. Trauma recovery is the same. You must feel safe (survival) before focusing on recovery (thriving).

SAFETY IS REQUIRED IN TRAUMA RECOVERY

If you take away one point from this chapter (or from this entire book, really) let it be this: forgiveness is not required to recover from trauma, but safety is. "The first task of recovery is to establish the survivor's safety," writes psychiatrist and trauma researcher Judith Herman. "This task takes precedence over all others, for no other therapeutic work can possibly succeed if safety has not been adequately secured."[1] Safety is the foundation of trauma recovery, and it must be established, maintained, and promoted. Recovery efforts built on a weak foundation will collapse. Fancy interventions used in therapy without established safety act as flimsy Band-Aids covering an open wound That's why it's important to spend time building safety in order to create a strong foundation to stand upon.

After I left my abusive husband, I realized that I had no foundation to stand on to recover from my experiences of childhood physical and emotional neglect. I was stuck in survival mode with no room for thriving. For years, I'd welcomed and tolerated unsafe people who benefited from my trauma responses. My husband had a wife who endured financial and emotional abuse, cleaned his home, paid his bills, raised his children, and didn't require emotional intimacy or reciprocity. My employer had an employee who worked longer hours and was more productive than any other clinician for less pay. My mother had a daughter who enabled her selfishness, victim identity, and utter lack of parenting without expecting any love in return. Society had a productive citizen who was a living example of the harmful myth "pull yourself up by your bootstraps." My trauma responses served these people, and so they actively prevented me from building a foundation of safety. They wanted me to remain the same, even though I was suffering. I'd like to say that my situation is unique, but it is not. Many survivors function in survival mode for years without being aware of it. For some of us, it's all we have ever known.

To engage in recovery, I had to reestablish safety by welcoming and embracing safer people in my life while restricting or ending relationships with those who were unsafe. These changes created a strong foundation that I could stand upon, and my brain became less focused on survival and began to consider the foreign experience of thriving.

SAFETY PRECEDES FORGIVENESS

To thrive, you must first survive. You cannot live a fulfilling life when you feel unsafe. Safety is also necessary for genuine forgiveness, as forgiving is a form of thriving. Therefore, you must feel safe before you can forgive.

"I know that what I am asking is almost too much for you, but without your answer I cannot die in peace," said a Nazi soldier on his deathbed as he asked Holocaust survivor Simon Wiesenthal for forgiveness.[2] Wiesenthal, who was asked for forgiveness while imprisoned in a concentration camp, did not forgive the Nazi. Instead, he was silent and walked away. Years later, Wiesenthal questioned whether he should have forgiven this dying man. He asked various people to comment on his decision, and he included their responses in his book, *The Sunflower: On the Possibilities and Limits of Forgiveness*. Some contributors wrote that Wiesenthal should have forgiven, others supported his decision not to forgive, and a few wrote that he did not have the authority to forgive on behalf of others (those killed by the Nazis). My perspective is a little different: I think Wiesenthal was incapable of experiencing genuine forgiveness because he was not safe. When asked for his forgiveness, Wiesenthal was imprisoned in a concentration camp. He could have been killed at any moment, and he knew it. Any forgiveness he gave this dying man would have been a survival response, nothing more. He was not in an environment where he could come to terms with his trauma because he was still living it. Wiesenthal could not have forgiven even if he wanted to, as survivors must reestablish safety before they can experience genuine forgiveness.

As in Wiesenthal's case, you may continue to be harmed or threatened by future harm from your offender(s). If this is the case, you are not safe. You must focus on survival, not forgiveness. And while it may seem a simple solution for survivors to reestablish safety by ending or decreasing their exposure to harm, this is far more difficult than most people recognize, as survivors are often in situations where escaping offender(s) is extremely difficult or even impossible. When caretakers abuse children, the children must decide if they will risk breaking up their family and perhaps placing themselves and their siblings in a situation that will bring about worse abuse. They have no guarantee that they will be safer outside the home, as children are abused in mental health treatment centers, group homes, foster homes, and detention centers. If you are a part of a marginalized group, you must overcome additional legal, societal, and financial obstacles to escape your offenders. If you are a survivor of domestic violence, you are more likely to be killed by your offender not while you remain in the relationship, but when you leave.[3] If you are in any of these precarious situations, you should not focus on forgiveness, as you cannot experience genuine forgiveness when all your efforts are justifiably focused on surviving.

When your offender(s) can't harm you now or in the future, you are safe. Can you forgive then? Like with all aspects of trauma recovery, the answer is not a simple yes or no. Safety isn't just about the reality of you *being* safe, but how safe you *feel*. You might *be* safe but not *feel* safe. This is a common experience, as trauma hinders the ability to assess one's safety accurately. Trauma tells us that we are not safe even when we are. Feeling is just as crucial in trauma recovery as being because these two experiences are often indistinguishable: for us, not feeling safe feels the same as actually not being safe.

After World War II ended, forgiveness advocates might have said to Wiesenthal, "You're safe now. You've survived. The Nazis cannot harm you. You should now be able to forgive." Yet if Wiesenthal experienced trauma and did not feel safe for years after he was liberated, that would have been impossible. Survivors must both *be* and *feel* safe before they can genuinely forgive.

FORGIVENESS WITHOUT SAFETY HARMS SURVIVORS

"He's a monster. He beat me and locked me in my room for days," Charlie shared during an Alcoholics Anonymous (AA) meeting. "I can't think about him without feeling angry."

Charlie began using alcohol at age ten to cope with their stepfather's emotional and physical abuse. By age twenty, they were hospitalized for alcohol poisoning twice and had been arrested for disorderly conduct, as well as for driving under the influence—multiple times. At age twenty-two, Charlie got sober, embraced their identity as nonbinary, and began attending AA meetings daily. AA helped Charlie to understand their trauma and use of alcohol as a coping mechanism, but the forgiveness advocates associated with AA nearly destroyed their recovery.

"You need to forgive him," was the message from Charlie's AA group members.

"If you don't forgive, you'll relapse, and if you relapse, you'll die," said Charlie's AA sponsor.

The AA group and the sponsor encouraged Charlie to forgive their stepfather by spending time with him. It did not matter to them that the stepfather continued to emotionally abuse Charlie; he often called them "a freak," "a drunk," and "a cunt." The group encouraged Charlie to ignore these harmful words and approach him with compassion and empathy. Charlie followed this advice and spent more time with their stepfather, expressing compassion and empathy in the hopes that this would ignite forgiveness, which they were told would help them recover from trauma and addiction. Instead, this exposure invited further trauma as their stepfather continued to abuse them emotionally and physically, resulting in Charlie needing to be hospitalized with a broken leg and ribs after their stepfather pushed them down a flight of stairs. The AA group's recommendation to forgive caused Charlie to place themself in unsafe situations, which led to retraumatization. As a result, Charlie stopped attending AA meetings, ended communication with their sponsor, and relapsed days later.

Attempting to forgive without safety threatened Charlie's survival. Some survivors have even been killed due to pressure to forgive their offender(s), which made them feel as if they needed to continue to participate in unsafe relationships. Psychologist Mona Gustafson Affinito writes, "Workers in the field of domestic abuse, for example, are familiar with victims returning to their abusers because they have been advised to 'forgive' the perpetrator. Physical and emotional injury, child abuse, and death of both victims and abusers have resulted."[4] Those who advocate for forgiveness should be aware that their recommendations might contribute to the deaths of survivors who are not safe. "How many battered women, for example, have returned to their batterers for more (and perhaps fatal) abuse because some counselor advised them to keep trying to save the marriage out of love and forgiveness?" asked philosopher Jeffrie G. Murphy. "I do not know what the answer to this question is, but I am worried that the boosters for universal forgiveness may not give ample thought to such issues."[5] Unfortunately, however, many laypeople and clinicians pressure, encourage, or recommend forgiveness to survivors without considering their safety.

Regarding the risks of forgiving when one is not safe, practitioners of forgiveness therapy say that it's not forgiveness that's the problem, it's reconciliation. They argue that reconciliation is to blame when forgiveness occurs without safety. "The argument seems to imply that forgiving is a way for the offender to keep a sinister control over the forgiver. If forgiving led automatically to reconciliation, then the argument would have weight," write Enright and Fitzgibbons.[6] They clarify their reframe with an example: "Suppose Alice forgives a husband who continues his pattern of abuse. Is she not now open to even deeper abuse? If she misunderstands forgiveness and confuses it with reconciliation, then, yes, she is open to further and dangerous abuse."[7] Many confuse forgiveness with reconciliation. People rarely know or communicate the distinction between these two concepts, and this mistake can cause harm. Practitioners of forgiveness therapy must be aware that though forgiveness is not reconciliation, forgiveness can *lead* to reconciliation, which may jeopardize a survivor's safety. Therefore, all clinicians must provide survivors with psychoeducation regarding the difference between forgiveness and reconciliation and consistently assess the safety of survivors pursuing forgiveness. But at the end of the day, a debate over semantics doesn't hold much weight when a recommendation to forgive could lead to a survivor's death. When forgiveness is dangerous, it should not be a part of recovery.

Of course, forgiveness without safety does not always lead to death. However, it can still harm in other ways. Forgiveness can encourage repeat offenses rather than deter them, giving the offender(s) the opportunity and incentive to continue their abusive behavior. Psychologist James K. McNulty conducted a study that found that the tendency to forgive correlated with continued psychological and physical aggression in marriage. He found that spouses who were more forgiving experienced greater psychological and physical aggression in their marriages over the first four years when compared to less forgiving spouses, who reported declines in psychological and physical aggression. McNulty expressed concern about how forgiveness can negatively impact relationships, writing that "the tendency to express forgiveness may lead offenders to feel free to offend again by removing unwanted consequences for their behavior (e.g., anger, criticism, rejection, loneliness) that would otherwise discourage reoffending."[8] Consequences are needed in relationships, but forgiveness can insulate offenders from the consequences of their actions, causing them to reoffend.

During the first month of Charlie's trauma therapy with me, they told me about their experience with their AA group and how their insistence on forgiveness had harmed them by encouraging them to reengage in an unsafe relationship with their stepfather. This prompted me to suggest, "What if you choose a new group that could better meet your needs?"

"I can do that?" Charlie asked, surprised.

"Why not?" I responded. "Your old AA group was no longer helpful. Why not see if another community could be more beneficial to you at this stage in your recovery?"

Charlie hit the ground running, and within two weeks, they found a new AA group and a new sponsor who considered safety, not forgiveness, the top priority. This group asked Charlie questions such as "What do you need to stay sober?", "What works for you?", and "Do you want to forgive him?" Charlie felt accepted by this group, and as a result, they continued participating in AA, which became vital to their recovery. Months later, Charlie decided to estrange themselves from their stepfather, which their AA sponsor, the group, and I supported, as Charlie reported that this estrangement was what they needed to feel safe. One year later, they received their one-year AA sobriety coin, and have since continued to make considerable gains in their trauma recovery.

You need to *be* and *feel* safe before you can forgive. If you are currently not safe, you cannot focus on forgiveness. You may be safe but do not feel safe, so forgiveness is currently out of reach for you as well. You may have never felt safe, and the experience of thriving feels foreign. However, it is entirely possible for you to both *be* and *feel* safe. The human brain prioritizes survival, but once this priority is met by reestablishing safety, the brain can refocus on thriving (recovery and possibly forgiveness).

FEELING SAFE ENOUGH

People often assume that certain types of traumatic experiences (physical or sexual abuse, combat exposure) are more impactful than others (financial, emotional, or spiritual abuse, abandonment, or neglect). Yet, studies indicate that children who experience emotional abuse and neglect develop the same or worse mental health issues as children who experience physical and sexual abuse.[9] Therefore, we cannot assume that one type of traumatic event will have a more or less significant impact on a survivor than another. What's more, response to trauma is highly dependent on the individual. I've worked with siblings who were close in age and lived in the same home throughout their childhoods, with the same abusive parents. These siblings never have the same experiences or the same trauma responses. They are always different. Comparing your traumatic experience with another's doesn't make sense; if trauma were a competition, every survivor would be a winner. All traumatic experiences are significant and valid, and so all types of safety are essential.

If you are currently safe but don't feel safe, you can begin to establish a sense of safety by accepting that all forms of felt safety are necessary. For instance, physical safety is not more or less essential than emotional safety. They are equally important. In the case of the former, you may need to feel that you are not in physical danger, and that the offender(s) or things that cause you harm cannot reach you. For the latter, the feeling of emotional safety might come when you are in an environment in which you can be honest about your emotions without feeling manipulated or invalidated. There is not one form of felt safety that should receive more or less attention or be taken more or less seriously. Every type of safety is essential in your recovery, especially since survivors often report lacking many different forms of safety. It's common for survivors to report feeling physically, sexually, emotionally, financially, and relationally unsafe.

Financial safety is a common theme in trauma recovery, which may be surprising. However, when you take a moment to think about it, it makes a lot of sense that this is so important. In most societies, financial security creates and sustains many other types of safety. Those with financial security can use their resources to support and promote their physical, sexual, spiritual, and emotional safety. Those without financial security are often the most vulnerable to experiencing trauma, less likely to be able to escape their offender(s), and less likely to receive treatment. In addition, those who do not feel financially safe often feel unsafe in other ways. For example, some survivors living in the United States do not feel physically safe because they cannot afford medical treatment if they become ill or experience an accident.

Some clinicians believe that you will never feel safe until you are fully engaged in the recovery process. In this view, it is impossible to reestablish safety at the beginning of recovery. Instead, these clinicians promote intense emotional processing interventions, such as forgiveness, before you feel safe or are able to tolerate processing, believing that safety will be reestablished along the way. This line of thinking only makes sense if one believes in the existence of perfect safety, a sense of security that never wavers during the pursuit of recovery. It assumes that once safety is achieved, it never goes away, and thus, the intense recovery process can continue uninterrupted. As nice as this would be, it's not how recovery from trauma works.

Some days you might feel safer than others, and the circumstances of your life can change to bring you closer to or further away from the unsafe situations or relationships you seek to avoid. There is always the possibility of a step back in recovery, and that's okay. It's a normal part of recovery. No one feels safe all the time, not even people who haven't suffered trauma. Safety cannot be a byproduct of recovery, something that happens once you start working. It must be the enduring foundation, and to lay such groundwork, the clinician must work with the survivor to establish safety before anything else. The truth is that recovery comes with safety, not the other way around. Perfect safety is unobtainable, but feeling *safe enough* is possible.

Events and experiences can and will threaten your safety. If you've ever had a pet, you've probably seen this play out. For instance, imagine your cat is asleep on your lap. Suddenly, the cat jumps up, looks at the corner of the room, and freezes. The cat's hackles are raised, as if static electricity has made their fur stand up. The cat is in survival mode; they heard something that caused them to feel unsafe. Then, after a few moments, the cat lays back down on your lap and falls asleep. The cat has reestablished a sense of safety and now feels safe enough to refocus on thriving (napping in the open).

All organisms have moments of feeling safe (focused on thriving) and moments of feeling unsafe (focused on survival). They go back and forth, course-correcting as they go. The goal for survivors is not to reestablish perfect safety; that is impossible, and they never had it in the first place (none of us do). The goal is to reestablish actual safety and a felt sense of safety, which promotes your survival and makes you feel *safe enough* to focus on thriving. As you progress in recovery, your clinicians hope to see you become more resilient as your sense of safety increases.

Reflections for Survivors

Survivors who question the importance of their safety can ask themselves the following:

- Am I safe? If not, can I prioritize reestablishing safety?
- Am I feeling unsafe? If so, can I prioritize reestablishing safety?
- Do I feel physically, emotionally, sexually, relationally, spiritually, or financially unsafe? Do I feel any other type of unsafety?
- Do I know what I need to support my actual safety and feelings of safety? If so, can I communicate these needs to my clinicians and those in my support system?
- Can I prioritize my need to feel *safe enough* over my participation in intense emotional processing interventions such as forgiveness?

Reflections for Clinicians

Clinicians working with survivors can ask themselves the following:

- Do I believe my client's safety is vital in their ability to progress in recovery?
- Have I assessed my client for all forms of safety (physical, emotional, sexual, relational, spiritual, financial, etc.)? Am I continuing to assess their safety at all stages of their recovery?
- Does my client always feel unsafe, or are these feelings triggered by something or someone?
- Am I helping my client reestablish both actual and feelings of safety?
- Am I prioritizing my client's sense of feeling *safe enough* before introducing processed-based interventions such as forgiveness?

PROMOTING AGENCY

There is no safety without agency. You must experience a sense of agency to feel safe, as the restriction of your agency was often a component of the initial harm that you experienced. "When we make voluntary actions, we tend not to feel as though they simply happen to us. Instead, we feel as though we are in charge," writes psychologist James W. Moore. "The sense of agency refers to this feeling of being in the driving seat when it comes to our actions."[10] You can exercise agency in the recovery process in many ways. You can choose what recovery methods you engage in, whether you engage in recovery at all, who you work with, and if you do or do not focus on forgiveness. Your agency creates empowerment that is needed in recovery. "Many benevolent and well-intended attempts to assist the survivor flounder because this fundamental principle of empowerment is not observed," writes psychiatrist Judith Herman. "No intervention that takes power away from the survivor can foster her recovery, no matter how much it appears to be in her immediate best interest."[11] Clinicians should never force survivors to engage in any intervention or method of recovery, even if they believe it's in their best interest. This includes the practice of forgiveness.

Advocates for forgiveness therapy will say that they promote the agency of their clients. Forgiveness therapy practitioners Enright and Fitzgibbons pay lip service to agency, writing, "Clinician enthusiasm for the concept of forgiveness does not mean that the client will share that view. Forgiveness always is a choice, one the client is free to try or to reject. There should never be subtle pressure on the client to forgive." However, they then contradict themselves: "At the same time, however, some clients blanch at the idea of forgiveness at first but then change their minds."[12] This is concerning, as it suggests that clinicians who provide forgiveness therapy only act as if they support a client's agency while expecting them to change their minds down the road and consent to forgiving.

Imagine that a survivor tells their therapist, "No, thank you. I do not feel safe enough to focus on forgiveness." The therapist responds, "Okay, I respect your decision. Let me know when you change your mind because eventually you will, and then we'll begin to focus on forgiveness." This is an example of pressuring clients to forgive. Sharon Lamb critiqued the practices of forgiveness therapists, saying, "They say nobody is pressuring anyone to forgive. But, of course, they are. There is pressure."[13] Enright and Fitzgibbons, in describing their methods of managing one's agency, openly admit to applying this pressure. They write, "Many decide to forgive their offenders with great reluctance, and they may state that they do not really feel like forgiving them at all. We usually inform these patients that as they grow to understand their offenders and their life struggles, eventually they will feel like forgiving."[14] It does not seem, from this description, that these patients have chosen to forgive at all. Instead, they are following the recommendation of clinicians who have convinced themselves that they know what's best for the survivor regardless of the survivor's wishes or needs. You need to be able to exert your agency in every stage of recovery to feel safe, and clinicians who nudge you one way or the other are actively preventing you from doing so.

Reflections for Survivors

Survivors who need to embrace their agency can ask themselves the following:

- Do I feel like I am or can make my own decisions regarding my recovery? If not, can I insist on making decisions?
- If I am receiving recovery recommendations, can I ask for options to choose from instead of feeling like I have to choose what my clinician wants me to pursue?
- Am I communicating my needs to all those involved in my recovery? When I communicate my needs, how do these people respond? Do they acknowledge and respect my agency?
- Am I aware that I can ask for a second opinion from mental health clinicians just as I can with medical doctors?
- Am I aware that I can end my participation in any recovery methods or therapeutic relationship with anyone who does not support or promote my agency?

Reflections for Clinicians

Clinicians working with survivors can ask themselves the following:

- Am I providing my clients with multiple recovery options and recommendations?
- Am I putting direct or indirect pressure on my clients to choose specific recovery methods or interventions?
- How do I respond when clients make decisions I don't prefer or agree with?
- Am I checking in with my clients and encouraging them to share their thoughts and feelings about their recovery with me at all stages of recovery?

- Am I giving my clients permission to express their concerns and provide me with feedback involving our relationship and their experiences in recovery? How do I respond when receiving feedback?

SEEING, HEARING, AND BELIEVING SURVIVORS

"Were you a neglected child?" asked my orthopedic surgeon while reviewing my X-ray.

"Yes," I responded. "How do you know?"

"I can see where you injured your knee as a child and that it was not treated. I can see how your body healed around it. It's a common sign of childhood medical neglect."

"Thank you," I whispered, holding back tears.

When I was forty years old, my doctor could see the eight-year-old girl who banged her knee on a fence and told her parents repeatedly that she was in pain. Her parents treated her as an inconvenience and shamed her for expressing her needs. Eventually, she stopped telling them about the pain and learned to live with it. My doctor could see me, hear me, and (thanks to an X-ray) immediately believed me. It meant the world to me, as it does for many trauma survivors who've had similar experiences with people who've created safe spaces and relationships for them to recover.

You may need to tell your story, and if so, you need capable people who can see, hear, and believe you. This doesn't always happen when survivors share their experiences with others. Judith Herman writes, "After every atrocity one can expect to hear the same predictable apologies: it never happened, the victim lies, the victim exaggerates, the victim brought it upon herself, and in any case it is time to forget the past and move on."[15] Many survivors have been silenced, minimized, manipulated, shamed, gaslit, or accused of lying. There are many instances in which survivors told their stories and warned people, only to be dismissed, which allowed their offender(s) to continue harming them and others. Some perpetrators were discovered years or decades after a survivor initially reported their actions to authorities. These survivors likely wondered, "Why did I say anything when it did nothing?" They were not seen, heard, or believed, and ultimately, these interactions negatively impacted their feelings of safety.

Forgiveness has played a negative role in this dynamic, as it is used as a tool to silence us. Many times, we have been told things like "It's in the past. It's time to move on," "Why are you still talking about this?", "You'll feel better if you just let it go," and "You need to accept their apology." Not everyone can or is willing to see, hear, and believe us. It takes courage for you to make yourself seen, heard, and believed, especially if you have encountered those who were unwilling or incapable in the past. You need capable and willing people to validate and believe you, people who will respect your experiences and act to support you. These relational experiences can reestablish your feelings of safety. As best-selling author Cheryl Richardson writes, "People start to heal the moment they feel heard."[16]

Reflections for Survivors

Survivors who need experiences of being seen, heard, and believed can ask themselves the following:

- Are there people in my life capable of seeing, hearing, and believing me? If so, have I allowed these people the opportunity to hear my story and to show me their support?
- Are there people in my life incapable of seeing, hearing, and believing me? Can I exclude or limit the involvement of these people in my recovery?
- Can I tell people what I need from them to feel safe enough to be seen and heard?
  o Examples of needs: "I don't need advice, solutions, or feedback; I just need you to listen," "I need validation and understanding," "I need empathy, not sympathy."

Reflections for Clinicians

Clinicians working with survivors can ask themselves the following:

- Am I capable of seeing, hearing, and believing my clients? If not, am I addressing the issues (countertransference, vicarious trauma, burnout, etc.) that are hindering my ability to be safe and present?

- Does my client need additional experiences of connection and acceptance in our therapeutic relationship? If so, can I provide these experiences?
- Does my client need additional experiences of connection and acceptance outside of our therapeutic relationship? If so, can I provide referrals (e.g., support groups, therapy groups, safe communities) to provide them with these experiences?
- Am I respecting my client's agency if they choose not to share their story with me?

DEVELOPING AND STRENGTHENING SOCIAL SUPPORT

One of the greatest resources in trauma recovery is relationships. Many clinicians believe that trauma recovery can only take place within relationships, and it's not possible to recover in isolation. The harm that causes trauma often occurs in unsafe relationships or due to isolation, and therefore recovery occurs in safe relationships. Neuroscientist Stephen Porges writes, "Safety isn't the absence of threat but the presence of connection."[17] In my experience, if you have a strong social support system, you are more likely to be able to reestablish safety.

Your social support system includes any safe and capable person (or animal). This include friends, family, community members, colleagues, pets, or anyone who is both safe and able to support you. Not everyone meets these criteria. Some people may be safe but incapable, while others may be capable but unsafe. You will have relationships with people who are not members of your support system, and these people are typically not involved in your recovery. For example, you might have a relationship with a family member who is not safe or capable and who you do not consider a member of your support system. For your recovery, you might instead seek out a friend, neighbor, or partner. You may struggle to determine if someone is safe and capable enough to be a member of your support system, especially if you have little to no experience with such people.

A safe person will not intentionally cause or contribute to further harm, and those who harm unintentionally will take accountability, make necessary changes, or admit that they are not capable of providing you with support. A capable person is able and willing to support you. They might be able to listen, express empathy, provide reassurance, give helpful feedback and advice, contribute resources, or simply be physically present. Members of a support system bring different strengths to their relationships with you. This is why I encourage survivors to embrace multiple support system members, not just one or a few.

Reflections for Survivors

Survivors who need to develop and strengthen their social support system can ask themselves the following:

- Who are the members of my support system? Are they all safe and capable?
- Is anyone in my life safe and capable and could be a more active member of my support system?
- Am I providing members of my support system opportunities to support me in my recovery?
  - Examples: Asking for help, allowing help to be given, telling them when I'm not OK.
- If I lack social support, what type of people do I feel safe welcoming into my support system?
- Are there people who are unsafe or incapable and should not be members of my support system? If so, do I have healthy boundaries with these people so I do not involve them in my recovery?

Reflections for Clinicians

Clinicians working with survivors can ask themselves the following:

- Does my client have a strong support system that's made up of safe and capable people? If so, is my client utilizing their support system in their recovery?
- If my client is not utilizing their support system, can I provide opportunities (group therapy, asking support members to join therapy sessions, modeling vulnerability, giving therapeutic assignments, etc.) for my client to utilize their support system?

- If my client does not have a strong support system, can I provide referrals (e.g., support groups, family and couples therapy, social groups) to assist my client in developing a support system?
- If my client has members of their support system who are unsafe or incapable, are we exploring the need for boundaries or other interventions to reestablish relational safety?

ESTABLISHING AND MAINTAINING BOUNDARIES WITH OFFENDER(S)—AND EVERYONE ELSE

There is no safety in relationships without boundaries. A boundary is a line that one cannot cross in a relationship without experiencing consequences. A few common boundaries in relationships are no tolerance of expressions of physical or verbal aggression, lying, stealing, or cheating. In addition to actions that need to be avoided, boundaries can also consist of actions that need to be taken. For example, a boundary might be that one must provide reciprocity, respect, empathy, attunement, and emotional vulnerability. When, whether through action or inaction, one crosses a boundary, there could be various consequences, such as needing to engage in the process of relationship repair, taking accountability, being exposed to expressions of anger or disappointment, receiving limited communication, or perhaps the end of the relationship. There is no healthy relationship without natural consequences, and there are no consequences without boundaries.

Boundaries determine our actions, not the actions of others. We cannot control others, but we can control our response. For example, if I do not tolerate verbal aggression in my relationships, I might immediately disengage from a discussion whenever someone expresses verbal aggression. My boundary is no expressions of verbal aggression, and the consequence is that the discussion will not continue as long as aggression is present.

When explaining boundaries, I often use the analogy of cows in pastures with electric fences. In the Midwest, cows are kept in pastures by fences composed of thin electric wires. Cows can easily break these fences and walk onto a highway, and if they do, both they and the motorists will be in danger. The cows will receive a mild electric shock, but it's not enough to deter them. You might think that cows are constantly roaming onto the road, but this rarely occurs, as the fence serves as a psychological boundary for them once they learn as calves not to cross the line. The fence helps them feel safe, as they know where they can and cannot roam. It also helps motorists feel safe, since they can drive without having to worry about cows venturing onto the road. Too often, people believe that boundaries are a punishment meant to restrict people in relationships, but that couldn't be further from the truth. Boundaries create safety for all those in the relationship by telling us where we can and cannot roam whether cows or people.

Offender(s) tend to despise boundaries, as they restrict their ability to cause harm and require them to change their actions or inactions if they wish to continue to participate in a relationship. Survivors often need help establishing and maintaining firm boundaries with their offender(s), especially if the offender is not a stranger. Many of our offenders are people that we know, such as family members, friends, lovers, spouses, coworkers, bosses, and community members. When we establish the boundaries that we need to feel safe, we are often criticized. This is especially true when those boundaries are stigmatized, like family estrangement. Some people would force, pressure, or encourage us to engage in relationships with genetically related family members who are offenders, regardless of whether we feel safe. To reestablish safety, we often need to identify, maintain, and sustain firm boundaries with our offender(s), and this may include family estrangements.

"Forgiveness releases our need for retaliation, not our need for boundaries," writes author Lysa TerKeurst.[18] Offenders may pressure us to forgive so they can avoid accepting and following our boundaries. However, genuine forgiveness often increases, not decreases, the need for boundaries in a relationship with an offender. "At the moment of the initial forgiveness, we begin building a new relationship that is different than the one before," says philosopher Leigh M. Johnson. "If you lie to me and hurt me, and I forgive you for it, I'm going to bury the hatchet and leave the handle sticking out of the ground." Johnson describes how forgiveness leads to burying the hatchet (letting go of resentment), yet by leaving the handle visible, they are embracing the new boundaries needed for this changed relationship to continue. Forgiveness does not create a clean slate in relationships; that's simply not possible. Instead, forgiveness makes way for a new relationship with new boundaries.

It isn't only offender(s) who need to accept boundaries in relationships with us; everyone else in our circle does too. Those who've experienced developmental trauma often struggle to identify and communicate their needs in their relationships, and as a result, their relationships tend to lack boundaries.

During recovery, this can change as we find ourselves becoming more capable of asserting our needs. I worked with a woman who was a survivor of childhood sexual assault. She had sex with her husband whenever he asked, as she felt it was her obligation as a wife. This was a belief that her parents taught her, and it was reinforced in all her sexual relationships as a teenager and young adult. During her recovery, the wife began to say no to her husband when she did not want sex. This was a new boundary in their marriage of thirty-five years. The husband felt angry, confused, and rejected. He believed therapy was making his wife worse. But with the support of their couple's therapist, the husband learned that his wife had not previously provided genuine consent, and she was not enjoying sex as he was. The husband wanted his wife to enjoy sex with him as much as he did, so he adapted to and embraced this new boundary in their relationship. As a result, my client began to feel sexually safer in her marriage, and their sex life drastically improved. We need members of our support system to understand that we will change during recovery, and as a result, our boundaries and relationships will also need to change. These new boundaries, if respected, will only lead to a healthier and happier relationship, as they enable us to assert our needs and see that they are met. This ensures that both parties are satisfied with the relationship, rather than just one.

Reflections for Survivors

Survivors who need to establish and maintain new boundaries with their offender(s) and everyone else in their lives can ask themselves the following:

- Do I need new boundaries with my offender(s) or anyone else to promote my actual and felt sense of safety? If so, what specific boundaries do I need? What are the consequences if my boundaries are not followed in these relationships?
- Can I communicate my new boundaries to my offender(s) and others to allow them the opportunity to adapt to the changes in our relationship?
- In regard to family members, am I restricting my boundaries because this person is a genetic relation? If so, what boundaries would I need if this person were not my genetic family member? Should I consider implementing these boundaries?

Reflections for Clinicians

Clinicians working with survivors can ask themselves the following:

- Does my client currently have healthy boundaries in their relationships (with offenders and nonoffenders)? If not, can I help them to explore how this impacts their actual and felt sense of safety?
- Can I help my client identify the boundaries they need in their relationships?
- Does my client know how to communicate (verbally and nonverbally) their boundaries to others? If not, can we address this in therapy?
- How do I feel about family estrangements? Am I addressing any of my obstacles (countertransference, vicarious trauma, stigma, my family relationships, etc.) that could impact my work with clients who may need or are engaged in family estrangements?

SAFETY IS REQUIRED—FORGIVENESS IS NOT

We need to feel safe enough to progress in recovery. Therefore, safety is required in trauma recovery without question, and clinicians and survivors must focus on reestablishing safety at every phase of the recovery process. Forgiveness may occur in trauma recovery, but unlike safety, forgiveness is not required. Forgiveness that is forced, pressured, recommended, or suggested without an elective spirit threatens safety. We need to feel safe enough to be capable of genuinely forgiving our offender(s), but the reverse is not true; we do not need to forgive to be and feel safe. Survivors who wish to forgive would be more effective if they focused on reestablishing safety before pursuing forgiveness, but they may not know this. Clinicians working with survivors who seek to forgive can help them by encouraging them to focus on their safety first. Focusing on forgiveness without safety can harm survivors, and this method is less likely to facilitate both trauma recovery and forgiveness.

CHAPTER FIVE

Destigmatizing and Embracing Anger

"I want him to die," Abigail said. "I know I'm not supposed to say that, but it's how I feel."

In 2022, a shooter fired into a crowd during an Independence Day parade in Highland Park, Illinois, killing seven people and injuring another forty-eight. Abigail was sitting along the parade route in the line of fire with her grandchildren.

"The worst thing is that people don't want to be exposed to my anger," Abigail elaborated. "They don't want to see it. They don't want to hear it. They want me to be calm and silent and grieve like a nice, sweet old lady. Well, I can't do that. I nearly lost my family to a madman. I'm angry, and everyone is going to hear it."

We live in an anger-phobic society, where people are afraid of your anger as well as their own. We're taught as children to avoid, restrict, and internalize our rage. We often hear phrases such as "Calm down," "There's no reason to get angry," "You're overreacting," and "Why are you so angry?" They imply that there is something terribly wrong with anger. In this environment that we have created for ourselves, we do not feel safe experiencing, expressing, processing, or integrating our anger. It has become a stigmatized emotion, and this has negatively impacted trauma recovery.

Research studies, psychology textbooks, and self-help literature label anger as a negative emotion, implying that it has less value or is less acceptable than positive emotions such as love, happiness, and gratitude. Our society is obsessed with the latter; there are thousands of self-help books devoted to accessing and embracing positive emotions and managing or eradicating negative ones. Meanwhile, anger has been successfully branded as an experience that must be fixed, neutralized, or treated.

Many people believe that anger harms survivors, offenders, and societies, and treat it like an illness that must be cured in order to avoid and manage harm. People who pathologize anger in this way often lack a clinical conception of the emotion. Though their beliefs and actions are well-intentioned, they aren't seeing the full picture, and attitudes like theirs create an environment in which recovery is difficult. For the sake of trauma survivors, it is crucial that we destigmatize the concept of anger in recovery, and this starts with having a clear understanding of what anger is and what it isn't.

ANGER IS NOT . . .

Clinical researchers, practitioners, and scholars can offer insight into what anger is *not*. A review of the literature reveals that it is not any of the following:

Violence or Revenge

Violence and revenge are actions; anger is an emotion. Violence occurs when any action, such as a physical or verbal assault, is taken with the intention to harm another. Revenge is any retaliating action that is taken with the intention to harm, spurred by real or perceived wrongs that one has experienced. There can indeed be a correlational relationship between anger and violence or anger and revenge. Our anger can drive us to lash out at others or repay the violence they have done to us in kind, but this correlation is not causation. Anger does not always, or even often, lead to violence. You have doubtless experienced this in your own life; someone might do something thoughtless or petty, such as make a snide comment about what you're wearing or cut in front of you in line, which makes you feel angry. But you choose not to act on this anger. As much as you'd like to fight fire with fire, perhaps firing off an insult of your own or shoving the line-cutter in the back, you do not. You instead sit with your anger, as uncomfortable as it is, and move on with your day, having decided that an offense so minor doesn't warrant your reaction. Similarly, we may feel intense rage directed at our offender(s) and never once engage in violence or revenge.

Emotions do not always lead to actions. When you feel happy (an emotion), you might smile (an action), but not always. For instance, if you are doing something that makes you happy yet requires intense concentration and focus, such as playing a sport, you might not smile. You'll be too focused on your performance, putting all your energy toward the game. Similarly, you can feel angry at your offender(s) and never express acts of violence or revenge.

Stories of trauma survivors who have engaged in acts of violence and revenge against their offenders are incredibly popular, but they are largely in the realm of fiction; this rarely happens in real life. "Although survivors are so often stereotyped as vengeful and excessively punitive, most of those I interviewed seem remarkably uninterested in punishment," writes Judith Herman, who conducted many interviews with a diverse group of survivors. "In general, they wanted justice to be centered more on themselves than on the perpetrator, more on healing than on just desserts."[1] My experience as a trauma psychotherapist is consistent with Herman's observations, as out of the hundreds of survivors I've worked with, not one has ever engaged in acts of violence or revenge against their offender(s). That is not to say that survivors don't entertain thoughts of revenge or violence. In fact, revenge fantasies are common among survivors. But there is simply no evidence that survivors who feel angry will engage in acts of violence or revenge or that their anger will always harm themselves or others.

Justice

"I feel like I'm doing something," said Abigail. "I know I can't bring anyone back or erase what happened, but these lawsuits make me feel like I'm actually doing something. It feels like I'm back in control."

Abigail participated in the criminal investigation that led to the shooter's arrest, and she joined other survivors in a lawsuit against the gun manufacturer for their unethical marketing campaigns, the two gun shops that sold the guns used in the shooting, and the shooter's father due to his negligence.[2] Abigail utilized her anger to seek justice for herself, her fellow survivors, those who did not survive, and others who may be harmed by gun violence in the future.

Justice, like violence and revenge, is something you do. It's a public collective action with the goal of establishing equitability and fairness. We can take action to pursue justice, such as participating in criminal or civil legal proceedings, seeking monetary damages from offenders, and changing legislative policies. There can be a correlational relationship between anger and justice, as one's anger might motivate one to seek justice. But just as in the case of anger and violence or revenge, this relationship isn't causational. There are survivors who've felt angry and have not sought justice, while many people have sought justice without feeling angry. In fact, lawyers, judges, and law enforcement officials are encouraged to seek justice as part of their jobs, which they are expected to do impartially and without emotion.

Typically, there is no justice for survivors. More often than not, offender(s) do not experience consequences for their actions. Rapists, even when reported and actually investigated (which can be rare), are often not arrested and charged with any crime and continue their lives without a blemish to their reputations. Many murders will never be identified. Soldiers who commit war crimes abroad return to their homes after the war is over and resume their normal lives. Abusive parents are often never reported, investigated, or held accountable and continue to harm their adult children. People in positions of power and privilege (e.g., politicians, CEOs, religious leaders) will almost never be held accountable, and many are praised and celebrated. Knowing that our offender(s) will likely never receive justice, we must find a way to take our anger with us as we navigate the recovery process.

A Psychiatric Disorder

There is no anger diagnosis in the *Diagnostic and Statistical Manual of Mental Disorders, Fifth Edition Text Revision* (DSM-5-TR). Certain psychiatric disorders are associated with feeling persistently angry, such as explosive disorder and oppositional defiant disorder. However, these diagnoses require action as well as emotional criteria. It isn't enough to feel angry; to qualify for a psychiatric diagnosis, you must also have a pattern of certain behaviors. In addition, many disorders in the DSM-5-TR list anger, irritability, or aggression as symptoms of the disorder, but the mere presence of anger alone is not nearly enough for one to be diagnosed with a psychiatric disorder.[3] Therefore, anger is neither a psychiatric disorder nor an illness that needs to be treated. It is an emotion, no more and no less.

Anger can certainly become a problem, but any emotion can cause significant psychological distress. It is not uniquely harmful, and demonizing it does not support trauma recovery. Anger management, a type of therapy that teaches people to experience, express, and cope with their anger, teaches that anger is a part of the human experience and should be embraced and processed, like every other emotion. This therapy does not at all suggest that anger is wrong or needs to be treated.

Any emotion that feels overwhelming or that you cannot process can cause psychological distress, even a supposedly positive one like happiness. Imagine that you feel happy all the time and are unable to feel anything else. You might struggle to relate to other people who aren't always happy, and your relationships will suffer. After all, if a friend comes to you feeling down about something, how could you possibly understand them? You may also notice a monotony in your everyday life, and your happiness may start to feel stale. "For a long time, there was this idea that being positive all the time was a life well lived, and that's what we should strive for," writes psychologist Heather C. Lench. "But there's more and more evidence that it's actually a life that's balanced by a mix of emotions that seems to be more satisfying and positive long-term."[4] Emotions, then, are like anything else: healthiest in moderation. They themselves—including anger—are not the problem. It's how they are experienced, expressed, and processed that impacts your quality of life.

Unforgiving

Practitioners of forgiveness therapy often equate anger with being unforgiving. They say that if you are angry with your offender, you have not forgiven them, and if you do not feel angry at them, then you have forgiven them. This interpretation is a vast oversimplification. My working definition of forgiveness, as laid out in chapter 2, is "a decision to open oneself to, or a certain level of receptiveness to, an emotional process that results in a reduction in negative emotions, thoughts, and behavioral dispositions toward the offender(s)." Reducing anger, which in this definition is a negative emotion, has a correlational relationship to forgiveness, as one who forgives is likely to feel less angry. However, eliminating anger does not cause forgiveness, and forgiveness is not automatically achieved when you are no longer angry. When you forgive, your anger may lessen without going away entirely. On the other end of the spectrum, you may feel no anger at your offender(s) and still choose not to forgive them.

ANGER IS A VALUABLE EMOTION

Anger, as we've established, is not good or bad or right or wrong; it's an emotion, no better or worse than any other. The APA defines anger as "an emotion characterized by tension and hostility arising from frustration, real or imagined injury by another, or perceived injustice."[5] Like all emotions, anger is a physical experience. When you're angry, you may notice a change not only in your emotional state but also in your thoughts and physical sensations. Your muscles might tense up, you might breathe rapidly, and your body temperature might rise. It can also come and go, quickly or gradually. You may be overcome with rage briefly, only for it to lessen as soon as it came. Sooner or later, it might disappear entirely and be replaced by another feeling. For instance, it's not uncommon for survivors in recovery to feel enraged one moment and then intense grief the next.

Emotions are meant to change, and going through the process of emotional change is like eating and digesting a meal. The composition of the food starts to change the moment you put it in your mouth, and it continues to change as it travels through your body. The accompanying sensations might not always be pleasant, as you may experience nausea, heartburn, or fatigue as you digest. Yet the food will pass through your system, being broken down and altered, until it eventually leaves your body entirely through energy or waste (a processed emotion) or gets stuck in your digestion system, such as with gastroparesis, and causes a slew of physical symptoms such as abdominal pain (an unprocessed emotion).

Anger is a vital part of trauma recovery. The stigmatization of anger can hinder recovery as it keeps us from recognizing when rage is helpful. Instead of rejecting anger as an inherently corrupting force, something to be stamped out, we are better served by acknowledging its importance and reflecting on its benefits.

Anger Promotes Safety

Anger is more than a knee-jerk response to real or perceived wrongs—it is a gift from nature that helps us to protect ourselves and others. As therapist Peter Allen writes, "Anger has been used in warfare, combat and defense since the dawn of time to give people courage, energy and motivation when they need it most—in survival situations."[6] When you feel unsafe, you can experience anger as an automatic physiological reaction. Trauma therapy practitioners call this reaction the *fight response*, and everyone acts on it differently. In a heated argument, you might yell obscenities, while another survivor may mutter sarcastic comments under their breath. When confronted by someone threatening physical violence, you might defend yourself by attacking preemptively, while another survivor may express an intimidating posture to dissuade the attacker before a fight breaks out.

Regardless of how you or others act on the fight response, its ultimate purpose is to promote safety, not threaten it. Imagine that you are standing on the sidewalk of a busy street. Next to you, an unsupervised child runs into the street and right in front of an oncoming car. If you experience the fight response, you might yell at the child to stop and pull them back onto the sidewalk. In doing so, you have saved the child's life.

Of course, you never would have yelled at the child and grabbed them in an ordinary scenario, especially a child you have no relationship with, but this was anything but ordinary. It was life-and-death, which is precisely why it triggered your fight response. Still, you may not feel good about it after. It's common for survivors to regret their behaviors while acting on their fight response, which is why it's so important to remember that the fight response is not a choice; it's an automatic response to feeling unsafe. That rush of anger gives us the strength and decisiveness to protect ourselves and others.

However, while the fight response might manifest as a feeling of rage, it is created and sustained by another emotion: fear. You might say that fear calls upon anger to keep us safe, a relationship that is important to keep in mind.

Anger Drives Social Change

Rage, resentment, and frustration have galvanized those who've fought for revolutionary social change. "Anger seems to have three valuable roles," writes philosopher Martha C. Nussbaum. "First, it is seen as a valuable signal that the oppressed recognize the wrong done to them. It also seems to be a necessary motivation for them to protest and struggle against injustice and to communicate to the wider world the nature of their grievances. Finally, anger seems, quite simply, to be justified: outrage at terrible wrongs is right, and anger thus expresses something true."[7] Anger helps you to recognize when you or others are being treated unjustly, and it can empower you to act. As Malcolm X said, "Usually when people are sad, they don't do anything. They just cry over their condition. But when they get angry, they bring about a change."[8]

"When we believe that we or others are being wronged in small or large ways, our anger can be incredibly effective at giving us the energy to make a change," writes therapist Peter Allen.[9] "A client who is angry about social justice issues may not need to 'manage' the anger as much as channel it." That is exactly what Abigail did. She was driven to combat the epidemic of rising gun violence in the United States and used her anger to create change. She contacted her mayor, senators, and Congress representatives to demand legislative actions supporting gun control. People criticized her efforts and tried to talk her out of her anger. She often heard phrases like "Calm down," "Don't make such a big deal out of it," and "You survived, isn't that enough?" It wasn't enough for Abigail, and she channeled her fury to fuel her efforts to prevent future mass shootings.

Those who oppose change feel threatened by the anger of the oppressed. They benefit if the oppressed fear their anger too; if you are too afraid to get truly mad, you may lack the motivation necessary to fight for change. Activist Audre Lorde cautions against fearing one's own anger, saying, "My response to racism is anger. My fear of anger taught me nothing. Your fear of that anger will teach you nothing, also."[10]

Anger Is Evidence of Self-worth

I rarely felt angry as a child or young adult. When asked to make sacrifices for my parents, I didn't feel annoyed or frustrated. When my value was measured by what I could provide to my mother, I didn't feel betrayed or disrespected. When my family's motto of *your mother matters, you don't* was reinforced, I felt no rage or resentment. How is this possible? The answer is devastatingly simple: I agreed. I believed that my mother had value while I did not. When my parents, family, and society communicated this belief, I felt validated. It was only during my recovery that I started to disagree. That's when I began to feel angry.

"What if you and your mother have equal value?" my therapist asked me. "What if, as a child, you had needs that should have taken priority over your mother's needs?"

These questions, although they made logical sense to me, initially felt blasphemous. How could I possibly matter when I had been taught otherwise all my life? Surely my entire family couldn't be wrong. I felt this way for much of my life, but over time, I began to consider that my value as a person might exist apart from how I could benefit my mother, and then the anger came. I began developing self-worth, and the more value I recognized in myself, the angrier I felt. It was as if my anger and self-worth were connected, and I could not have one without embracing the other.

Anger tells you that you are being harmed or were harmed in the past. "Feeling anger (and variants such as indignation) when appropriate may be a condition of self-respect, and so failure to feel appropriate anger may be a sign of insufficient concern for one's rights and dignity, insufficient self-respect," writes philosopher Jerome Neu.[11] It's common for survivors with low self-worth and pervasive feelings of shame to not feel angry when they are harmed.

Imagine that you are sitting on a train and someone takes the seat next to you. As soon as they sit down, this person proceeds to spread their arms and legs and put all their belongings at your feet, encroaching on your personal space. If you believe that you have the right to take up space in the world (self-worth), then you are likely to feel annoyed by their actions. However, if you believe that you have fewer rights than others or consistently feel the need to put their comfort ahead of your own, you probably won't mind. In fact, you might try to take up as little space on the train as possible, both appearing and feeling small. Your anger signals that you are being treated in a manner that does not align with your self-worth. In contrast, the absence of anger when treated poorly is an indication of your lack of self-worth.

Anger Shields from Vulnerable Emotions

"Hatred, I learned quickly, was the antidote to sadness. It was the only safe feeling," writes survivor Stephanie Foo. "Hatred does not make you cry at school. It isn't vulnerable. Hatred is efficient. It does not grovel. It is pure power."[12] Foo's experience is not unique, as many survivors hold onto their anger because it feels safer than experiencing those devastating, overwhelming, frightening emotions that often lie in wait. You may use anger as a shield against grief, betrayal, loneliness, guilt, shame, and fear.

We can choose to use our anger to protect us, or it can be an automatic trauma response. When we embrace our anger, it eventually runs its course. It often steps aside and allows those vulnerable emotions to rise to the surface. The goal in accepting anger is to eliminate our need for it as an emotional shield, but we cannot discard it before we're ready. Until we can truly confront our deep-seated, vulnerable emotions, our anger keeps us safe.

Anger Supports Trauma Recovery

When I began recovery, I was unable to access emotions associated with my experiences of childhood neglect and emotional abuse. My therapists wisely started by focusing on anger. They encouraged me to embrace whatever anger I could feel, even if it was slight. Slowly, I began to experience more and more rage. I became angry at my parents for being incapable of caring for me, angry at my relatives for not protecting me, and angry at a society that encouraged me to believe that I had less value than others. Then, as I embraced my fury, I became better able to access those vulnerable emotions that often lie in anger's wake.

Grief was hands down the most difficult emotion that I experienced in recovery. I could handle anger, anxiety, and numbness, but I met my match with grief, which fell on me with unrelenting force. It smacked me in the face when I watched children's movies with scenes of parental love—the love I didn't and would likely never have. It curled my body into the fetal position as I hid under blankets, hoping it would leave me in peace. My grief stalked me at night when I was alone and made me cry so hard that I vomited and had migraines days afterward. I was grieving a lifetime of losses that I never expected to feel: both my parents, my extended family, a brother, my childhood, my identity development, and all those lost years. Anger helped me slowly open the door to grief. It held the key to unlocking the most challenging and life-changing experience of my life.

Anger is vital in trauma recovery. It starts by shielding us from those frightening, overwhelming, and devastating emotions that are waiting for us behind that door. We can hold onto that shield until we feel safe enough to open the door and cross the threshold; then, anger turns from a shield to a key. It allows us to access emotional pain in a way that we can experience, express, share, process, and integrate. Of course, there will be times when our anger must change back from a key to a shield; we may need to put that shield back up again, only lowering it once we have reestablished safety or feel ready to continue. Anger is both a protector and key master, staving off threats to our recovery and unlocking it when we are ready.

ANGER VS. FORGIVENESS THERAPY

Anger and forgiveness are often pitted against each other as if they are and always have been archrivals. In this contest, forgiveness is cast as the hero, while anger is cast as the villain. Forgiveness therapy practitioners embrace and perpetuate this manmade rivalry by insisting that survivors must forgive to reduce, manage, or eliminate their anger. "If strong feelings of anger emerge, the patient is encouraged to spend time each day forgiving the offender and working toward understanding and forgiving others from the past who have caused similar hurt," write Enright and Fitzgibbons.[13] This therapeutic intervention illustrates the belief that anger is an obstacle that must be conquered and that forgiveness is the conqueror.

What forgiveness therapy advocates fail to recognize is that the goal of trauma recovery is to integrate trauma, not conquer anger. "A potential solution to these unhelpful conceptions of anger may be that forgiveness or the lack of anger should be set aside as a goal," writes philosopher Georgina H. Mills.[14] "Instead, allowing the victim to come to terms with the harm that they have suffered should be the goal, which may entail letting go of anger in some cases. In this way, the goal is not to control the victim's feelings or communication, the goal is the victim's own well-being." Forgiveness therapy's stringent focus on the contest between anger and forgiveness can sabotage recovery; it obscures the true purpose of recovery, leaving us in an unsafe environment with no way out.

Forgiveness therapy practitioners who follow the Enright forgiveness process model do allow survivors to experience and express anger, at least for a time: During the first phase of the model, the uncovering. In this phase, survivors can acknowledge the offense(s) they suffered and the impact that these offense(s) have had on their lives. This appears to be the only phase that allows anger to be present. The goal of the process model is to complete all four phases, which allegedly results in forgiveness. Once they pass phase one, survivors are encouraged not to dwell in anger any longer. Enright and Fitzgibbons write that people "lose their motivation to continue the process of forgiveness because they want to experience, own, and discuss at length their anger regarding the offender before they are willing to let it go."[15] Although the model does not indicate any specific timelines, the aim is for survivors to move on to the next phase in a timely manner. Unfortunately, what constitutes a timely manner might be decided by the practitioner rather than the survivor.

Imagine that you have been raped, and your therapist says, "You can feel angry for five days, but then you need to reestablish your motivation to forgive your offender." This kind of restriction clearly doesn't work for trauma survivors because trauma recovery doesn't exist on a timeline, and we cannot pick and choose which emotional experiences we will allow into the process and which we will exclude. "All emotions should be acceptable," says Sharon Lamb. "When therapists start to advocate for forgiveness, right away they're saying your vengeful feelings and anger are unacceptable. Or it's acceptable temporarily but it's only appropriate because it produces forgiveness down the line."[16] Clinicians can sabotage recovery when they promote forgiveness. Psychotherapist Bonnie Burstow puts it another way: "By treating forgiveness as necessary, therapists effectively pathologize anger, close down the survivor's own process, and reinforce social messages."[17]

Forgiveness therapy practitioners claim that they welcome anger, as it has a part in achieving forgiveness. However, they *only* welcome anger to the extent that it supports forgiveness, and then only for limited periods of time, which restricts emotional processing and hinders recovery. For instance, if you are participating in the process model and progress to phase three, what happens if you experience anger—which is only permitted in phase one? You would return to phase one, as anger's place in the process model is only at the beginning of the model. It is an obstacle that must be overcome at the start as opposed to a valuable emotion that is welcomed throughout the recovery process. Can you imagine having to go back and repeat phrase one due to experiencing an emotion that is a natural part of your recovery process? You may feel as if you are being punished or perhaps come to believe that you are not trying hard enough to forgive. When anger is seen as a sign of failure, recovery is hindered rather than facilitated.

Enright and Fitzgibbons provide therapists with suggestions on how to help clients who insist on experiencing and expressing their anger: "When clients learn that they may be controlled by the offenders for the rest of their lives if they do not let go of their anger, many finally decide to work at forgiveness with clenched fists and white knuckles."[18] This method, though well-intentioned, is manipulative. Imagine your therapist saying, "Let go of your anger and forgive, or else your offender will control you for your entire life." You may feel forced to choose between your anger and future forgiveness, if it's even possible for you to make that choice. What if you insist upon embracing your anger at all phases of recovery? "With the hostile, mistrustful, depressed patient who misdirects anger regularly, it may be necessary at times to refuse to continue the therapy unless a commitment is made to try to let go of resentment," writes Enright and Fitzgibbons.[19] Their answer, in other words, is to kick the survivor out of forgiveness therapy. Though this is hardly ideal, it might be the best thing for your recovery. Therapy in which forgiveness is seen as optional rather than inevitable is far more effective in trauma recovery.

EMBRACING ANGER IN TRAUMA RECOVERY

"I still want him dead," said Abigail. "I'm doing so much to change things for the better, and it's helped, but I'm still so angry at him."

"How do you feel about leaning into your anger in this moment?" I asked.

"You mean, just let myself feel angry?"

"Yes, and if it ever feels like too much, we can take a step back."

Since the shooting, Abigail had had little opportunity to experience and express her anger in a safe environment. She either felt obligated to protect others who were also impacted by the mass shooting or she felt judged for feeling angry. When we create an environment free of judgment, where we have the time and space to sit with our own feelings, we embrace anger as a valuable emotion that is important in trauma recovery and allow it to be experienced, expressed, shared, processed, and integrated.

Here are a few methods that survivors and their clinicians can consider to help embrace anger in recovery.

Establishing and Maintaining Safety

Your safety is always the top priority. You must feel safe enough before any therapeutic intervention can be effective. Therefore, safety must be established and consistently maintained before you embrace anger, and clinicians should focus on safety before encouraging survivors to dive into intense emotional processing. "I believe that the establishment of safety—real physical, emotional and spiritual safety—is the primary task of counselors working with clients who are angry," writes therapist Peter Allen. "When anger is protective, we cannot expect people to remove their armor if the arrows are still flying."[20] Vulnerability cannot come without safety. It will be painful either way; there's no avoiding that. But when you feel safe, that pain goes from feeling threatening to uncomfortable.

"It doesn't feel like too much. But, if I let myself get angry, truly angry, will you think that I'm going to kill him?" asked Abigail.

"Are you having any thoughts or plans of harming him?"

"No, I wouldn't actually do it. That's not who I am."

"Are you having any thoughts of hurting anyone else or yourself?"

"No, I wouldn't hurt anyone else and never myself."

"It sounds like you have no intention to act upon these thoughts. Do you feel safe enough to allow yourself to feel angry in this moment?"

"You know what, I think I do."

I had this conversation with Abigail five months after she began trauma therapy. During that time, we focused on building safety, which included establishing a trusting therapeutic relationship, increasing her ability to utilize her support system, learning coping skills to manage overwhelming emotions and trauma responses, and taking steps to reinforce her agency and feelings of empowerment.

There is no normal length of time it takes to establish safety. It can take weeks, months, or years—and there is no endpoint where you can just stop. It is an ongoing process, as safety must be maintained or it will fade away. Sometimes, it can even disappear in an instant; you might feel safe experiencing intense anger one moment and then unsafe the next. Whenever you feel unsafe, it's OK to pause your emotional processing to focus on reestablishing a felt sense of safety. Once you feel safe enough again, you can resume processing. This pattern of starts and stops is common in recovery, and although it can be frustrating at times, it's more successful than trying to just push through it. If you become too overwhelmed, your brain will work overtime doing what it needs to do to protect you, and your emotional processing will cease until you feel safe once again. Trying to bullishly force your way past your emotions without first establishing safety will only waste your time, and it can even put you at risk of retraumatization.

As discussed earlier, however, anger is not always productive. If clinicians have reason to believe that survivors will act on their rage and harm others or themselves, they should focus on establishing safety, not embracing anger. Clinicians should feel free to conduct safety assessments whenever needed. I conducted a safety assessment with Abigail, and she denied having any thoughts or plans of homicide, suicide, or self-harm. This intervention was not new to Abigail; I established my intent to assess her safety and informed her of the limits of confidentiality from the very start of our relationship. I made it clear that if I believed she might pose a danger to herself and others, I would have to take action. This transparency created the trust that I needed to assess Abigail's safety throughout the recovery process.

Expressing Curiosity and Validation

"Allow yourself to feel angry at him," I encouraged Abigail.

"There's a lot of it."

"Can you feel it in your body?"

"Yes."

"What does it feel like?"

"It's hot and hard, like a red stone."

"Where is that hot, hard, red stone in your body?"

"My chest, it's always in my chest."

"Can you feel it now?"

"Yes."

"Is it okay to just let yourself feel it?"

"Yes."

"Notice that hot red stone of anger in your chest."

"I really hate him. I wish he were dead."

"Yes, that stone is hot with anger. Feel it."

Expressing genuine curiosity without judgment welcomes anger into the recovery process. We can be curious about thoughts, physical sensations, revenge fantasies, and memories associated with anger. Just being curious is not enough, however; while curiosity helps welcome anger, validation gives it an invitation to stick around so that it can be processed and integrated. Abigail wasn't used to receiving validation when feeling angry, as after the shooting, she was often told to calm down. People urged her to "stop talking like that," said "You don't really mean that," and even gave the most unfortunate response: "If you forgive him, you'll feel better." Many people, including clinicians, give these unproductive responses to manage their own fears surrounding anger. We need to express curiosity and provide validation to ourselves and others so that anger, which is already a part of the recovery process whether we like it or not, can feel welcomed and included.

Exploring Revenge Fantasies

"I want him to die," said Abigail.

"Can you imagine his death? The death that you want him to have?" I asked.

"I imagine it often."

"Talk me through it. How would it happen?"

"It's not that hard to have someone killed in jail. You only need to get to an inmate or a guard who wants money and either believes they can get away with it or doesn't care if they get caught. I would pay someone to have him killed. I don't care how it's done. I'd just want him to know that I was the one who paid them. I was the one who killed him. He tried to murder my grandbabies, and now I've murdered him."

"Imagine doing that."

Abigail closed her eyes, and her face twitched.

"What does it feel like?"

"Empowering."

Talking about revenge is taboo. "Even when we're really angry, resentful, and filled with desire for retribution, we dare not use that name revenge to justify our own behavior toward our attackers for fear of seeming petty, base, immoral, or just plain evil," writes psychologist Michael McCullough.[21] Our struggle to separate thought from action is harmful here, as revenge fantasies can be beneficial in trauma recovery. They bring significant catharsis and reestablish a sense of empowerment after one has been made to feel powerless.

As Judith Herman defines it, "The revenge fantasy is often a mirror image of the traumatic memory, in which the roles of perpetrator and victim are reversed."[22] This is not an inherently bad thing. It can help survivors regain some semblance of power and control over their lives, which in turn reduces the power the fantasies have over them. When I've witnessed survivors explore their revenge fantasies, I've noticed that once power is restored to them, the fantasies lessen or are no longer present. George Orwell phrased it quite succinctly: "Revenge is an act which you want to commit when you are powerless and because you are powerless: as soon as the sense of impotence is removed, the desire evaporates also."[23]

You might be afraid to explore revenge fantasies because you don't want to be tempted to act upon them. This fear is why a focus on establishing and maintaining safety must occur *before* revenge fantasies can be explored. "I have sat with clients who created the most horrendously delicious visions of tortures they would like to inflict on wrongdoers, knowing they had no intention, or even ability, to carry them out," writes psychologist Mona Gustafson Affinito.[24] Similarly, Abigail had no intention of harming the shooter, and when I asked her about it, she gave replies like, "That's not who I am," "His death won't change anything," and "What's done is done." Although she made it sound so easy in her imagined scenario, Abigail had no means to harm him in reality. She had no connections to anyone in the prison system and had no idea how to make such connections. This was good evidence that she was safe to explore her fantasies.

"Notice that empowering feeling. Where is that in your body?"

"In my chest."

"What does it feel like?"

"It's like water, flowing water. It's cooling the stone."

"What does the stone feel like now?"

"It's turning blue, and there's smoke coming off of it as it cools down."

"Notice those changes in your body."

Abigail's eyes grew soft, and she began to cry.

"I couldn't save them. I watched them die, and I couldn't save them." That was the last time that Abigail had a revenge fantasy about killing the shooter, and the first time that she was able to access her survivor's guilt, the emotion that her anger was likely shielding her from.

Abigail's anger paved the way for her to experience, express, share, process, and integrate her grief and guilt. Over the next few months, she focused on grieving and exploring her survivor's guilt, both of which lessened over time. When her therapy came to an end, she hadn't forgiven the shooter, yet her anger had significantly decreased and, when accessed, often turned into grief. She told me, "When I feel angry at him, that's the sign that I need a good cry." Though her anger was largely absent, Abigail continued to engage in creating social change by advocating for victims of gun violence.

There are many ways to explore revenge fantasies, and the method is often determined by how you best access and process your emotions. Ask yourself what helps you connect with your emotions when you are angry, anxious, or sad. Consider what gives them space to change. Does it help you to speak out loud? Write? Engage in movement? The answers will almost certainly be different for each survivor. For instance, survivor Nancy Richards created violent Mother's Day cards, which she never sent, that helped her to embrace her anger at her abusive mother.[25] There is no wrong method; it's about finding what works best for you.

Here are a few ideas of methods you can use to explore revenge fantasies for the purpose of embracing your anger in recovery.

- Verbalize your revenge fantasy out loud (with or without a safe and capable person present).

- Write out your revenge fantasy in detail.
- Write your offender(s) a letter or card expressing your anger and/or revenge fantasy. Do not send this to the offender unless your goal is to involve the offender in your recovery and you believe your safety will not be compromised. It is possible to achieve emotional processing without the involvement of your offender(s). In fact, many survivors never involve their offender(s) in their recovery at all.
- Imagine that you are acting out your fantasy by moving your body. For example, you might hit or kick a soft surface and imagine that it is your offender(s), or you might use your arms and hands to push your offender(s) away from you.
- Create an art project (e.g., compose a song, paint, draw, collage) representing your revenge fantasy.

The goal of exploring revenge fantasies is to embrace anger for the purpose of facilitating your emotional processing. This method is not beneficial for everyone in recovery and could cause feelings of unsafety in those who aren't prepared. "Repetitive revenge fantasies are known to increase distress," writes psychologist Michelle P. Maidenberg. "Violent, graphic revenge fantasies may be as arousing, frightening, and intrusive as images of the original trauma."[26] If you do not feel safe exploring revenge fantasies or if exploring these fantasies makes you feel unsafe, stop and reestablish safety. If you explore your fantasies and notice no emotional movement—in other words, if you are just as angry as you were before, or even more so, and no other emotions are coming to the surface—this method may not be effective for you. Many survivors report that they feel safer exploring their revenge fantasies with a trained clinician or a trusted member of their support system than they do by themselves.

ANGER AND FORGIVENESS: A TRUCE?

Anger is a valuable emotion that shouldn't be feared or stigmatized in trauma recovery but rather embraced. It can protect us, shield us, show us our self-worth, open doors to unprocessed emotions, and help us change our world. Anger was never the villain; it was always a misunderstood ally. Forgiveness was never the hero, only an experience that was pitted against anger.

How can we call a truce between these artificial enemies? It starts by acknowledging that they both have value and a purpose and can exist in recovery as needed. We do not need to choose one over the other. We can allow them both to occur however and whenever necessary. They might come together, and we can have both; one may be stronger than the other, or one may stick around simply because the other is no longer needed. We don't need to perpetuate the belief that one is good and the other is bad or that one is right and the other is wrong. Perhaps, as it was for my relationship with my mother, anger and forgiveness can have equal value.

CHAPTER SIX

Shame Obstructs Forgiveness

"I'm bad," said sixteen-year-old Owen.

"How long have you believed that you're bad?" I asked.

"Since forever. I was a bad baby and a bad kid, and I'm still bad. That's why my mom did what she did. She knew. Now you know too."

Owen's mother physically abused and neglected him for years, starting when he was three. She locked him in his room for days without food and water, forcing him to urinate and defecate in his closet. She would slap, punch, and kick him whenever she perceived him as misbehaving or when he cried. The abuse continued until he was eight, when he was removed from his home and brought to live with relatives. His mother died a year later of a drug overdose. At thirteen, Owen started instigating physical and verbal fights at school and at home. He skipped classes, ran away from his relatives, and started experimenting with drugs.

Owen completed three years of individual, family, and group therapy and had moderate success before he was referred to me for trauma therapy. His family needed additional help; Owen continued to express defiant behaviors, and when he was asked why he acted out, he consistently responded, "Cause I'm bad." His relatives suspected that his trauma wasn't being addressed in therapy. They were correct, but his mental health struggles weren't so simple. Something else was harming him, something that had been completely overlooked: shame.

SHAME IS DESTRUCTIVE

In trauma recovery, shame is not defined by the emotions of embarrassment or feeling ashamed but by a much more detrimental experience. Shame researcher Brené Brown defines shame as "the intensely painful feeling or experience of believing that we are flawed and therefore unworthy of love and belonging—something we've experienced, done, or failed to do makes us unworthy of connection."[1] Shame is created by our emotional and cognitive response to an experience, an action, or a lack of action.

"Can you tell me all the reasons why you're bad?" I asked.

"You want a list?" Owen smiled.

"Sure, give me a list."

"One, I was born," he said, counting on his fingers. "I shouldn't have been born because I was a mistake. My mom would have been happier if she had got an abortion. Two, I made my mom the way that she was. I was bad, and I made her angry, so she hurt me. Three, I didn't stop her, so she got angrier, and she got worse, and I made her worse."

Shame is often confused with guilt, and the two concepts are often used interchangeably. However, they are very different experiences. Shame is the result of how you feel and what you believe about *yourself*, whereas guilt is the result of how you feel and what you believe about *your actions*—or lack thereof—and how they impact others.

Try this simple exercise. Point your finger at your chest. This movement represents shame, as it is directed at yourself. Now, point your finger away from yourself. This movement represents guilt, which is directed at what you did or did not do and how it impacted something or someone. Shame is inward; guilt is outward. Thoughts of shame are along the lines of, "I'm bad, and that's why I acted that way." Guilt, on the other hand, sounds like, "I did that, and I feel bad about it. Yet, I know that I'm still a decent person."

We can experience shame and guilt together or separately. Neither feels particularly good, and both together can be unbearable—but guilt, if channeled correctly, may help rather than harm us. Guilt is more useful than shame, as it enables us to change our behaviors. To feel guilty is to recognize the consequences of our actions and acknowledge moments in which we fail to live up to our standards. Reckoning with that helps us decide what we want to do and who we want to be, paving a path to self-realization.

Let's say, for instance, that you're taking the train back home. It's late; you've had a long day, and you're dead tired. So, you find a seat and sit down. It feels good to get off your feet, but at the next stop, a pregnant person gets on. They move slowly and unsteadily. Every other seat is taken, and no one, including you, gets up for them, so they are forced to stand. Afterward, you feel bad about your inaction. What do you do with that feeling? The next time you're taking the train and someone comes on who needs your seat more, you give it to them. Of course, the path to behavioral change that guilt lays out for us might not always be so straightforward, but you'll find it if you look hard enough.

Shame, on the other hand, does not help us change our behaviors, as shame is focused on our self-worth rather than our actions. This distinction is mind-blowing to those who subscribe to the outdated belief that shame is productive. These are people who practice shame-based parenting, teaching, and leadership methods, guided by the misconception that shame positively influences changes in behavior. Their rationale is that people will be motivated to act in certain ways to avoid that awful experience of shame, but this theory falls apart when you look at how people behave in the real world.

Psychologist June Tangney interviewed 550 children and their parents at three points in their lives: during the fifth grade, the eighth grade, and at age eighteen. She found that children who were prone to shame were more likely to engage in behaviors such as unsafe sex and alcohol abuse and were less likely to apply to college. The children prone to guilt, however, were less likely to engage in harmful behaviors. Her work demonstrated that shame does not teach us valuable lessons or motivate us to change for the better. Instead, shame prompts behaviors that are often self-destructive. As Tangney says, "Shame is not useful or protective. Guilt is moderately preventive."[2] Brown has a similar view of shame, writing, "I think shame is much more likely to be the source of destructive, hurtful behavior than the solution or cure."[3] Instead of helping us improve our behaviors, then, shame makes them worse.

Shame is also self-perpetuating. You're more likely to act in ways that support your shame than ways that challenge it. For example, if you believe you are unlovable, you are more likely to engage in unloving relationships, and you may even sabotage loving relationships. When we are motivated by shame, we seek to confirm rather than challenge that feeling; we are driven to prove that we do not deserve to be happy or loved.

Psychologist Linda M. Hartling's research on shame indicates that we cope with shame in three specific ways. First, we move away from people by separating ourselves from relationships. We might socially isolate, withdraw, and lack emotional vulnerability. Second, we move toward people by seeking to appease or please them to secure or survive relationships. We might dance around our feelings or outright lie about them, avoid conflict at all costs, and engage in people-pleasing while sacrificing our needs. Third, we move against people by directing our anger at those who we believe are the source of our shame. We may express anger, rage, or resentment.[4] Owen, for instance, instigated verbal and physical fights with his peers, teachers, and family. These actions only served to perpetuate his shame. When asked why he engaged in these behaviors, Owen consistently replied, "Because I'm bad," or "They think I'm bad, so I'll show them bad."

TRAUMA PRODUCES SHAME

When our offenders harm us, they clearly communicate their perception of our value. They may perceive us as having less value than themselves or others or as having no value at all. Owen doesn't remember his mother ever calling him bad. She didn't have to; she made it clear how she valued him—or rather, how she didn't—through her actions. As philosopher Jerome Neu writes, "Wrongdoing is in part a communicative act, an act that gives out a degrading or insulting message to the victim—the message 'I count, and you do not, and I may thus use you as a mere thing.'" Through her violence and neglect, Owen's mother taught him that he had no value. She began conveying that lesson when he was three; why would Owen believe any different?

We are not born with an inherent sense of self-worth. Instead, we learn our worth based on our relationships and interactions with others. When we soothe an infant or child, we communicate to them, "You are valuable." When we ignore or mistreat a child, we communicate, "You have little to no value."

Self-worth is a factor in determining whether you will view mistreatment as demeaning or as just. Developmental trauma, which occurs over a period during childhood, often creates shame, as a child's self-worth is undeveloped and particularly susceptible to outside influence. When an adult with a strongly developed sense of self-worth is wronged, they may experience confusion or anger instead of shame, as their offender's actions do not align with their perception of their value. However, a child who has undeveloped self-worth can interpret mistreatment as a reflection of their lack of value, especially if that mistreatment is a constant in their life. As they grow up and internalize what they've been taught about their self-worth, they express behaviors, such as moving away, moving toward, or moving against, that reflect their shame. These behaviors create relational experiences, which reinforce shame. For example, Owen hit his friend because he believed that his friend thought he was a bad friend. Then, Owen's friend stopped talking to him, which proved to Owen that he was, in fact, a bad friend. This shame cycle can go on for years, even a lifetime, as the child's shame (the core issue) is often left unaddressed because the focus of their recovery is usually on changing their behaviors. Soley focusing on changing shame fueled behaviors is like placing Band-Aids upon an inflected wound. You must address the wound, the shame, head on.

For children, the explanation that they are inherently worthless is very accessible, more so than the alternative: acknowledging and accepting that their offender, who is usually an adult, was wrong and that the fault lies with the offender. Children struggle to conceive of this. After all, what if their offender is someone they love? How could that person possibly be wrong? "To preserve her faith in her parents, she must reject the first and most obvious conclusion that something is terribly wrong with them," writes psychiatrist Judith Herman. "She will go to any lengths to construct an explanation for her fate that absolves her parents of all blame and responsibility."[5] Few children have the cognitive and emotional capabilities to acknowledge and accept that their parents or other adults are offenders or that they are capable of making nonoffending mistakes. It is far easier for them to blame themselves for their abuse.

When we are mistreated, we often ask ourselves two questions. The first is, Why? The second is, Why me? For those trauma survivors, adults or children, the easy answer to both is often that we deserved it. We may struggle to acknowledge and accept that our offender(s) are to blame. Sharon Lamb writes, "It is as if we so want to believe in the goodness or righteousness of the other that we would rather sacrifice our belief in ourselves than our belief in them."[6] It can feel easier, safer, or more morally sound to blame ourselves.

Shame allows us to preserve our positive view of our offender(s), even if it comes at a high cost. It can also keep us from having to reassess our beliefs about the world. "From the 'just world' perspective of the victim, it would be easier to see oneself as blameworthy than to give up the more important belief that the world is a fair place and that people get what they deserve in life," writes Lamb.[7] When your shame is challenged, you might feel as if you need to choose between your perception of the world and your offender(s), and your perception of your own value.

However, none of this is to say that shame is an inevitable result of trauma. It is entirely possible to go through traumatic experiences and hold onto your sense of self-worth. "Shame comes when you think that his [the offender's] behavior is about you—about your unworthiness, your defectiveness, your unlovability," writes Janis Abrahms Spring.[8] If you have developed a strong self-worth prior to trauma, you may be less likely to succumb to shame, and more likely to perceive the offender's behaviors as a representation of their flaws, not your lack of value.

Shame is also not unique to trauma survivors. Everyone has experienced shame at some point in their lives. It is possible to experience trauma and develop short-term shame, experiencing it temporarily as you process a traumatic experience. When someone is wronged, it can challenge their self-worth, and they can experience shame for seconds, minutes, hours, days, or months. Pervasive shame, however, can last for years, decades, and even a lifetime, and this is the kind of shame that trauma survivors are particularly susceptible to.

WHO'S TO BLAME?

"You believe that because you're bad, your mom hurt you."

"Yeah, why else would she have done it?"

"What makes you bad?"

"Everything. I deserved what I got."

I had to restrain myself from responding. I desperately wanted to tell Owen the truth: he was not to blame for his mother's actions, and he didn't deserve mistreatment. But I didn't say that, because I knew it wouldn't be effective. Shame doesn't retreat with well-intentioned words. You cannot talk someone out of their shame. When you try, they will almost always react with disbelief. They might accept that your words reflect how you feel about them, but that's as far as they'll go. Nothing you can say will make a dent in their internalized belief that they lack value. Instead, like a good novel, the best way to get your point across is to show rather than tell. That's exactly what I did with Owen. Over the next year, I focused on showing him his value within our relationship and his relationships with his family, friends, and teachers. Eventually, he was ready to begin challenging his shame.

A year later, Owen asked me, "Do you think I'm bad?"

"What do you think I'm going to say?" I responded.

"No, because you're my therapist."

"You think because I'm your therapist, I don't think you're bad?"

"Cause if you think I'm bad, you'll get fired." He smiled.

"That's probably true." I returned his smile. "Why do you want to know if I think you're bad? Does that matter to you?"

"Cause if I'm not bad, then that means my mom was bad. But that's not right."

"Does one of you have to be bad?"

"Yeah, it's someone's fault. So, I guess it's mine."

When shame is present in recovery, there is often one question that needs answering: Who's to blame for your trauma? Is it you? Is it your offender? Or are you both to blame? I felt compelled to tell Owen that it wasn't his fault. How could a three-year-old child be blamed for the actions of a thirty-year-old woman? Yet, I knew that my well-intended words wouldn't challenge his shame. In fact, they could even be interpreted as disempowering. As Sharon Lamb writes, "If we truly listen to victims and honor their perspectives, we see that by advocating a cognitive view of their experience that is so at odds with what they themselves are feeling, by telling them that we know more about their agency in the world than they do, and by informing them that they are sadly mistaken in their perception of choice and free will, we do them an injustice."[9] But while I couldn't convince Owen that he was not to blame, I could help him discover this fact on his own.

When assessing and assigning blame, Lamb states that survivors can embrace one of three explanations: "1) Being entirely to blame for what happened to him or her, 2) Either not having been an agent at all or having made no contribution whatever in his or her actions, 3) Having acted in a way that was both blameworthy and foolish but does not in the least diminish the blameworthiness of the person who took advantage of this."[10] Essentially, we can take all the blame, none of the blame, or some of the blame.

Accepting No Blame

"It's not just me, you know. My grandpa thinks it's my fault," Owen clarified.

"Did he say that?" I asked.

"He says that I should have told someone."

"Do you think it's your fault because you didn't tell someone?"

"A good kid would have told someone. I didn't tell anyone. He also says that I'm a man, and my mom was a woman, and I should have protected myself."

"Do you think you could have protected yourself?"

"Hell yeah! Look at my muscles." Owen rolled up his sleeve and showed me his bicep. He was tall with an athletic build. He might have been able to protect himself now, but not at three years old, and not under the influence of a parent.

There are people who want us to take all the blame because it benefits them in some way. These people can include family members, friends, community members, religious communities, and people in positions of power. There are many reasons why these people might want us to take all the blame. They may need to sustain dysfunctional family, community, or societal dynamics; they might be trying to avoid their own emotional experiences or they might be the offenders themselves, trying to avoid accountability. When someone needs a survivor to blame themselves for their offender's actions or inactions, they will inevitably find real or imagined evidence to support that story. They will provide explanations or pose questions to encourage you to take full blame. My clients have reported receiving the following messages from influential people in their lives:

- You should have told someone.
- You overreacted.
- Why didn't you fight back? You could have stopped them.
- You shouldn't have fought back. You made it worse.
- You made them angry.
- Why didn't you just leave?
- You shouldn't have left. You made it worse.
- Weren't you the one who started it?
- Didn't you see the red flags?
- What were you wearing?
- You shouldn't have been drinking/using drugs.
- Why did you put yourself in that situation?
- Why didn't you report it to the police?
- You can't act that way around men.
- She's a woman. You're a man. Why didn't you protect yourself?
- You should have known.
- You weren't an easy child.
- You need to understand that it was a different time.

These statements and questions encourage us to blame ourselves for the actions or inactions of our offenders, which perpetuates our shame. It takes a great deal of insight and social support to be able to recognize the true intent of these harmful messages and overcome their influence. Owen was unaware that the messages he received from his grandfather were inaccurate and more about meeting his grandfather's emotional needs than his own.

Assessing Your Past Capability

When my clients struggle to place appropriate blame, one of my most successful interventions is helping them assess their past capabilities. Could you really have done anything different? What were you realistically capable of at that time? What were you incapable of at that time? These aren't easy questions to answer. First, you must be honest and realistic. Second, you need to answer these questions based on your capabilities when the trauma occurred, not afterward. It is neither possible nor fair to assess your past capabilities based on who you are now. Often, we ascribe our current capabilities—including our knowledge, skills, insights, experiences, resources, relationships, and feelings of safety—to our past selves. As a result, we appear far more capable and powerful in our recollections than we were in reality. Because of this, we erroneously believe we could have done things differently in the past and hold ourselves unfairly responsible for the actions of our offenders. We take all the blame based on false beliefs about ourselves.

"Can you draw me a picture of you as a three-year-old?" I asked Owen, presenting him with paper and colored pencils.

"Three years old?" he asked.

"Yes, you as a three-year-old living with your mother."

Owen presented me with a simple black and-white drawing of a six-foot-tall man with six-pack abs and bulging biceps.

"Now, can you draw me a picture of a three-year-old who isn't you?"

"Like, some kid?"

"Yes, a typical three-year-old that you may see in public."

Owen presented me with a colorful image of a small child, about three feet tall, with a teddy bear in his arms. Then, I placed the two images next to each other. "Are these both three-year-olds?"

Owen was silent. We sat looking at the two pictures for a long time. I waited, feeling his confusion as his shame was directly challenged. I held my breath as I prepared for his possible responses: anger, avoidance, shock. Owen was contemplating if he, at three years old, really could have protected himself or told someone about his horrific abuse. This process isn't easy. After all, as Judith Herman writes, "To imagine that one could have done better may be more tolerable than to face the reality of utter helplessness."[11] Who wants to admit that they are helpless or powerless?

"Where's my teddy bear?" Owen asked in a high-pitched child's voice, a drastic change from the deep tone he'd affected earlier. "I needed a teddy too." Then, he placed his head in my lap and cried.

Over time, Owen realized on his own that he was not to blame for his mother's actions. He was a three-year-old boy with no bodily strength, social support, identity, safety, self-worth, or teddy bear (which he came to realize represented love). As a result of this shift, Owen was able to blame his mother and embrace his anger at her, which helped him to progress in his recovery.

If you have taken full blame for your offender's actions, ask yourself these questions:

- When you were mistreated, could you have changed anything or done anything differently? If so, what?
- What were you realistically capable of at that time? What were you incapable of at that time?
- Are you assessing your capability, knowledge, skills, insights, experiences, resources, relationships, and feelings of safety based on your capabilities back then or based on your present-day capability?

Accepting Some Blame When Appropriate

Blame is not a zero-sum game. It doesn't all have to be laid at your feet or at the feet of your offender. You can recognize your mistakes without using them as an excuse to absolve your abuser. This is the third option that Sharon Lamb describes, one that applies a more nuanced lens to trauma. This view isn't always appropriate, as there are situations where there is truly nothing we could have done differently to spare us someone else's abuse. Owen, as a three-year-old, could not be blamed for his mother's abuse. When I was a child, neither could I. I couldn't take care of myself; there was nothing I could have done to prevent or report the neglect and emotional abuse my parents put me through. However, as an adult, I do accept accountability for some aspects of our relationship.

When I was twenty-three, my mother hired a family member to remodel her house. This man took her money and never finished the remodel. In addition, he convinced her to give him additional money to pay backdated court-ordered child support so that he wouldn't go to jail. Months later, he stopped communicating with her entirely, and it was clear that he wouldn't pay her back. I was furious. I contacted him and threatened to sue him and his family in civil court and destroy his life. I said some horrible things, and I caused harm. Unfortunately, my mother played both sides, as she was encouraging me to fight and to protect her while acting confused and apologizing for my behaviors when concerned family members questioned her. Luckily, I soon realized that I was reinforcing my family's motto of *your mother matters; you don't*. I was enabling her at my own expense, as I had done in childhood. But now, as a grown woman, I had the wherewithal and power to do something different.

In the end, I didn't pursue any legal action, and I became estranged from a family member I'd idolized as a child. Some may think that my mother was completely to blame, as she created the dynamic that impacted my actions, but that doesn't feel right to me. I had the capacity to respond differently and not act on my anger, yet I let it take over. I was not incapable in the same way I was as a child, and it was important to acknowledge that so I could stay true to myself and my values. I felt guilt, not shame; I regretted my actions without taking them to be reflective of my value as a person. My guilt was productive, as I learned to cease actions that harmed others in order to enable my mother.

While accepting some blame can be helpful in recovery, you can only do so when you feel safe. "It bears repeating that the survivor is free to examine aspects of her own personality or behavior that rendered her vulnerable to exploitation only after it has been clearly established that the perpetrator alone is responsible for the crime," writes Herman. "A frank exploration of the traumatized person's weakness and mistakes can be undertaken only in an environment that protects against shaming and harsh judgment."[12] If you do not feel safe, it's not the time to explore any contributions you may or may not have made to your traumatic experiences and circumstances. You must undertake this exploration only when it's in *your* best interest. If someone else prompts you to assess and assign your culpability, it might be a ploy for them to meet their own needs at your expense. Perpetrators and other self-interested parties often use manipulative methods such as blame shifting, victim blaming, and gaslighting, and these will only reinforce your shame.

Accepting some blame when it's justified and safe to do so can have a positive impact on challenging shame. It helps us gather information that we can use in the future to keep ourselves safe and improve our relationships and quality of life. As philosopher Jerome Neu explains, "Clarifying the part you actually did play could show you something you could change if you wish in order to avoid having someone else treat you in this way."[13] I learned not to enable my mother, as this causes harm to me, to her, and to others. Sadly, more family members have chosen to estrange themselves from me as a result of this change in our relationship, as they need me to enable her because they need our dysfunctional family dynamic to remain intact. This is common when one breaks a cycle of trauma or refuses to participate in a dysfunctional family dynamic; they become the black sheep.

Shame is the bane of my existence both as a trauma therapist and as a survivor, as it is one of the most difficult obstacles to overcome in recovery. It can masquerade as guilt, pessimism, or having a low opinion of yourself, but the reality is that it's much more damaging and invasive, as shame erodes the fabric of our self-worth and identity. Shame also prevents us from assigning appropriate blame, which hinders our recovery. And, importantly, shame can make forgiving our offender(s) impossible.

SHAME OBSTRUCTS FORGIVENESS

Self-worth must precede forgiveness; you need some level of self-worth before you can forgive. "Within the definition of forgiveness is the implicit idea that people possess at least a moderate degree of self-respect, self-esteem, or perhaps, ego strength to be able to forgive," writes forgiveness researcher Nathaniel Wade and his colleagues.[14] Shame corrodes self-worth, and without self-worth, we may not be able to forgive, even if we want to. One precondition of forgiveness is that you must be able to take on the perspective of another person: your offender. This requires a foundation (self-worth) to stand upon. If you believe that you have value and someone wrongs you, you're not only able to recognize that you've been wronged but can also consider the offender's experience. If you don't believe that you have value, it might be impossible for you to consider the experience of your offender, as you are blocked by shame. "They're right and I'm wrong" will likely be the extent of your consideration.

When I was thirty-two, my boss assigned me the smallest, darkest therapy office in the building. My colleagues assumed that I would be angry, as I was given what they called "Satan's Closet." Instead, I was resigned. I didn't bother considering my boss's intention; I believed that I deserved the worst office because I had little value. A few years later, when I was thirty-six, my boss reassigned me to a small, windowless office in a new building. Meanwhile, therapists who were newly hired, less experienced, and served fewer clients were assigned larger, more beautiful offices with windows. This time, I felt angry. I had completed three years of trauma recovery, and I believed I had value and that I was being treated unfairly. I questioned my boss, who informed me that I was "more adaptable and flexible," whereas my colleagues were "pickier and high-maintenance." Although I was still upset, I was able to understand that my boss was attempting to make her employees happy and avoid conflicts. She wasn't trying to harm or disrespect me.

My self-worth and lack of shame helped me to consider my boss's experience, and I was able to empathize with her. I quickly forgave her and informed her that I would need a new office, as she had underestimated my needs and expectations—a reminder that forgiveness and boundaries do not conflict. My boss was receptive, and a month later, I moved into a lovely new office with some of the largest windows in the building.

Shame can become a significant roadblock in forgiving your offender(s), as it is the antithesis of self-worth. If you do not believe you have been harmed but rather brought harm upon yourself, you will not even consider forgiveness. After all, in that view, you're the one at fault. To forgive, you must first be secure in your own value as a person. Forgiveness advocates, however, believe it's the process of forgiving that supports self-worth. "With forgiveness, a client's self-worth is restored because they respect themselves enough to admit what was done to them was wrong," writes forgiveness researchers Suzanne Freedman and Tiffany Clark-Zarifkar.[15] This theory may apply if you did not experience shame before or after being wronged. But if you did, shame will most often prevent you from acknowledging and accepting that you were wronged. How can we forgive our offenders if we absolve them of blame? I didn't realize that my boss wronged me by assigning me Satan's Closet, because I believed that's what I deserved. So, there was nothing to forgive. I could not forgive her as a method to restore my self-worth; shame made that impossible.

Shame does not have a correlational relationship with forgiveness. Psychologist Varda Konstam and her colleagues collected data from 138 graduate students and found that guilt-proneness, not shame-proneness, had a positive relationship with forgiveness. Participants who were prone to guilt were more likely to engage in conflict resolution and forgiveness, while those prone to shame were less likely to engage in forgiveness.[16] Therefore, experiencing guilt can possibly motivate you to forgive, but experiencing shame may not. In fact, I've noticed that my clients who experience shame are more likely to act in ways antithetical to forgiveness, such as avoiding or instigating conflicts, sabotaging relationships, or isolating themselves socially.

WHEN FORGIVENESS REINFORCES SHAME

If you plan to have any type of relationship with your offender(s), they must make changes, or your forgiveness will reinforce your shame. Psychologist Laura B. Luchies and her colleagues investigated how forgiveness impacts self-worth. They conducted two experiments and two longitudinal studies to measure what they called *the Doormat Effect*, which is the idea that your self-esteem will be negatively impacted if you forgive an offender who makes no behavioral changes and they continue to harm you. They found that forgiveness can be beneficial if offenders meet certain conditions. They wrote that the perpetrator needs to act "in a manner that signals that the victim will be safe and valued in a continued relationship with the perpetrator, and examples of appropriate actions are acting in a generally agreeable manner and making amends."[17] Therefore, if your offender makes authentic and consistent positive behavioral changes, and you then forgive them, your self-worth is unlikely to be negatively impacted. In conjunction, the researchers found evidence of the Doormat Effect. If your offender doesn't make positive changes and you forgive them anyway and they continue to offend, your self-worth will likely be diminished and your shame reinforced. Luchies and her colleagues write: "Victims' self-respect and self-concept clarity are determined not only by their own decision whether to forgive or not but also by their perpetrator's decision whether to act in a manner that signals that the victim will be safe and valued or not."[18] Offenders will often try to force, pressure, or encourage victims to forgive without making any meaningful changes in their behavior or attempting to repair their relationship. These offenders want to have their cake and eat it too, so to speak: they seek absolution without acknowledging their responsibility, putting the burden of blame solely on the survivor.

Forgiveness advocates will never admit that forgiveness can reinforce shame. Instead, they maintain that withholding forgiveness will harm you, even when your offender(s) do not make authentic and consistent positive changes. Enright writes that "an offended person who refuses to forgive until certain contingencies are met suffers twice: once in the original offense and again as he or she is obligated or retain resentment, along with its concomitant negative cognitions and perhaps even negative behaviors . . . To forgive, then, is to show self-respect."[19] This guidance is common among forgiveness therapy practitioners and advocates, and it's damaging to those who experience shame. Well-intentioned though they may be, these practitioners and advocates reverse the order; forgiveness is a result of self-worth, not the other way around. Advice like Enright's is tantamount to telling victims that they have no self-respect unless they forgive, and if they cannot forgive, then they will fail to achieve self-respect.

Enright's position is unsurprising given his failure to recognize the role shame plays in recovery; his forgiveness process model does not adequately address the impact of shame on one's ability to forgive. In the process model, shame is briefly addressed in the uncovering phase, but it is completely absent in the remainder of the phases. This brief intervention might be effective if you don't experience shame, experience little shame, or have a strongly established self-worth. If you experience shame on any meaningful level, however, the model will be completely ineffective.

Whether or not we are trauma survivors will have a tremendous impact on the way our shame impacts our ability to forgive. Practitioners of forgiveness therapy often warn against clinging to anger and resentment, believing that such feelings only harm the victim, but they fail to realize that this conceptualization cannot be applied to trauma survivors. Activist David Bedrick puts it quite clearly: "Much of the counsel is downright offensive, suggesting that if we can't forgive, we are dwelling on the past, focusing on negative emotions, holding on to grudges, filled with retribution and revenge, addicted to adrenaline, marrying our victimhood, recoiling in self-protection rather than mercy, or poisoning ourselves with non-forgiveness."[20] How can these messages not reinforce our shame?

Forgiveness has its place, to be sure, but that place is not as important as its advocates maintain. For the good of their clients, I wish forgiveness practitioners and advocates would admit that forgiveness therapy was not created to meet the needs of trauma survivors who experience pervasive shame and therefore should not be used in trauma recovery.

"Grandpa says that I should forgive my mom," said Owen.

"What do you think?" I asked.

"He says that it's not right to be angry at her 'cause she's my mom, and she's dead. He says if I don't stop being angry, it'll hurt me in the end."

"What do you think?"

"I don't know. I tried to forgive her, but I couldn't. I know all that stuff she did wasn't my fault. But now I feel like because I can't forgive her, and I'm supposed to, now that's my fault. It makes me feel like I'm bad all over again."

Owen's shame was reinforced by his grandfather's well-intentioned attempts to help him by encouraging forgiveness—a forgiveness he could not offer. This is a common response when we are forced, pressured, or encouraged to forgive when our shame is keeping us from doing so. "Everywhere I turned, I heard the same words: 'You have to forgive,'" writes survivor Nancy Richards. "They came from my family, my counselors, and the religious community alike. I saw myself as a complete and utter failure. As though my self-esteem wasn't low enough from years of abuse, try as I might, I couldn't even get forgiving right!"[21] If you are told over and over that you need to forgive to move past your shame, but you can't bring yourself to do it, the most intuitive explanation will be that there is something wrong with you. This only exacerbates your shame, moving forgiveness further out of reach.

IDENTIFYING NEGATIVE CORE BELIEFS TO ASSESS SHAME

We've already seen how destructive shame can be; it can wreak even more havoc on your mental and emotional well-being if it goes unnoticed. That's why it's paramount that we recognize shame within ourselves. If you already know that you experience shame, it may help to have words to identify and express it. If you don't, you can spot it by being on the lookout for certain thoughts.

There are many ways to assess whether you experience shame. One of the most successful interventions that I use is to identify negative core beliefs, which are core truths that you believe about yourself or the world. Core beliefs are strong and less likely to be changed by external evidence. For example, if you have the negative core belief of "I'm stupid," you would believe this regardless of whether you received a high or low score on an intelligence test. If you got a high score, you'd tell yourself that the test was too easy. If someone told you that you're smart, you'd think they were being polite, or they just didn't know the truth. You may logically understand that you are smart, but you won't believe it instinctually or in your emotional core. The existence of negative core beliefs about yourself is often an indication that shame is present.

Consider if any of these common negative core beliefs feel true to you. Remember, don't ask yourself if these beliefs are *logically* true. Instead, ask yourself if they *feel* true.

- I'm bad.
- I'm worthless.
- I'm unlovable.
- I'm inadequate.
- I'm not good enough.
- I'm undeserving.
- I'm broken.
- I'm ugly.
- I'm unimportant.
- I don't matter.
- I'm stupid.
- I'm not smart enough.
- I'm a disappointment.
- I should have done something.
- I deserve to die.
- I deserve to be miserable.
- I don't belong.
- I'm powerless.
- I'm helpless.
- I'm weak.

- I cannot be trusted.
- I cannot trust myself.
- I cannot trust my judgment.
- I cannot protect myself.
- I'm a failure.
- I'm abandoned.
- I have to be perfect.
- I have to please others.

Negative core beliefs are common, and everyone has at least a few. Those who experience shame tend to have many negative core beliefs or a few that are very strong. Owen's negative core beliefs were "I'm bad," "I'm weak," "I'm unlovable," "I can't protect myself," and "I'm broken." These beliefs became the words he needed to conceptualize and express his shame. As Owen progressed in recovery, he started asking himself the question, "How would I act if I completely believed that I am good/loveable/strong?" This helped him to explore how his actions challenged or supported his shame, and eventually he was able to engage in actions that promoted his emerging self-worth.

"Can you list all the reasons why you're good enough?" I asked Owen during his last session with me, as he was ready to graduate from therapy.

"I can, 'cause I actually believe it now. First, I'm strong, both physically and mentally." He counted on his fingers. "I know I can protect myself if I need to. But I can also ask for help. I think I still need to work on that one. Two, I'm kind, and people like me 'cause they always want to talk or hang out with me. Three, I'm funny, and not everyone has a sense of humor. Four, I can count at least eleven people who love me, and all those people can't be wrong."

ADDRESS YOUR SHAME BEFORE YOU SEEK TO FORGIVE

Shame is a part of the web of trauma that ensnares us. You may have a long list of negative core beliefs that hold your web in place. They may feel unbreakable, but these strong silk fibers can be loosened and untangled while being interwoven with beliefs that are more accurate, like "I'm good enough," "I'm lovable," and "I have value." One day, you may notice that your web looks and feels different, as self-worth has become a foundational aspect of your identity.

Four years after Owen's graduation, I received an email from him. He started a carpenter apprenticeship program and was engaged to be married. "I'm a dog dad!" he wrote. He attached a picture of himself and his fiancé surrounded by three large golden retrievers. "And by the way, you want to hear something crazy," he wrote. "I forgave my mom. It just happened one day. Crazy, huh?" Forgiveness was elective in Owen's recovery, as he was free to explore whether he felt ready to forgive his mother or not. While in therapy, he didn't forgive her. Four years later, he did. Owen needed to address his shame before he could take that next step.

If you want to forgive but can't bring yourself to do so, you may be experiencing shame. If you are, it's best to address your shame before you pursue forgiveness. Survivor Nancy Richards says it best, "We have all heard 'You must forgive in order to heal.' It is my experience that you must heal in order to forgive."[22] Once your self-worth is restored, you may find that you are better able to forgive or that you might not need to forgive at all. I've witnessed many survivors report a decrease in shame and improved self-worth. Some forgave, and others didn't; most made progress in recovery.

CHAPTER SEVEN

Recognizing Religious Influences

It's impossible to explore the concept of forgiveness in trauma recovery without acknowledging the impact of religion, as forgiveness and religion can be so tightly interwoven that to speak of one is to speak of the other. In my research, I interviewed theological scholars and religious leaders associated with Buddhism, Christianity, Judaism, Hinduism, and Islam to explore the role of forgiveness in each religion and its influence on survivors in recovery. But first, a few considerations.

AVOID MAKING ASSUMPTIONS

There are no two survivors who share identical religious beliefs, even if you identify with the same religion. One Muslim does not have the exact same perspectives, practices, and ideologies as another. This is true of all religions, as people, by nature, are diverse and complex. Moreover, a single religion often has different denominations or sects. For example, Catholicism and Protestantism are two denominations of Christianity. A Catholic and a Protestant both identify as Christian, yet their religious beliefs are not the same, nor are their conceptualizations of forgiveness within Christianity.

Religious beliefs will also differ between two survivors in the same denomination. One Catholic survivor might believe that forgiveness can only be granted by God after the offender confesses. Therefore, they feel they do not need to forgive, as only God has this privilege. In contrast, another Catholic survivor may believe that they must follow God's forgiving nature by offering their offender forgiveness. Making assumptions based on anyone's identified religion, or lack of religion, is a mistake. Instead of assuming, try engaging in genuine curiosity to discover your and other's unique religious interpretations, beliefs, and practices related to forgiveness's role in recovery—if it plays a role at all.

ACKNOWLEDGE THE PREVALENCE OF RELIGIOUS TRAUMA

There is no denying that religion can cause and exacerbate trauma. Millions of people have been killed in the name of religion. Trusted religious leaders have abused their power to harm and exploit others. Religious organizations have contributed to the oppression of women, children, and many marginalized populations. Offenders have even reported that their religious beliefs had an influence on their harmful actions. Religious scholar Darren M. Slade and his colleagues wrote, "Religious trauma results from an event, series of events, relationships, or circumstances within or connected to religious beliefs, practices, or structures that is experienced by an individual as overwhelming or disruptive and has lasting adverse effects on a person's physical, mental, social, emotional, or spiritual well-being." Slade and his colleagues conducted the world's first and currently most exhaustive sociological study on religious trauma. They found that as many as one in five adults in the United States experience symptoms of religious trauma.[1] To put it another way, someone who grows up in the United States has a 20 percent chance of developing religious trauma throughout their life. This study, then, implies that religious trauma is not a rare occurrence. If you are a survivor of religious trauma, you may have unique experiences, conceptualizations, and needs related to forgiveness in recovery.

BE MINDFUL OF SAMPLING LIMITATIONS

In chapter 3, I detailed the sampling limitations that exist in forgiveness therapy research, which include small sample sizes and self-selection bias. These same sampling limitations are present in this chapter. I interviewed eight people and included research and insights from an additional ten.

This is a small sample size, and therefore cannot be used to generalize how Buddhist, Christian, Jewish, Hindu, and Muslim survivors view forgiveness. The information in this chapter is not a substitute for learning about your or anyone else's unique religious interpretations, beliefs, and practices.

In addition to a small sample size, this chapter has a strong self-selection bias. The scholars and religious leaders I interviewed chose to participate because they agreed that forgiveness should be elective in trauma recovery. The people I contacted who did not agree either did not respond or refused to be interviewed. One religious leader responded to my interview request by writing, "Your book is going to destroy our society. I suggest that you abandon this ridiculous project and focus on actually helping people. I will pray for you." I wish they had consented to an interview so I could include their perspective; it would have allowed me to better represent the diverse beliefs regarding forgiveness in religious circles.

Since no one with dissenting viewpoints agreed to an interview, there will be few rebuttals in this chapter. Therefore, you should keep in mind the impact of sampling limitations. If you seek to have a balanced debate, I suggest you review resources that discuss forgiveness in the context of your specific religion or a religion that interests you.

BUDDHISM

In Buddhism, forgiveness is seen as a way to end suffering. "From a Buddhist orientation, forgiveness is a matter of responding to suffering with compassion and loving-kindness," says Paula Arai, professor of women and Buddhist studies at the Institute of Buddhist Studies in Berkeley, California. "The root assumption in the Buddhist tradition is someone who causes harm does it because they are suffering. This includes the pain we inflict on ourselves. We harm ourselves when we are suffering. The Buddhist tradition is focused on how to stop suffering, the suffering of others and ourselves. A Japanese Buddhist woman explained forgiveness to me in a profound way. She said, 'I know I am healed when I am kind.'"[2]

In Buddhism, forgiveness can occur in simple daily tasks. "The Buddhist forgiveness process is like gently making space between knots of yarn," says Arai. As she describes:

Imagine a ball of yarn that a cat's played with, and it's now a shape-less mess that's lying on the floor. To undo all these knots, you must create space between the strings. You slowly start pulling this yarn to loosen it up, undoing each knot and creating space. This space can come from breathing deeply, inhaling the positive, and exhaling the negative. You can create space by doing the little things in daily life with the intention of patiently caring. For example, when cutting carrots, take care to nourish yourself with as much of the edible portion as possible, as opposed to mindlessly lopping off parts of the vegetable that could be eaten. Such little actions demonstrate to yourself how kind you are, and the warmth that you give to yourself can help to loosen those knots. This is what forgiveness is like in Buddhism.[3]

Buddhism does not require its practitioners to forgive. "The foundation of Buddhist practice, or engagement, is to see clearly what is happening around us, no matter what that is, to have the bravery, the wisdom, the compassion, to look at the world and yourself and to see what's going on," says Eli Brown, dharma teacher at Midwest Buddhist Temple in Chicago. "Therefore, the whole point of any Buddhist practice is that we're not looking for an expected result. For example, if I meditate, I'm not focusing on the goal of calming or increasing productivity or even forgiveness. I'm focused on seeing clearly what is going on at this moment. So, expecting forgiveness is setting myself up for failure. Forgiveness can arise during the process of healing or not. It's not the goal of any Buddhist practice."[4]

If you're a Buddhist survivor, ask yourself these questions:

- How does Buddhism impact your life? Your trauma recovery?
- Do you have an adequate support system? If not, can you focus on building a support system?
- Are you utilizing your support system in your recovery? If not, can you begin to rely on your support system during your recovery?
- Have you experienced forgiveness-related stigma in your recovery? If so, how has this stigma impacted your recovery?
- Can Buddhist organizations provide you with resources to support your recovery? If so, are you or could you utilize these resources?

- Do you need to work with a clinician who understands or is accepting of Buddhism? Do you need to work with a clinician who identifies as a Buddhist?

Here are some considerations for clinicians working with Buddhist survivors:

Explore what being Buddhist means to each survivor. Buddhist survivors, in particular, may differ in their perception of the self. "It's important to understand that survivors in the West may have different perceptions and experiences than those shaped by an Asian Buddhist culture," says Arai. "Western culture cultivates an individualistic concept of self. Buddhist culture cultivates a relational concept of self, where we are interdependently interacting in a flux of causes and conditions. Therefore, a Buddhist concept of forgiveness would likely have different dynamics and textures than a Western concept of forgiveness."[5] Clinicians should assess not only a survivor's associations with Buddhist beliefs but also if these beliefs exist within an Asian or Western cultural context, as the different cultural perceptions of self may impact views on forgiveness. To assess what being Buddhist means to each survivor, clinicians can ask the following questions:

- Do you identify as Buddhist?
- How does being a Buddhist affect your life?
- Do you identify more with Asian or Western Buddhist culture, or perhaps another culture?
- How does Buddhism impact your conceptualization and experiences with forgiveness?

Follow the survivor's lead. "I've been working with people for over twenty years, and it's easy for me to believe that I have specific recipes that I can just change up to meet someone else's needs, such as handing them options, like forgiveness, and trying to get them to pick one of my choices," said Brown. "If I do that, I'm not opening up to what they need or are looking for, and even with the best intentions, I'm limiting my openness, and the healing isn't cocreated. Instead, I follow their lead, and I often find that what they need isn't necessarily what I thought they needed."[6] Instead of encouraging or discouraging forgiveness, then, clinicians should consider engaging in a partnership when working with Buddhist survivors, staying open to the survivor's needs rather than prescribing methods for healing based on their own beliefs.

Assess a survivor's social support system. "Healing in a Japanese Buddhist paradigm would suggest that the more you feel connected to others who suffer similarly, the more healing will occur," says Arai. "You are a victim, but keeping yourself stuck there generates more suffering. The more you can perceive yourself as a whole person who had this horrible thing happen, the more you can turn that horror into a way to connect to other people who also know this horror. You can extend your loving-kindness to others who have been traumatized and experience that very intimate connection."[7] A strong support system is vital for survivors in recovery, and Buddhist survivors are no different. Clinicians should assess a survivor's current social support system to determine if there is a need to create or strengthen that system to promote recovery.

Be aware of the stigma experienced by Buddhist survivors. Others may believe that Buddhist survivors must forgive to end their suffering, and survivors may feel the pressure of this expectation. "Buddhist trauma survivors might feel like they have to want everybody to be happy and free even if these people harmed them," says Brown. "Yet, there are infinite ways to free people, and that has to start from a genuine place of having all those intentions and feelings for yourself. So, if a Buddhist survivor is feeling limited in the ways that they have to forgive people, they need to know that there is no shame."[8] Because of this, Buddhist survivors may experience shame when they are not able to offer forgiveness to their offenders, and clinicians must be aware of this possibility and be ready to help their clients deal with these feelings should they arise.

CHRISTIANITY

Christianity began with the belief that God is the only one capable of providing forgiveness. Judith Herman, referencing the work of scholar David Konstan, writes, "The modern concept of interpersonal forgiveness is of relatively recent origin. It is not found in classical antiquity or even, surprisingly, in the Old or New Testament. In the Bible and in the works of Jewish and early Christian theologians, only God has the authority and the grace to forgive."[9] Some Christians do not believe that people can and should forgive; instead, they maintain that forgiveness can only be offered by God, who sees the hearts and minds of offenders. "The main message is that we are forgiven by God," says John Blackwell, a retired United Methodist pastor and scholar. "You aren't God. We are not God. I am not God."[10] Therefore, Christian survivors may believe that they are not required to forgive their offenders, as only God can forgive them, and that it falls to their offenders to seek forgiveness from God.

That said, the concept of interpersonal forgiveness does exist in Christianity and is reflected in the life and death of Jesus Christ. "Jesus is considered to be the symbol of grace and forgiveness as he, the Son of God, made the ultimate sacrifice when he died for our sins," says Chaplain Kenna Hollingshead. "Christians are encouraged to walk in the footsteps of Jesus, who forgave, and follow his teachings."[11] Inspired by Jesus's forgiveness of humanity and those who harmed him, some Christian survivors may believe that they too must forgive their offenders. However, as forgiveness is not a necessary part of trauma recovery, it should not be required for all Christians; in fact, expecting all Christians to be able and willing to forgive can be counterintuitive to their recovery. "God is forgiving; this is a core tenant of Christianity," clarifies Blackwell. "The question becomes, would it be helpful for me to be forgiving also? Forgiveness is not the goal; healing and wholeness is the goal. Forgiveness is a tool in the toolbox for some people, and it may not be a useful tool for others."[12] This is why Christian survivors' conceptualizations of forgiveness tend to vary.

The phrase *turn the other cheek*, which refers to suffering insult or injury without retaliation, is strongly associated with Christian practice and deeply embedded in Western culture. It is a sentiment often associated with nonresistance and pacifism. However, it should not be taken to mean that Christian survivors must endure their suffering without taking measures to keep themselves safe. They can forgive their offenders while also protecting themselves; the two are not mutually exclusive. "Biblically, I don't think there has to be a fine line between forgiving someone who has harmed you and protecting yourself," writes social worker Leslie Vernick. "When someone harms you, forgiving him (or her) doesn't mean you automatically trust him or allow him to continue to harm you, does it? For example, if someone raped you, in time, you might forgive that person so you don't get eaten up with bitterness, but you wouldn't hang out with this person or ever allow him near you, right? Biblically, he is classified as an enemy, and although Jesus tells us to forgive our enemy, even love our enemy, he doesn't ask us to trust our enemy or give them a moment to harm us further."[13] Christian survivors should not be expected to choose between forgiving and their personal safety. You can, and should, have both.

If you're a Christian survivor, ask yourself these questions:

- How does Christianity impact your life? Your trauma recovery?
- Do you believe that you were created in God's image? If so, how does this impact your self-worth and feelings of shame?
- Have you experienced coercion or pressure to forgive in your Christian community? If so, how have experiences impacted your recovery?
- Are you aware of the existence of Christian privilege as it impacts you and others who are not Christian? Has your Christian privilege ever been challenged? If so, how did this impact you?
- Can Christian organizations provide you with resources to support your recovery? If so, are you or could you utilize these resources?
- Do you need to work with a clinician who understands or accepts Christianity? Do you need to work with a clinician who identifies as a Christian?

Here are some considerations for clinicians working with Christian survivors:

Explore what being Christian means to each survivor. Christianity is highly diverse, with many denominations and a wide range of beliefs within those denominations. For example, Baptists differ from Lutherans, and both are considered Christian. Methodists and Presbyterians differ, and both are considered Protestant. Simply knowing that a survivor is a Christian is not enough information to determine how their religious beliefs influence their conceptualization of forgiveness. Clinicians must dig deeper. To assess what being a Christian means to each survivor, they can ask the following questions:

- Do you identify as Christian?
- How does being a Christian affect your life?
- Do you identify with a certain denomination of Christianity?
- How does Christianity influence your conceptualizations of and experiences with forgiveness?

Reflecting upon God's love can promote self-worth. "As a Chaplain, I've worked with many people who've experienced trauma, and they almost always have trouble with self-worth," says Hollingshead. "Relearning to love oneself after trauma is something that you must home in on. For Christians, it may be important to honor the concept that we've all been created in the image of God, and there's a little bit of God in everyone."[14] To support Christian survivors, Hollingshead recommends clinicians ask survivors questions such as: "What do you think God loves about you? Why do you think God created you? Do you believe that God made you in his image?" These questions can help Christian survivors utilize God's love as an anchor in developing and strengthening their self-worth.

Be aware that Christian communities can pressure survivors to forgive. "Christian communities can brush over things because they are hard and uncomfortable to talk about," says Hollingshead. "So, they say that you need to forgive because Jesus would. But Jesus would also sit with you while you cried and sit with you in those dark places. Christian communities must be willing to sit in those dark places with survivors before they can get to the point of forgiveness. Forgiveness has to be something that one decides for themselves. It cannot be decided by or for a community. It can't be something that's forced or presumed by a community, even if they have good intentions."[15] Blackwell elaborates on the dangers of forced forgiveness, saying: "Coercion to forgive in the name of Christianity doesn't aid healing. All coercion is anti-therapeutic and an obstacle to healing."[16] Clinicians should be aware that Christian survivors may have experienced coercion or pressure to forgive in their communities, and these experiences may have a negative impact on recovery.

Acknowledge the existence and impact of Christian privilege. "Christian privilege is a set of advantages that benefit Christians, but not people who practice other religions or no religion at all," writes author Maisha Z. Johnson. "That means that American Christians—even those who aren't particularly religious—can openly express their faith, while people affiliated with other religions or no religion are othered and marginalized for practicing theirs."[17] This privilege manifests in many ways. In the United States, Christians are more likely to get time off work for religious holidays (Christmas, Easter), are less likely to be the targets of violence and oppression, are more likely to see images representing Christianity in public spaces (work, school, government), and are more likely to have people in positions of authority (government officials, law enforcement, corporate leaders) who share their religious beliefs. In addition, there is a misconception that the United States is a Christian nation. While Christianity has been an influential religion in the United States over the past several hundred years, this has never been the case, and to assert this erroneous idea is to overlook the diversity of religious beliefs and practices that exists within the country.

When their privilege is challenged, Christians can be emotionally impacted. Some Christians express anger, fear, and grief when Christian symbols are removed from public spaces, Christian prayer is forbidden in public schools, when people say "happy holidays" instead of "merry Christmas," and when other religions appear more frequently in the media we consume. There are those who view this increase in inclusivity and secularism as a personal attack and an attempt to limit their religious freedoms. Clinicians should be aware of the existence of Christian privilege, as it can negatively impact both Christian and non-Christian survivors in their recovery.

JUDAISM

"Forgiveness is a core concept in Judaism that's ever-present," says Rabbi Aaron Finkelstein. "Traditionally, Jews pray three times a day. One prayer is, 'Blessed are you, God, who desires forgiveness.' We say this three times a day, every day."[18] In addition to consistent prayer, religious Jews celebrate Yom Kippur, a holiday dedicated to forgiveness and repentance. "In Judaism, we have a forgiveness holiday, Yom Kippur, which is known as the holiest day of the year," says Rabbi Rishe Groner. "The root of Yom Kippur is not forgiveness; it's atonement. Yom Kippur is a day of clean slating oneself between you and the Divine."[19] Yom Kippur is a time of reflection in which Jewish survivors may focus on seeking forgiveness from God and others. "We do a personal spiritual accounting," describes Finkelstein. "You're looking back at your deeds of the last year and asking people and thinking to yourself, *Who have I hurt? Who do I need to ask forgiveness from?* These can be people in my life that I might need to apologize to and ask for forgiveness."[20] During Yom Kippur and in their prayers, Jewish survivors may focus intentionally on seeking forgiveness from God.

In order to be forgiven by God, Jewish survivors are sometimes driven to pursue self-improvement. This dedication to working on oneself is internal, not external, meaning that Jewish survivors may seek personal, mental, and emotional growth. "The idea of Yom Kippur is that if you do the work on yourself, then the forgiveness, the pardoning, and the erasing comes automatically from God," says Rabbi Groner. "But, you have to do the work on yourself. This takes place during the Ten Days of Teshuvah, the ten days of returning. *Teshuvah* is the Hebrew word for returning. It's returning to myself. In Jewish culture, the idea that you are supposed to take the time to make amends and work on yourself is very strong."[21]

Although forgiveness is an important aspect of the Jewish faith, Jewish survivors should not be expected to forgive any more than practitioners of any other religion. "There is a tradition that if you ask someone for forgiveness three times and they don't forgive you, you've done what you can," says Finkelstein. However, he also asserts that forgiveness is often more complicated. He illustrates this point through a story:

There are cases where real trust is betrayed and real trauma is done. There is a story in the Talmud of a rabbi who offended another rabbi. The offending rabbi went thirteen times for thirteen years before the High Holidays to ask for forgiveness. The rabbi, who was offended, refused to forgive. The conclusion is that this rabbi was being exceptional, as most people only need to ask three times. But, in this context, it could be interpreted in another way: there are times when many treaties are required and perhaps still not sufficient. There is a difference between apologizing and forgiveness. The perpetrator may apologize and be sincere, but not be forgiven.[22]

Jewish survivors may believe they are obligated to forgive if their offender asks for forgiveness three times, while others may feel no such obligation. In the case of the former, clinicians should understand whether Jewish survivors genuinely believe that forgiveness will aid their recovery or are being pressured into doing so.

If you're a Jewish survivor, ask yourself these questions:

- How does Judaism impact your life? Your trauma recovery?
- Do you experience the effects of intergenerational trauma? If so, how does your intergenerational trauma impact you and your recovery?
- Have you experienced antisemitism? If so, how have these experiences impacted you and your recovery?

- Can Jewish organizations provide you with resources to support your recovery? If so, are you or could you utilize these resources?
- Do you need the support of a trauma-informed rabbi? Have you considered participating in rabbinic counseling?
- Do you need to work with a clinician who understands or accepts Judaism? Do you need to work with a clinician who identifies as Jewish?

Here are some considerations for clinicians working with Jewish survivors:

Explore what being Jewish means to each survivor. "Judaism is not just a religion, it's a people," says Rabbi Groner. "You might have people who don't practice Judaism regularly, but they have certain experiences built into their culture, without it being something that makes them an actively religious person. In other religions, if someone identifies themselves as Christian or as Muslim, you might generally assume that they're actively practicing. If someone identifies themselves as Jewish it can be more of a national identity, rather than a practicing Jew."[23] In order to assess what being Jewish means to each survivor, clinicians can ask the following questions:

- Do you identify as Jewish? If so, is your Jewish identity a representation of your national identity, religion, culture, or another aspect of your identity?
- How does Judaism affect your life?
- Do you identify with a particular denomination of Judaism?
- How does Judaism impact your conceptualization of and experiences with forgiveness?

Acknowledge the impact of intergenerational trauma. The Jewish people have a history of persecution that goes back millennia. This is true of other religious and ethnic groups as well, but the Jewish diaspora may feel the effects of their peoples' history particularly keenly. "My grandmother was traumatized by Stalin," says Rabbi Groner. "I cannot forgive Stalin but I can let the story of Stalin have a less of an impact on me and on my generation. There is a lot of resentment, fear, and anger that gets held onto for generations. Letting go of that is the deepest work that people can do not only in their lifetime but for the generations that come after them, as it carries through. There is an aspect of letting it go that is really important for me, my generation, and my family." [24] Clinicians need to be aware that Jewish survivors may experience the impact of not only their own trauma but intergenerational trauma as well. As one of my Jewish clients told me, "Everyone thinks it's just about the Holocaust. It's not. Antisemitism existed long before the Nazis appropriated it. Jewish trauma is ancient trauma."

Recognize the existence and impact of antisemitism. There is a myth in the United States that antisemitism ended with the Holocaust. This is far from the truth, as modern-day antisemitism is alive and thriving. The Anti-Defamation League's Center on Extremism reported that antisemitic incidents in the United States reached their highest count in 2022.[25] Jewish survivors and their families continue to be murdered, harassed, and oppressed. Clinicians who deny the existence and impact of antisemitism create an unsafe relationship with and environment for Jewish survivors. Instead, clinicians should actively assist survivors in exploring the effect antisemitism has had on their trauma and recovery.

Refer survivors to Jewish resources when needed. "There's a lot more trauma-informed rabbinic practitioners and teachers out there who are open-minded and available for rabbinic counseling and pastoral counseling," says Rabbi Groner. "They can reach out to a rabbi but not everyone today is a member of a synagogue or has a rabbi. Clinicians can invite them to reach out to someone they know or to find teachings online. This could help them to learn more about a Jewish approach so that they don't think that forgiveness in Judaism is a black and white situation."[26] Access to multiple resources, then, can assist Jewish survivors in their recovery, and clinicians are uniquely positioned to encourage survivors to seek and engage with these resources.

HINDUISM

The act of forgiveness in Hinduism has many layers. "The Sanskrit word for forgiveness is Kṣamā—which can be split into two; kṣa = to decrease and mā = measure or degree—so basically forgiveness is the decreasing of the degree to which we are indebted to the one who has wronged us or persecuted us," writes dharma teacher Rami Sivan.[27] Meanwhile, theologian Olusegun Obasanjo has another interpretation:

Hinduism recognizes two sides in the act of forgiveness. Each side is a multi-layered structure. The first side is the seeker of forgiveness; the other side is the one who extends and delivers forgiveness. The act of seeking (prar-thana) forgiveness (kshama, daya, krupa) may be carried out unilaterally, without the presence, permission, or expectation of the other side. The act of extending deliverance (anugraha-pradana) or forgiving (karunya, advesha, ab-haya) may also take place unilaterally without the presence, permission, or expectation of acceptance from the other side. The theological basis for forgiveness in Hinduism is that a person who does not forgive carries a baggage of memories of the wrong, of negative feelings, of anger and unresolved emotions that affect their present as well as future.[28]

Hindus may choose to forgive or not. "Forgiveness is not required as in Christianity," writes Sivan. "The paradigm of sin–forgiveness–justification–redemption is completely foreign to Hinduism." Yet Hindu survivors are encouraged to forgive if it's needed. "Every positive and negative transaction with another person causes a karmic debt or bond known as runa-anubandhana," Sivan writes. "Depending on the strength of this connection we will be compelled to encounter that person again and again in future lives until the debt is required and the bond dissolves. So, the act of forgiveness in which we let go of the pain, vengefulness, sorrow, and regret liberates us from the runa-anubandhana to that person."[29]

Hindu survivors who cannot or will not forgive, however, have another option. "There is forgiveness and unforgiveness, and I propose a third category: letting go," says Hinduism scholar Abhishek Ghosh. "If someone, out of bad intention or sheer accident, placed a bunch of hot coals in my hand, I wouldn't brood on it. I wouldn't feel like holding onto the coals, thinking I would get revenge one day. If you ask me if I can forgive the person who put the hot coals in my hands, I won't be able to do it. But am I able to let the coals go? Forgiveness and detachment are two different things. Pain is inevitable, but suffering is optional."[30] In this way, a Hindu survivor may feel as if they have many options outside the binary of forgiveness versus unforgiveness.

When most people think of Hindu beliefs, they most often think of karma. This concept has become so ubiquitous that it is an English loan word, used by atheists and practitioners of other religions alike. Therefore, there is a risk that an uninformed layperson or clinician may misunderstand karma and use it to pressure people who are suffering into a certain course of action. "One of the cruelest explanations is Karma, that something happened to someone because of their Karma," says Ghosh. "Karma acknowledges that there is some kind of retribution in the universe. However, it is not a tool to beat yourself or someone else up. Telling someone who is suffering, 'That's your Karma!' is one of the cruelest statements one can make. People fail to notice the other side of Karma, which is compassion. Karma is the explanation of the problem; compassion is the solution."[31] Karma should never be weaponized against Hindu survivors.

If you're a Hindu survivor, ask yourself these questions:

- How does Hinduism impact your life? Your trauma recovery?
- What's your conceptualization of karma in relation to forgiveness and trauma recovery?
- Do you have dharmic duties? If so, what are they, and how can these duties support your recovery?
- Do you have an adequate support system? If not, can you focus on building a support system? If so, are you utilizing your support system in your recovery? If not, can you begin to rely on your support system during your recovery?
- Do you need to integrate your support system into your mental health treatment? If so, have you considered participating in couples, family, or group therapy?
- Do you benefit from self-help or holistic techniques (medication, yoga, stories, etc.)? If so, are you using these techniques often in your recovery?

Here are some considerations for clinicians working with Hindu survivors: *Explore what being Hindu means to each survivor.* Clinicians should never make assumptions about the beliefs of Hindu survivors. Hinduism is a highly diverse religion, and no two Hindu survivors will have the same experiences or beliefs. "Hinduism is more than a religion; it's a culture," says Ghosh. "99 percent of Hindus in the world have very little knowledge of the details of ancient Hindu texts, although that is changing. They are Hindus because they are ethically Hindus, and follow the festivals, rituals, and customs. There are 1.3 billion Hindus, and everybody believes in something different even though they may belong to the same group or share common identity markers like a sacred thread or a home puja shrine."[32] To assess what being Hindu means to each survivor, you can ask the following questions:

- Do you identify as Hindu?
- How does Hinduism affect your life?
- Do you identify with a particular sect of Hinduism?
- What's your conceptualization of karma in relation to forgiveness?
- How does Hinduism impact your conceptualization of and experiences with forgiveness?

Understand and support dharma. "Dharma refers to codes of appropriate behavior within Hinduism and is specific to each person depending on their stage in life, i.e., the dharma of a student is to attend school, respect their teachers, and be studious, while the dharma of a parent is to provide and care for their children and raise them to become upstanding citizens," writes Dr. Narmi Thillaninathan. "Hindus believe that by following a Dharmic way of life they will avoid attracting negative karma or suffering in the future. Therefore, by reminding the client of the importance of their current actions and directing the client to focus on their Dharmic duties, the practitioner can facilitate change and healing through counseling. The importance of social systems and the individual's responsibility to the community are central themes in Hindu philosophy."[33] Because it plays such an important role in determining how practitioners of Hinduism feel they should behave, clinicians need to know how dharma impacts survivors and can benefit their recovery. To support the concept of dharma and community involvement, clinicians can provide Hindu survivors with referrals and recommendations for family therapy, couples therapy, group therapy, and support groups. They can also invite members of the survivor's social support group into their therapy sessions, which may benefit their recovery.

Discover the benefits of stories. "Lots of people can't afford therapy; they don't have the resources or the means," says Ghosh. For these people, stories and religious texts often take the place of therapeutic interventions. They help Hindu survivors to overcome personal hardships. As Dr. Ghosh states:

The wisdom they get from religious texts and their experiences from religious practices can help alleviate the suffering when they cannot forgive. A version of narrative therapy can be seen in ancient Hindu texts like the *Bhagavata* or the *Bhagavad Gita*. It appears to be blending a little bit of what we know today as CBT (cognitive behavioral therapy) with cognitive reframing. The *Bhagavata*, in particular, is a very popular book in India, showcasing many individual adversities of past role models and how they cope. This book has often filled the role of a therapist for some Hindu survivors.[34]

Clinicians can better serve Hindu clients when they recognize the role that stories play in their emotional well-being. They may benefit from therapeutic interventions incorporating stories, like narrative therapy and bibliotherapy.

Embrace self-help techniques. "Hindus have also been conditioned to use self-help methods and self-training through the system of yoga, meditation, etc.," writes Dr. Thillaninathan. "Counselling approaches could harness and utilize these techniques and accommodate the Hindu meditative and contemplate approach with its emphasis on the interior life."[35] Hindu survivors may bring their own self-help techniques to therapy, and part of working with them means embracing those techniques while introducing them to additional self-help methods. Many self-help techniques can be integrated into trauma recovery and used to support a survivor's success without overriding the practices that give Hindu survivors comfort.

ISLAM

Forgiveness is a vital aspect of Islam. "In the noble Qur'an, 'forgiveness' and 'mercy' are mentioned around 100 and 200 times, respectively," writes faith columnist Murtada Muhammad Gusau. "An entire chapter of the Qur'an is devoted to the quality of mercy that is (Surah Rahman)."[36] In Islam, there are two types of forgiveness: forgiveness granted by the Divine and forgiveness granted by a human. Muslims can seek forgiveness from the Divine or a person," says Muslim chaplain and theologian Omer Mozaffar. Mozaffar offers a detailed breakdown of the process of seeking forgiveness, both from a person and the Divine:

When seeking forgiveness from the Divine, we consider the tests of sincerity, which are the following questions that we ask ourselves:

1. Do I regard the act or violation as wrong?
2. Do I stop doing it?
3. Do I hate to go back to it?

If we can say *yes* to all three of those questions, we can assess that our own request for forgiveness is sincere. If we're not able to say *yes* to all those questions, then, if we are being honest with ourselves, we might need to do something further. If we don't regard the action as wrong, it means that we may need more knowledge to understand what was wrong. If we're not able to stop doing it, maybe we need training of some form in order to stop. If we don't hate to go back to it, we may need more knowledge and more training. The general principle is that if we can say *yes* to all three of these questions, then the Divine has forgiven us. When we are seeking forgiveness from a person, then there's also a fourth question we must ask, which is:

4. Do I try or am I trying to reform whatever it is that I've broken? Do I try to fix it if that's a possibility?

If we can say *yes* to all four of these questions, there is no obligation on the victim to grant us forgiveness. The benefit of the victim granting forgiveness is primarily for them to be able to clean their own heart or whatever they are feeling. But it is not an obligation.[37]

Muslim survivors, therefore, are not required to forgive. "I wasn't asking about forgiveness; I was asking about healing," says Muslim author and trauma survivor Umm Zakiyyah. Zakiyyah's process of healing and reckoning with forgiveness was as follows:

I knew that I was trying to figure out a way to heal. This put me on my own journey of looking inward and studying my own faith with my own eyes, and there was none of this forced forgiveness in my faith. Some Christians have told me that, like Muslims in my own faith community, they don't feel that they have to forgive, but their spiritual teachers and congregations do, and they push forgiveness as if it's a part of faith itself. This put me on a journey of studying to discover if I had to forgive, and I realized I don't. If you look at the Qur'an and prophetic teachings, there is no question that forgiveness is not an obligation.[38]

In Islam, the nuances of forgiveness go beyond human versus Divine. Whether you are oppressed or privileged also influences the process; there are a different set of expectations for the former than the latter. In describing her journey to forgiveness, Zakiyyah draws on the Qur'an's teachings:

In the Qur'an, there's a difference between the privileged and the oppressed. For the people who are oppressed, the first thing you need to do is stand up for yourself. After you stand up for yourself, then you can forgive, but it's not obligatory. When it comes to those who are privileged, they are first encouraged to forgive. For example, the Qur'an says, 'And let not those among you who are blessed with graces and wealth swear not to give (any sort of help) to their kinsmen, the poor [and needy] and those who emigrated in the cause of Allah. Let them [instead] pardon and forgive. Do you not love that Allah should forgive you? And Allah is 'Oft-Forgiving, Most Merciful' (24:22). If you look at society, it's the opposite; it's the oppressed who are told to constantly forgive. Yet, in the Qur'an, if you are opposed and being wronged, you need to stand up for yourself before you can consider forgiving. For example, the Qur'an describes the true believers as those 'who, when an oppressive wrong is done to them, they help and defend themselves' (42:39).[39]

If you're a Muslim survivor, ask yourself these questions:

- How does Islam impact your life? Your trauma recovery?
- Have you experienced Islamophobia, stigma, or discrimination? If so, how have these experiences impacted your recovery?
- Do you experience the effects of intergenerational trauma? If so, how does your intergenerational trauma impact you and your recovery?
- Are you a part of a privileged or oppressed population when compared to your offender(s)? Does this distinction influence the process of forgiveness for you?
- Can Islamic organizations provide you with resources to support your recovery? If so, are you or could you utilize these resources?
- Do you need to work with a clinician who understands or accepts Islam? Do you need to work with a clinician who identifies as Muslim?

Here are some considerations for clinicians working with Muslim survivors:

Explore what being Muslim means to each survivor. As with every other religion, clinicians cannot assume that two Muslim survivors will have the same beliefs and experiences within Islam. The Pew Research Center interviewed thirty-eight thousand Muslims from thirty-nine countries and found that Muslims "differ significantly in their levels of religious commitment, openness to multiple interpretations of their faith and acceptance of various sects and movements." This report found that geographical location and generational status were the most prominent differences between Muslims.[40] To assess what being Muslim means to each survivor, clinicians can ask the following questions:

- Do you identify as Muslim?
- How does Islam impact your life?
- Do you identify with a particular sect of Islam?
- How does Islam impact your conceptualization of and experiences with forgiveness?

Be aware of the stigma experienced by Muslim survivors. Despite being the second-largest religion in the world, there are many stigmas about Islam that negatively impact Muslim survivors. One such stigma is that Islam is a violent religion that promotes terrorism. "There are people who sincerely view themselves as Muslims who have committed horrible acts in the name of Islam," writes the Anti-Defamation League. "These people, and their interpretation of Islam, are rightly called 'extremist'; they are a minority within Islam, and the vast majority of Muslims reject their violence and consider their interpretation a distortion of the Muslim faith."[41] Nearly every religion has extremists who do not represent the religion or its followers. For example, members of the Klu Klux Klan (KKK) often identify as Christians and use crosses as symbols of white supremacy, and they do not represent Christianity. No clinician would assume that a Christian client is inherently violent because of their religion. Making that assumption of Muslim survivors is discrimination, pure and simple, and only serves to hinder their recovery.

Be aware of the existence and impact of Islamophobia. Georgetown University defines Islamophobia as "an extreme fear of and hostility toward Islam and Muslims which often leads to hate speech, hate crimes, as well as social and political discrimination. It can be used to rationalize policies such as mass surveillance, incarceration (imprisonment), and disenfranchisement, and can influence domestic and foreign policy." Islamophobia is not an opinion or a criticism of Islam, as its actions have "the sole purpose of advocating social and political measures that discriminate against and violate the rights of Muslims."[42]

Clinicians must be aware that Islamophobia exists and impacts the safety of Muslim survivors. "By the time that a Muslim comes in front of a non-Muslim clinician, they had to go over so many hurdles just to get to that space," says Zakiyyah. "There is a fear of Islamophobia. There is a fear of the white person teaching 'the lower person' about their religion."[43] Clinicians who deny the existence and impact of Islamophobia create an unsafe relationship with and environment for Muslim survivors. Instead, they should actively assist survivors in exploring the impact Islamophobia has had on their trauma and their recovery.

Refer survivors to a variety of Islamic resources when needed. Clinicians may need to provide Muslim clients with resources to assist them in exploring forgiveness within Islam. "When someone is in that in-between space where you know that you don't have to forgive, but you don't have proof that you don't have to forgive, and you're struggling with it, it's important to give them room to explore their options on their own," says Zakiyyah. This is especially important for non-Muslim clinicians, who may not understand that Muslim survivors are seeking a way to reconcile their forgiveness or unwillingness to forgive with their religion. Encouraging them to review multiple resources concerning forgiveness in Islam will allow them to choose what's best for their recovery as it relates to their beliefs. Zakiyyah details the dangers of an insensitive approach and the importance of resources:

> As a clinician, it's most important to offer support to them as they engage in spiritual self-discovery. Sometimes, pushing a person too fast into understanding they don't have to forgive can be just as triggering as pushing them to forgive, especially if you are a non-Muslim clinician working with a Muslim. What ends up happening is the trigger can become that much deeper because it comes from a mental health professional. It can come across as 'you guys are inferior, and I'm going to teach you a better way to live.' This happens to a lot of Muslim clients; they are guilted out of their faith. My personal opinion is that it's important for all survivors to be given resources of different perspectives from different platforms so that the journey of forgiveness or non-forgiveness remains personal rather than forced.[44]

RESPECTING AND ACCEPTING RELIGIOUS
BELIEFS IN RECOVERY

Those who support trauma survivors need to be aware of the impact of religious influences on a survivor's conceptualization and practice of forgiveness, and they must be willing to work within, not opposed to, those influences. If a survivor's religious beliefs compel them to forgive, this must be acknowledged, respected, and accepted by those who seek to be a part of their recovery. The opposite is also true: survivors who believe that they do not need to forgive deserve the same level of respect, acknowledgment, and acceptance. Codes of ethics bind clinicians to respect and accept the religious beliefs of survivors. As a psychologist and religious researcher, Brian E. Eck writes: "Ethical practice includes and requires that therapists recognize the central role religion and spirituality play in the client's life, and they demonstrate a sensitivity, awareness, and respect for the client's beliefs, practices, and values."[45] Of course, it's just as important for survivors themselves to be aware of how their faith influences their healing.

As a survivor, you should also be able to stand up for yourself when you feel that your religious beliefs are under attack or are hindering your recovery. You would benefit from asking yourself these questions, which may help you to explore your unique religious perspectives, ideologies, and practices related to forgiveness and trauma recovery:

- Do you identify with any religious beliefs or organizations? If so, how do your beliefs influence your conceptualization of and experiences with forgiveness in recovery?
- Were you raised in a religious group, environment, or culture? If so, how do those experiences influence your conceptualization of and experiences with forgiveness in recovery?
- Do you feel comfortable correcting people, including clinicians, when they make assumptions about you based on your religious affiliations?
- Have you had any negative experiences associated with religious groups or communities, or have you experienced religious trauma? If so, how have these experiences impacted your ability to navigate the concept of forgiveness in recovery?

- Has a religious community attempted to force or pressure you to forgive? If so, how has this impacted your perceptions of forgiveness in recovery?
- Are you aware that having a shared religion with another person does not automatically result in a shared understanding and implementation of that religion? If so, how have you embraced your own interpretation and practice of your religion?
- Are you aware of the existence of Christian privilege in the United States? If so, has Christian privilege impacted you?
- Have you been exposed to stigmas associated with your religious beliefs or experienced religious discrimination? If so, how have you challenged or managed the impact of these untrue assumptions?
- If you are working with a clinician, do you feel as if they respect and accept your religious beliefs?
- Do you need more information about your religion to help in your recovery? If so, can you connect with religious leaders such as a rabbi, priest, minister, chaplain, or spiritual teacher? Or can you review various resources associated with your religion and the practice of forgiveness?
- Do you feel like a part of a community within your religion? If not, do you need to be a part of a religious community to aid in your recovery? If so, can you connect with religious organizations online or in your community?

Your religious beliefs, or lack thereof, will impact the role that forgiveness plays in your recovery. You may or may not believe that you are required to forgive your offender. Regardless of where you stand in regard to required or elective forgiveness, your religious beliefs deserve acknowledgment, respect, and acceptance if the recovery process is to be successful.

CHAPTER EIGHT

Forgiveness and Social Justice

We are not perceived or treated equally. The attributes with which you are born, or the material conditions into which you are born (your sex, sexuality, gender, class, race, ethnicity, ability, and so on), largely shape your social position in American society, how others (mis)perceive and (mis)treat you, and your professional and economic possibilities. Such markers of identity are also markers of social marginalization and oppression, and therefore they are not only often a source of trauma but are also factors that limit one's access to treatment and support. Trauma is not only inflicted and reinforced by individual offenders but also by social systems and institutions that operate at a level that transcends individual agency and yet are preserved by silent bystanders and enablers, passive collaborators, uncritical apologists for the status quo, and in general those who—whether or not they consciously recognize it—benefit from the oppression of others. In the United States, many trauma survivors are members of oppressed groups who experience systemic persecution, which can include racism, sexism, sizeism, classism, ableism, antisemitism, cisgenderism, heterosexism, xenophobia, and ageism. Suppose you are a survivor and a member of an oppressed group. In that case, you are not only more likely to experience trauma, but you are also more likely to feel pressure from society to forgive your offender(s).

When forgiveness advocates pressure, recommend, or encourage you to forgive your offender(s), how often do they consider whether you're a member of an oppressed group? And if you are an oppressed survivor, how often do they consider how your experiences of oppression may impact your willingness and capability to forgive? Forgiveness advocates and theorists rarely examine such matters, as they insist that forgiveness benefits everyone no matter who they are or what their position in society is (thus, it is not surprising that such advocates are predominately white, heterosexual, able-bodied, middle/upper-class, Protestant men). "Some give an exemption to Holocaust survivors, claiming that some injuries are too great to forgive," writes Sharon Lamb. "But rarely does a theorist consider how a belief in the virtue of forgiveness might affect African Americans in relation to Whites; women in relation to men; or abuse victims in relation to perpetrators."[1] This diminishment of matters of social identity, oppression, and privilege is harmful, as it implies that forgiveness occurs in a social and political vacuum or independently of any historical or material context in which entrenched power imbalances shape the relationships we occupy. Social inequalities not only affect how one processes trauma but can also themselves be, partly if not entirely, the cause of one's trauma in the first place. We cannot separate forgiveness and social inequality in trauma recovery, as forgiveness, trauma, and trauma recovery always occur in a social and political context—one that is fraught with inequality.

FORGIVENESS AND JUSTICE

There may be instances when an offender and a survivor have equal standing in society. Yet, often they do not. Factors such as race, ethnicity, sex, sexuality, gender, age, class, education, disability, religion, position of social authority, or genetic relationships shape a person's standing or power in society. A society's construction of your "value" directly impacts the amount of power that you have in that society. For example, a white Protestant middle-aged heterosexual man from a middle-class family who is a CEO has more power than a Black nonbinary retired atheist from a lower-class family. The amount of power that you have in society impacts your ability to seek and receive justice from your offender(s).

What if your offender has more power in society than you do? First, others may not believe you. People tend to listen to and accept information from those with greater societal influence and standing. If you have less power than your offender, you may be unable to safely make a report to law enforcement, seek justice, or protect yourself. If the Black nonbinary person in the previous example reported that the white CEO raped them, who would be more likely to be believed? We want to believe that the crime will be reported and investigated and that the evidence will show us who is telling the truth. Yet, we assume that the survivor feels safe enough to report the crime, that the crime will indeed be investigated, and that the CEO's expensive lawyers won't find a way for him to escape accountability. The truth is that the white cisgender CEO has more power and influence in society than his Black nonbinary victim, who is less likely to be believed.

If one of the people in the list below is an offender and the other is a survivor, and they both have conflicting accounts of a crime, who is more likely to be believed or given the benefit of the doubt?

- A child vs. their parent
- A civilian Black man vs. a white police officer
- A lower-level employee vs. their CEO
- An Asian gay man vs. a white heterosexual man
- A low-income Latina woman vs. a wealthy white woman
- A person with Autistic Spectrum Disorder vs. a neurotypical person
- A transgender woman vs. a cisgender woman
- An older disabled man vs. a middle-aged able-bodied man
- A civilian vs. the president of the United States

Those mentioned first are less likely to be believed or afforded the benefit of the doubt than those mentioned second, as society has conditioned us to associate socioeconomic power and privilege with *credibility*. Philosopher Myisha Cherry describes "testimonial injustice" as "failing to give victims credibility because of their gender, race, or class." She writes, "We doubt what they report, not because we detect falsehood, but simply because we are conditioned to provide certain speakers with less credibility than others."[2] If you are not believed because of your lack of power in society, you are less likely to seek justice and receive justice.

"I'm just some Black kid, and he's a white cop," said Maya. "Of course they didn't believe me. They didn't even do a rape kit."

When Maya—a Black lesbian girl from a low-income family—was fifteen, she was raped by a police officer as she was walking home from school. Her offender—a white heterosexual middle-class man who occupies a position of authority that is shielded from accountability by a number of institutional systems—had much more power she did. When she reported the rape, she was questioned by one officer and told that they would contact her to follow up; however, they never did. When Maya reached out to them, she was informed that they had found no evidence to support her claim and that if she made false reports in the future, she would be charged with a crime. Like many survivors, Maya had the deck stacked against her and never received justice.

At the end of many movies about survivors who seek justice in a court of law, the soundtrack cues, and we hear that one word we've been waiting to be spoken for the entirety of the film: *guilty.* Justice is served, and the survivor and society can begin to recover. Unfortunately, such Hollywood endings rarely happen in real life. Many offenders are never reported, reported offenders are not always investigated, and those who are investigated rarely experience legal consequences. Moreover, offenders who have more wealth or power than their victims are more likely to be able to evade justice. Some offenders are even praised and celebrated after they are reported, as they continue to thrive as successful politicians, former presidents, movie directors, athletes, singers, and celebrities.

"He's the commissioner now. Can you believe that?" said Maya. "They appointed a rapist as their police commissioner. There is no way that he's stopped raping people, and now he's got more opportunity to do it. Sometimes, I really wish that I would have fought harder to get justice. But a part of me is relieved that I didn't have to testify or go through all that. I know people who have, and the whole thing is traumatizing."

To put it lightly, the legal system in the United States is decidedly not trauma-informed. It was never created to support survivors and has not been changed to do so. In fact, the legal system itself can often trigger trauma responses. "Indeed, if one set out intentionally to design a system for provoking symptoms of traumatic stress, it might look very much like a court of law," writes Herman. "Victims need social acknowledgement and support; the court requires them to endure a public challenge to their credibility. Victims need to establish a sense of power and control over their lives; the court requires them to submit to a complex set of rules and bureaucratic procedures that they may not understand and over which they have no control."[3] It's no wonder why some survivors choose not to report crimes, as the justice system does not promote their agency or emotional safety. Offenders are encouraged to deny all fault (even and especially when they are guilty) to avoid legal consequences. Too often, this strategy leads to blaming or attacking the survivor's credibility. And if you are an oppressed survivor, this tactic is usually more successful than it would be if you were a nonoppressed survivor. "Our legal system was not designed initially to redress the harms done to women or to enslaved or Indigenous people," writes Herman. "Often, in fact, it has been an active instrument of those harms. So perhaps it is not surprising that both women and the descendants of enslaved people remain to this day deeply alienated from the legal system."[4] If you belong to a historically oppressed or marginalized group, you are less likely to seek and receive justice within the American legal system, as that system was constructed on the basis of, and largely with the implicit purpose of, sustaining foundational socioeconomic inequities.

Restorative Justice

The one form of justice that attempts to meet the needs of victims is restorative justice, which occurs after an offender has been found guilty by the legal system. Restorative justice does not replace the legal system, as the two have different goals. The legal system seeks to discover whether laws were broken and, if so, who is culpable for breaking them and what punishment is warranted for having done so. In short, the legal system pursues *punitive* justice. Restorative justice programs, on the other hand, aim to redress harms in a survivor-centered, rehabilitative, and interpersonal way. They seek to determine who was harmed and how best to repair those harms. Their aim is to support survivors and work toward rehabilitating the offender by getting the offender to understand and take responsibility for the harms they caused. These programs, which can be used with both juvenile or adult offenders, assemble the survivor, the offender, a facilitator, and community members (people from both the survivor's and offender's support systems) for one or more meetings.[5] The Bureau of Justice Assistance describes these meetings as follows: "The process begins with the victim's account of what happened and the impact of that incident. The second part is identifying the victim's needs for repairing the harm, which could range from repayment for items taken and an apology to a demonstrated, long-term turnaround in values and lifestyle by the young person responsible for causing harm. The final result is a restorative plan developed by both parties and their supporters that addresses the root causes for the harm (such as unstable housing, financial instability, gang interaction, etc.) and meets the needs of those harmed."[6] Is restorative justice beneficial for survivors and offenders? First, let's consider offenders.

Researcher Yotam Shem-Tov and his colleagues found a negative relationship between restorative justice and recidivism. They conducted a randomized control study with offenders aged thirteen to seventeen who either completed a restorative justice program or engaged in the traditional juvenile justice system. After six months, the restorative justice group was rearrested at 19 percentage points lower than the traditional group. This may imply that restorative justice is more successful in preventing future crimes than the juvenile justice system. More studies need to be conducted in order to determine the extent to which restorative justice benefits offenders and reduces recidivism.[7]

Restorative justice may provoke genuine emotional responses from offenders, which may elicit positive changes in their behavior. The program gives offenders the opportunity to be directly exposed to the effects of their actions upon survivors. Rather than learning about the impacts of their actions from others (prosecutors, judges, law enforcement), offenders hear it from the survivors themselves in a setting that encourages them to listen and accept. This exposure may initiate emotions of empathy, compassion, guilt, and remorse; emotions that might not be felt in a traditional justice setting. These experiences may give offenders the opportunity to engage in the work that's required of them not only to change their actions but also to improve their lives.

Next, let's consider survivors. Restorative justice may have some benefits for survivors. You may have the opportunity to be seen, heard, and believed by your offender and by members of your community. You could create a more cohesive trauma narrative by collecting information from your offender. You can also be a part of your offender's restorative plan, whereas in traditional legal proceedings, you would have little input regarding what happens to your offender. "Victims who participate in restorative justice have reported feeling more heard and validated and have experienced a greater sense of closure and healing," writes psychologist and attorney Robert Goldman. "They also reported feeling more satisfied with the outcome of the process, believing that justice was served and that the offender took responsibility for their actions." Depending on the facilitator, restorative justice can be a trauma-informed experience. "Restorative justice can use a trauma-informed approach by recognizing the impact of trauma on both the victim and the offender and addressing those effects in the process of restoring harm and repairing relationships," writes Goldman.[8] However, restorative justice programs are not the best fit for every survivor, as they have limitations.

Restorative justice programs are rare and only accessible to a few offenders who are chosen by law enforcement and legal officials. Lindsey Pointer, Principal Investigator of the National Center on Restorative Justice, fears that giving judges and police officers the power to determine who qualifies for these programs creates room for bias based on the offender's race and gender. Pointer says, "We have something that's shown a lot of promise in terms of reforming the system, but we run a significant risk if we have these referral structures that could be replicating the same bias that we see elsewhere."[9] Therefore, offenders from oppressed or marginalized groups may be less likely to be chosen as participants and as a result their victims will also be unable to participate.

Restorative justice programs can inadvertently pressure survivors to forgive because some facilitators may require the offender to offer an apology to the survivor in order to make amends. These apologies may not be genuine (as they're mandatory), and the environment in which they take place can feel coercive for both the offender and the survivor.

"She apologized to me in front of everyone," said Issac. "What was I supposed to say? 'No, I won't forgive you'? That would have made me look evil, so I told her I forgave her, but I didn't."

Isaac—a seventeen-year-old Latino boy who was a struggling student from a low-income family—was the victim of revenge porn when his ex-girlfriend—a sixteen-year-old white, straight-A student from an upper-middle-class family—sent nude pictures of him to her classmates after their relationship ended. Authorities initially considered charging her with the distribution of child pornography, but the prosecutor and families decided it was best to engage in restorative justice. I can't help but wonder whether differences in race, social class, and academic performance impacted this decision. Isaac, his mother, Isaac's ex-girlfriend, her mother, a school counselor, and a facilitator participated in three meetings.

"She admitted everything, which was good because I was being blamed because I sent her the pictures in the first place," Isaac said. "She had to do a bunch of community service, and she wasn't able to be our class president anymore, which was good. I don't know if her apology was real or not because she was supposed to apologize. But the fact that I was asked to forgive her was just wrong. I should be the one to decide if I forgive or not—not her, our parents, or the program."

Although forgiveness is not a requirement of restorative justice, you might feel pressured to forgive your offender in such a scenario, just as Isaac did. "If we're going to think about forgiveness in terms of restorative justice, the only morally and politically careful way to do that is to recognize the legitimacy of the unforgiving victim," argues philosopher Alice MacLachlan. "Not forgiving is a legitimate response to being seriously harmed."[10] There are restorative justice facilitators who carefully ensure that forgiveness is elective and that apologies, if appropriate, are authentic rather than performative. If you are interested in participating in restorative justice, you may need to advocate for your needs regarding apologies and forgiveness. Facilitators of restorative justice should allow survivors—and only survivors—to decide whether they wish to express forgiveness, unforgiveness, or nothing at all in response to an apology from their offender(s).

"BLACK PEOPLE ARE EXPECTED TO FORGIVE SO THAT WHITE PEOPLE CAN SLEEP AT NIGHT."

Systemic racism refers to the policies and practices within a system (e.g., organization, institution, society) that are harmful or unfair to some people based on their race while providing advantages to others based on their race. This type of racism does not depend on whether people in a system are themselves racist but rather the existence of methods within a system that ensure or perpetuate discrimination based on race. For example, imagine that the leadership of a corporate American company is not composed of any racists but is plagued by policies and practices that are systemically racist. This is a common occurrence. Many American citizens report that they are not racist, yet American society is plagued with systemic racism.

Systemic racism causes and perpetuates trauma. Developmental psychopathology researcher Nathalie M. Dumornay and her colleagues studied 9,382 children ages nine to ten in order to discover whether there were any differences in the brain structures of white and Black children impacted by childhood adversity. They found that Black children overall experience more childhood adversity, as their parents are more likely to have lower incomes, lower levels of education, and higher rates of unemployment than their white counterparts, and they are generally exposed to more family conflicts, material hardships, neighborhood disadvantages, and traumatic events when compared to white children. As a result, Black children participating in the study had comparatively lower volumes of gray brain matter in their amygdala and hippocampus and in several subregions of their prefrontal cortexes. The changes in these specific brain regions are observed in people with PTSD. This study suggests that childhood adversities (which Black children are more likely to experience than white children) change the physical structures of the brain that are consistent with those who experience trauma.[11] Therefore, if you are Black, you are more likely to experience the impacts of systemic racism throughout your life, which can cause trauma as well as compound other existing traumas, such as racial trauma.

Psychologist Jude Mary Cénat defines *racial trauma* as "dangerous experiences related to threats, prejudices, harm, shame, humiliation, and guilt associated with various types of racial discrimination either of victims directly or through witnesses."[12] Racial trauma can be caused by either explicit actions (such as murder) or covert actions (such as expressing microaggressions). We don't know how many survivors suffer from racial trauma, as these experiences have not been adequately researched or treated. "Similar to complex trauma, racial trauma surrounds the victims' life course and engenders consequences on their physical and mental health, behavior, cognition, relationships with others, self-concept, and social and economic life," writes Cénat.[13] Forgiveness advocates should avoid pressuring or requesting Black Americans to forgive their more powerful offenders, as these efforts may reinforce racial trauma.

"I said that I forgave him, but I didn't," said Maya. "White and Black people kept telling me to forgive him, and when I wouldn't, they blamed me. So, I had to say I forgave the white cop for raping me so they wouldn't turn against me."

Maya expressed inauthentic forgiveness to protect herself. "For Black people in America, forgiveness has almost never been a choice," writes author and survivor Umm Zakiyyah. "It has been a coping mechanism."[14] Black Americans have been murdered, assaulted, persecuted, isolated, and moralistically criticized for not forgiving racially motivated injustice. In chapter 4, I argued that safety is a precondition for forgiveness. Can Black Americans authentically forgive their offender(s) if they are unsafe in their social and political environment? Black Americans are not safe in American society; they are not only more likely to experience racial trauma but are also more likely to be arrested, prosecuted, charged, and convicted (with longer sentences), and murdered by officials associated with the justice system. Forgiving your offenders is challenging when you are not safe or do not feel safe, or when your offenders inherently have more power over you owing to the long history of racial oppression from which they benefit and all the institutions of privilege from which they receive support at the continual expense of your livelihood, dignity, and socially perceived value and credibility. Therefore, it's readily understandable why Black survivors may need multiple coping responses—including expressing inauthentic forgiveness—in order to promote their own safety. "It took me some time to realize that my emotional triggers in environments of forced forgiveness were at least partially due to having lived daily in a culture that taught me that only white people mattered," writes Zakiyyah. "As an African-American woman, I subconsciously understood that my social acceptance in wider American society, as well as my emotional and physical safety in predominately white environments, depended almost entirely on my filtering all experiences with racism (by myself and other African Americans) through one of four lenses: denying that any racism was involved, blaming the victim (even in cases of murder), acknowledging the wrong but emphasizing the good intentions of the aggressor, or forgiving any aggression, no matter how horrific."[15] Expressing forgiveness can be a way for Black survivors to ensure their own safety. Unfortunately, such forgiveness can be misperceived as authentic forgiveness and an invitation to white Americans to solicit or expect it from Black survivors.

Black Americans are constantly asked and even expected to forgive offenders who have much more power than they do. Those who do not forgive risk their safety or, as political writer Chauncey DeVega writes, risk "being branded with the veritable scarlet letter of being an 'angry' Black man or 'angry' Black woman, [which] can result in their life opportunities being significantly reduced."[16] DeVega describes the destructive pattern of white society demanding Black forgiveness:

> On the one-year anniversary of the death of an 18-year-old Black teenager named Michael Brown by a (now confessed racist) white police officer named Darren Wilson in Ferguson, Missouri, Brown's mother, Lezley McSpadden, was asked if she forgave Darren Wilson for his cruel and wanton act of legal murder. She told Al Jazeera that she will 'never forgive' Darren Wilson and that 'he's evil, his acts were devilish.' Her response is unusual. Its candor is refreshing. Lezley McSpadden's truth-telling reveals the full humanity and emotions of Black folks, and by doing so defies the norms which demand that when Black Americans suffer they do so stoically, and always in such a way where forgiveness for racist violence is a given, an unearned expectation of white America.

The expectation that Black people will always and immediately forgive the violence done to them by the State, or individual white people, is a bizarre and sick American ritual.[17]

Society's pattern of demanding Black survivors to forgive is not only a reflection of overt and systemic racism within society but also a strategic method to shield those who feel uncomfortable when acknowledging these realities.

"I have a friend who was raped by his elementary school teacher, and no one ever asked him to forgive," Maya reported. "His rapist, like mine, was never charged. But no one asked him to forgive. Why? It felt like people couldn't stand it if I, a Black girl, didn't forgive, but they were fine if he, a white boy, didn't forgive. It's unfair. Black people are expected to forgive so that white people can sleep at night."

Maya's experience is not uncommon. Philosopher Myisha Cherry found many examples of Black survivors of high-profile cases being publicly asked to forgive their white offenders, while white survivors are rarely publicly requested to forgive Black offenders. For instance, Michael Brown, Samuel DuBose, and Eric Garner were Black men murdered by white men. Reporters asked all of the victims' families if they could forgive.[18] In contrast, there are few examples in which the families of white victims in high-profile cases are publicly requested to forgive Black offenders. Why the double standard? As Cherry explains, "The forgiveness request can be read as a way to escape the racial discomfort that white violence and Black victimhood have introduced. If the victim forgives, we can all move on from the uncomfortable race conversation. White discomfort departs when we introduce forgiveness. Unfortunately, this move ensures that we do not deal with the underlying racism and injustice that give rise to the wrongdoing."[19] Pressuring, demanding, or encouraging forgiveness from Black survivors may be used as a method to avoid the realities of systemic racism and racial trauma and used as a substitution for enacting substantive social justice.

Forgiveness is often weaponized by the white establishment in order to shift the burden for remedying the social injuries and rifts engendered by the long history of white supremacy and colonialism onto the shoulders of Black survivors. Our working definition of forgiveness consists of internal changes in the survivor's thoughts, emotions, and actions—not the offender's. Therefore, requesting Black forgiveness is requesting Black Americans to change without requiring any changes from their offenders or from society, which does more harm than good. If white offenders are "forgiven" by Black survivors and by colonized peoples, then they don't need to reorganize or dismantle status quo social, political, juridical, and educational institutions, redistribute wealth or pay reparations, give back stolen land, and so on. Those who advocate for Black survivors forgiving their white offenders may intentionally or unintentionally be contributing to the preservation of systemic racism.

Forgiveness advocates need to consider not only the impact of systemic racism and racial trauma on Black survivors' capability, willingness, safety, and need to forgive but also the fact that withholding Black forgiveness may indeed lead to societal changes that would benefit Black Americans. "Expectations of forgiveness are raced and gendered," says legal scholar Martha Minow. "They're also about class. They're about power, but that's partly because forgiveness is one of the powers of the weak. To claim the ability to forgive—and let's be clear, to not forgive—is to claim the position of equality and dignity."[20] Black survivors may not forgive in order to reclaim their equality, dignity, and to create societal change. Instead of demanding or requesting Black Americans to forgive, forgiveness advocates should consider embracing elective forgiveness, which could foster rather than hinder social justice.

"WOMEN ARE EXPECTED TO FORGIVE, EVEN IF IT KILLS THEM."

"He won't get raped; you will," my father told me when I was thirteen years old, after I asked why my brother did not have a curfew but I did. "You have to do everything that you can not to get raped."

"But that's not fair," I said.

"That's how it is," he replied, nonchalantly.

This was how I discovered that I am not socially equal to men; I realized that my gender marked me as *less-than*. My father's advice reflected the ideology of a patriarchal society—that is, one that structurally and unapologetically centers and privileges men and subjugates and devalues women. My father was not telling me that I *could* be raped; he was informing me that I *would likely* be raped, and he was correct. Moreover, he was telling me that it was my responsibility to make sure that such a likelihood did not come to pass, rather than placing the responsibility on rapists or society as a whole. Herman writes that "rape, battery, and other forms of sexual and domestic violence are so common a part of women's lives that they can hardly be described as outside the range of ordinary experience."[21] Statistics show that women are much more likely to experience sexual assault and domestic violence than men, and this clearly reflects the social construction of women's inferiority.[22] Sexual assault is not about sexual attraction or sex, just as domestic violence is not a private dispute or family matter. They are both always about *power*. The fact that women are so often sexually assaulted and abused in their own homes signifies their offenders' implicit devaluation of them as human beings, and the fact that this abuse occurs so often and without legal repercussions is a clear indication of society's devaluation of women. My father's way of "protecting" me was telling me that I was likely to be victimized because I was born and identify as female, and that it was my responsibility—and mine alone—to prevent it. My father never discussed sexual assault with my brothers (society's future men), likely believing that they would never be victims of sexual assault; he also never taught them that they are equal to women, which would help counteract future violence against women. Instead of teaching my brothers to respect women and practice consent, he taught me to avoid being assaulted; instead of teaching my brothers not to victimize women, he told me not to "allow myself" to become a victim; instead of telling my brothers not to rape, he told me not *to get raped*. My father, I later discovered, was a rapist himself. So, he knew firsthand the dangers that his daughter faced living in a society that allowed people like him to assault women without consequences.

The United States is a patriarchal society, that is, a society in which men systemically dominate women; it is a society in which men hold more positions of authority and power, and in which women are structurally relegated to marginalized and subordinate positions within social institutions. Simply put, patriarchy is a social hierarchy in which men, purely in virtue of being men, are at the top, and in which women, purely in virtue of being women, are at the bottom, and this is reflected in the United States not only by its history but also by its present social policies and legal system. The United States is lacking in maternal healthcare, parental leave, and reproductive rights, and there continues to be a pay gap between men and women (with women currently earning eighty-two cents to every dollar earned by men).[23] This oppression is far worse for women who are not white. In 2022, Black women earned 70 percent as much as white men and Hispanic women earned 65 percent as much as white men.[24] In the household, women are more likely to be responsible for childcare, food preparation, and household chores compared to their male partners, regardless of whether women are employed or not.[25] Society continues to view women as primary caretakers, and their caretaking—though essential for the functioning of society—is rarely compensated. The responsibility of providing care for children, aging parents, disabled family members, and community members often falls to women. When we examine this oppression, it's no wonder that women are more likely to experience crimes (e.g., sexual assault and domestic violence) that are motivated by the offender's need, desire, or perceived right to exert power and control over them.

It should be noted that patriarchal societies harm both women and men, as men who experience sexual assault and domestic violence are less likely to report and seek treatment for their trauma due to the roles and pressures that society places upon them. I rarely trust statistics measuring men as victims of sexual assault and domestic violence, as I know that it's a gross underrepresentation of reality. In addition, patriarchal societies promote an oppressive view of masculinity, which has caused and perpetuated trauma. Men who are raised and live in patriarchy are often taught to engage in emotional detachment and encouraged to suppress their emotional responses and expressions. As a result, men are susceptible to becoming offenders and survivors.

"Women are expected to forgive, even if it kills them," said April. "They would rather I die and forgive him than not forgive him and live."

April left her physically, sexually, and financially abusive husband for the final time. It was her third attempt at leaving and what she called "my last Hail Mary." She moved in with her sister, ceased all communication with her husband, and filed for divorce. Her husband attempted suicide and was hospitalized. April's family, friends, and church members begged her to forgive him so that he wouldn't harm himself again.

"They keep saying, 'You don't have to go back to him, just talk to him, just forgive him,'" April said through tears. "It's funny how I'm supposed to be the bigger person. The woman is always expected to sacrifice, be better, and forgive, even if it's not what's best for her."

American society can pressure women to forgive when it's not in their best interest. Women are socialized, taught, and expected to have superior relational skills, which include expressing empathy, humility, and compassion, resolving conflicts, and managing their emotions for the benefit of others. Women in this role are considered "nice girls" or "good women." Those who do not subscribe to or are incapable of embracing this role risk being judged, ostracized, or excluded from valuable opportunities. Society penalizes women who express anger, are direct or blunt, or who dare to establish and maintain firm boundaries that promote their safety and happiness. How often have you heard epithets such as "cold," "angry," "dramatic," or "bitch" used to refer to women who were simply standing up for themselves, speaking their minds, or expressing confidence and ambition? Men would surely not be disparaged for speaking or behaving in similar ways, and such a double standard is rooted in patriarchal constructions of masculinity and femininity. Many women do embrace the "good woman" role in order to promote their safety, maintain relationships, and advance in society. Unfortunately, this role often requires that they forgive even when such forgiveness would be inauthentic or not in their best interest. Rabbi Susan Schnur writes, "We say 'I'm sorry' to a fault—even when we're the ones being victimized! Forgiving is easy for us; it's not forgiving that's the struggle. We are over-socialized to stay connected, to 'make peace,' to make sure nobody is offended, to forget to ask if we ourselves are offended. Indeed, this is perhaps the core of our gender socialization."[26] Therefore, women in American society are expected to forgive if they are to be considered "good" women.

Women are not only expected to embrace the "good woman" role in society but also the role of the "good victim." As Sharon Lamb writes, "Being a victim affords a woman an instant purity and sympathy, if not martyrdom, and all too often, the public has trouble with victims when they do not live up to this idealized standard."[27] Women must be "pure" enough when they are victimized, or else they might be blamed for their offender's actions, and they must also show sympathy for their offender after being harmed in order to be a "good victim." Lamb elaborates that "to maintain her role in the dichotomy as the 'good one,' the victim will need to forgive and show compassion. It would not be consistent with her victim role to be angry, resentful, and retaliatory."[28] If your response to harm is anger rather than forgiveness, you are not acting as a "good woman" or "good victim." Society's moral and relational expectations of women pressure them to forgive their offenders, even if doing so puts their safety at risk.

As was pointed out for Black Americans, women may express forgiveness in order to promote their immediate physical and emotional safety by placating oppressive social norms. "For women raised to fear, too often anger threatens annihilation," writes Audre Lorde. "In the male construct of brute force, we were taught that our lives depended upon the goodwill of patriarchal power. The anger of others was to be avoided at all costs because there was nothing to be learned from it but pain, a judgment that we had been bad girls, come up lacking, not done what we were supposed to do. And if we accept our powerlessness, then of course any anger can destroy us."[29] Women have been belittled, socially marginalized, and punished for expressing their anger or not being able to avoid or manage the anger of men. It's not uncommon for women to be expected to remain calm, speak softly, and verbalize forgiveness in order to manage someone else's anger. Unfortunately, when women embrace the role of the "nice girl" or "good woman," they often place themselves in danger. "A woman who fights back gains an 86% chance of avoiding the rape and incurs little chance of additional injury," reports IMPACT Chicago, an organization that teaches self-defense to women, girls, and people with disabilities.[30] Self-defense classes teach women how to appear as if they *will* fight back, to scream and yell when attacked, and how to fight back physically; all qualities or behaviors that a "good woman" would never embrace. However, it's precisely these interventions that have saved women's lives. "Most injuries occur before the woman starts fighting back. Women are most likely to stop an attack if they act immediately and use multiple strategies," IMPACT reports.[31] Many women survivors have participated in self-defense programs and classes to support their recovery. Self-defense facilitators must be careful to avoid perpetuating patriarchal beliefs that blame women by overemphasizing a woman's responsibility to resist being assaulted rather than a man's responsibility not to commit assault. One of IMPACT's slogans is *One day 'no' will be enough*, emphasizing that their ultimate goal is social change.

"They don't get it. If I talk to him or if I forgive him, I'll go back to him, and if I go back, he'll kill me," said April. "If I protect myself and don't forgive, then I'm a bitch who's no better than him. But if I forgive, then I'm a dead woman who should have left before she got herself killed. I just can't win."

Forgiveness can harm women who forgive their offenders, as doing so in cases of domestic violence increases the possibility that they will continue to participate in relationships with their offenders and therefore expose themselves to further abuse. Forgiveness might make further abuse more likely because, provided one extends forgiveness to one's offender without conditions, the offender may simply continue to behave abusively because they know that every time they do so, they'll simply be "forgiven." Some couples counselors, who are trained to support relationship reconciliation rather than termination, will refuse to work with couples who have domestic violence occurring in the relationship, as reconciliation or the continuation of the relationship would be harmful to one or both parties. There are some couples counselors who will work with these couples if the goal is to help them to terminate their relationship safely. Those who encourage forgiveness must remember that safety must always precede forgiveness, as you cannot authentically forgive when you do not feel safe. Safety also takes priority over forgiveness because you cannot forgive your offender when you are dead.

Forgiveness therapy practitioners and advocates may take advantage of society's expectations of women to extend forgiveness to those who wrong or harm them. The few studies that measure the impact of Enright's process model of forgiveness upon trauma survivors include only female participants, and most of them forgave. Such biased samples render the results of these studies scientifically dubious, but I can't help but wonder if they were intentional. Would they have found similar results if men had been included in their studies? To be clear, forgiveness *can* benefit women, but only when it is on their terms and in their best interest—not when it is in the interest of their offender, and not when it is performed merely to appease social norms. Forgiveness therapy practitioners and advocates shouldn't reinforce patriarchal double standards and pressures by encouraging women to forgive so that they will let go of their anger. "Forgiveness professionals play into stereotypes of the 'good' woman when they help her to experience her anger and then move beyond it," writes Lamb. "Instead, the integration of anger and aggression with their identity, even as a compassionate, caring person, is ideal for women who have been brought up in this culture."[32] Forgiveness advocates should be aware of the social expectations placed upon women and consider offering *elective* forgiveness in order to avoid perpetuating oppressive gender norms and support the genuine needs of their clients.

Expecting women to forgive also reproduces gendered inequality in society. As Lamb writes, "For women, refusing to be angry historically has kept them in a position of subordination; realizing and acting on anger has led to greater rights and freedoms."[33] As we explored in chapter 5, the stigmatized emotion of anger has many positive benefits, which include promoting social change. Women may need to embrace their anger in order to challenge patriarchy and work to bring about the changes that are necessary for a just society.

Lamb worries that the pressures impressed upon women to forgive, and that the moral value of forgiveness in general, have "kept them reading self-help books rather than marching in the streets."[34]

FORGIVING WITHOUT EQUALITY

Can you authentically forgive your offender when you are not considered their equal in society? Forgiveness therapy practitioners argue that you can and should forgive your offender because doing so will help you perceive yourself as an equal, for in doing so you "take your power back from them." As Enright writes, "A forgiver who knows that the act was unjust can see his or her own status as equal to the other person, regardless of the other's stance toward that offended person. Resisting the act of forgiving until the offender somehow changes is giving great power to the offender."[35] This remark clearly indicates that forgiveness therapy is oblivious to the reality of social inequality. You cannot use forgiveness as a method to establish equality with your offender in a society that already views you as having less value than them. Forgiveness will not give you equal power to your offender in a society in which you are systemically oppressed and they are systemically privileged. The cliché sentiment that "you are giving them power over you if you don't forgive them" has in fact not only been weaponized to center the interests of offenders rather than survivors but also promotes the deep-rooted power irregularities that prevail between them and that are often at the motivational basis of the harms committed by offenders in the first place. Maya—a low-income Black lesbian girl—cannot achieve the same value and power in society as her rapist—a white heterosexual police commissioner—merely by forgiving him. April's "good woman" forgiveness won't protect her from her husband; on the contrary, she reported that forgiving him would likely lead to her murder. It is possible to forgive an offender who has greater value and power in society than yourself, but such forgiveness should never be requested, pressured, recommended, or encouraged; rather, it should always be *elective*.

FORGIVENESS CAN HINDER SOCIAL JUSTICE

Can you, an oppressed survivor, authentically forgive your privileged offender (who has made no positive changes) without reinforcing your own subordination and oppression? Perhaps you can. However, this question must be seriously considered, as forgiveness can strengthen and sustain social inequalities. When we, oppressed survivors, forgive our privileged offenders, we might be inadvertently maintaining the status quo in America and hindering social justice. Karl Marx famously wrote that religion is "the opium of the people" because he feared that certain religious teachings pacify oppressed people into submission to their own oppression, or that they serve to mystify the real material conditions of their exploitation and misery.[36] I fear that a culture of compulsory forgiveness similarly serves as an "opiate" that prevents oppressed survivors from engaging in emancipatory social action.

Forgiveness is used as a method to manage anger; as such, it might benefit some people, but it can also cause social harm by suppressing the kinds of attitudes that motivate and inspire agitation for social justice. Rather than encouraging social progress, it may in fact encourage social stagnation. Conditions of inequality, exploitation, and oppression are sustained when people feel comfortable and complacent, and they are challenged when people feel appropriately angry about them and are motivated to act for change based on that anger. Society typically requests, expects, or pressures forgiveness from oppressed survivors, yet does not expect or demand any commensurate amends, concessions, or substantive changes from those in power. As survivor Umm Zakiyyah writes, "It is no accident that these oppressive systems required love and forgiveness only from those they continuously harm, but not from themselves as the oppressors. In other words, by establishing a one-sided culture of forced love and forgiveness (no matter how egregious their own crimes), oppressors ensure that their systems of hate and injustice will never be meaningfully challenged."[37]

Forgiveness has been and will continue to be used as a weapon against oppressed survivors in order to maintain social inequalities, which causes further trauma. Thus, philosophers Luke Brunning and Per-Erik Milam write:

Forgiveness can seem like a powerful practice to which the oppressed, as regular victims of wrongdoing, have unimpeded access. In fact, the opposite is the case. The oppressed are less able to forgive and less able to do so successfully. Moreover, because of the mismatch between its perceived power and its actual effectiveness, forgiveness is likely to be misused by those who need it and misunderstood by those who 'police' it, whether as recipients of forgiveness or bystanders to the practice.

Rather than helping oppose oppression, forgiveness may stem from, reflect, and exacerbate it.[38]

Like all human experiences, forgiveness does not exist in a vacuum but within a larger social context. Social inequalities directly impact your ability and willingness to forgive and determine whether forgiveness is beneficial or detrimental. Forgiveness is not a substitute for justice, and indeed it is often an obstacle to it. Forgiveness does not alter political policies or foment institutional change; *people* do, and they often do so precisely when they refuse to forgive those in power for the policies and actions that have wronged them. More specifically, it's often oppressed trauma survivors who have led the most successful social justice movements in American history, survivors who are commonly moved by anger, resentment, and rage—not forgiveness—toward those who are responsible for their oppression and trauma.

CHAPTER NINE

Responding to Forgiveness Advocates

Those who overtly pressure trauma survivors to forgive often expose their intention to harm. But the intentions of those who recommend or encourage forgiveness are much less clear.

The truth is, those who promote forgiveness often have many different intentions. Specific intentions might be perceived as right if they have the survivor's best interest in mind, and as wrong if they carry the malicious intent to cause harm, but it's not always that simple. The intentions of forgiveness advocates lie on a spectrum, existing somewhere between the abstract concepts of right and wrong. Muddying the waters even further, advocates may not even be aware of their true intentions. They may not interrogate their intent thoroughly or at all, recommending forgiveness without pausing to ask themselves "Is it my place to recommend forgiveness?", "Why do I need to encourage them to forgive?", and "What is my honest intention in promoting forgiveness?" Advocates must be able to identify, accept, and communicate their intentions for promoting forgiveness if they seek to support trauma survivors. In turn, you must be prepared to respond to advocates in ways that promote your safety and support your recovery.

I've compiled some of the most common intentions of forgiveness advocates, which I've encountered in my work as a trauma psychotherapist, and questions that advocates can ask themselves to identify their honest intentions and scripts for you to use when responding to them.

"YOU'LL FEEL BETTER."

Many forgiveness advocates genuinely want to help you. These advocates have been sold the product of forgiveness as a panacea that heals all emotional pain caused by trauma. They have read articles, watched videos, and listened to experts who speak about the healing power of forgiveness. Why wouldn't they recommend it to someone in emotional pain?

Sasha's father abandoned him when he was eight years old. His father started using methamphetamines and abruptly left the family one day. Sasha came home from school to his mother screaming, "What are we going to do now?" When Sasha was thirty-six years old, his father, now sober, reconnected with the family. His mother and siblings invited him back with open arms. They never thought they would see him alive again. Sasha, however, was angry and refused to speak to him.

"You need to forgive him," Sasha's brother said. "It's not for him; it's for you. You need closure."

"You're only hurting yourself by not forgiving him," Sasha's aunt wrote in an email. "It's time to move on. I hate seeing you like this."

"Forgive," texted Sasha's sister. "I promise you: you'll feel better."

Sasha believed that his family members had good intentions. They wanted to help and genuinely believed they were doing so by encouraging forgiveness. However, this encouragement had the opposite effect. Sasha stopped reaching out to his family for emotional support. When they asked him how he was doing, he reported, "okay," "fine," and "hanging in there." But Sasha was not okay. He was experiencing severe nightmares, depressive symptoms, and panic attacks.

"I need to protect them," Sasha told me during a therapy session. "If that means I must sacrifice myself, so be it." Sasha was convinced that his struggles were harming his family, and they needed him to forgive so that they would feel better. Sasha could not forgive, so he felt that he needed to keep them at a distance, and he ceased all communication with his family.

Encouraging survivors to forgive may be less about the needs of survivors and more about the needs of the encouragers. It hurts us to see loved ones struggling; we are compelled to try to fix or heal their pain however we can. But, in doing so, we are also trying to escape our own suffering. Recommending forgiveness is a method people use to avoid the anguish it causes them to see the ones they love in pain. Forgiveness advocates may also recommend forgiveness to give survivors access to an escape route. "They don't know how to hold space for people's pain," said psychologist Rosenna Bakari when I asked her why people promote forgiveness. "They don't understand that once survivors are given the space to experience and understand their pain, that's when the healing begins."[1] Forgiveness is not a method to bypass or avoid the long and at times brutal recovery process. The truth is that there is no shortcut or escape route. You cannot go around or avoid recovery, as the only way forward is through. Advocates cannot rescue you from your emotional and physical pain, as processing that pain is an essential part of recovery. This difficult truth can devastate those close to you, who must simultaneously hold space for your pain while managing their own emotional responses.

It can take a significant amount of emotional and physical energy to hold space for another's pain. We must stay in our window of emotional tolerance, the space we need to remain emotionally regulated and present, while also sitting with their pain. To help them, we must cope with our own emotional reactions and possibly our own trauma responses. We must resist the urge to fix them or to rescue them. The more we care about them, the harder this can be to achieve.

Those who encourage forgiveness might experience guilt or shame if they cannot provide survivors with the emotional support they need. There are many valid reasons why they are incapable of this, such as their own trauma being activated, their emotional needs not being met, feeling overwhelmed by the stressors in their own life, shouldering the burden of a sole support system for a survivor, et cetera. In addition to coping with the difficulty of bearing witness to another's pain, they may also encourage forgiveness to assuage their own feelings of inadequacy, guilt, or shame.

Self-reflection for Advocates

Advocates who believe forgiveness will help trauma survivors to feel better can ask themselves the following:

- Am I struggling to bear witness or hold space for the survivor's pain? Is this why I'm promoting forgiveness?
- Am I attempting to rescue or fix them instead of being present with them in their recovery process?

- Are my trauma responses becoming activated as I attempt to support them?
- Do I feel guilty or shameful that I cannot support them as much as I would like to?

Responses for Survivors

Survivors who encounter advocates with the intention that forgiveness will make them feel better can consider using these responses:

- Thank you for your thoughts. I know what's best for me.
- I cannot forgive. Do you have any other suggestions?
- This isn't helpful. Would you like to know what would be more helpful?
- Instead of encouraging me to forgive, I need you to _____ [a behavior that would be more helpful, such as listening, being present, empathizing, validating, accepting, proving physical touch, etc.).

"IT HELPED ME. I KNOW IT'LL HELP YOU."

Those who encourage forgiveness may be motivated to recommend it because forgiveness has helped them. They intend to help you based on their experiences and testimony. To them, encouraging forgiveness is no different from recommending a coping skill that has been successful for them in the past. Meditation, deep breathing, and yoga are coping skills that are often recommended to trauma survivors. Some have benefited from these interventions, and some have not. Just as with the practice of forgiveness, no single intervention works for all survivors.

"It helped me. I know it'll help you," Sasha's aunt told him repeatedly. "If you forgive your father, you'll be just like me and Alexi. We are both so much happier now."

Sasha's aunt was raped by her cousin Alexi. She forgave Alexi and was able to have a friendly relationship with him. Forgiveness helped her, and she wanted Sasha to experience the same benefits. Sasha's father abandoned him; Sasha could not forgive him. After Sasha became estranged from his family, his aunt continued promoting forgiveness as she sent him books about how to forgive, asked family friends to speak to him, and found a family therapist who agreed to work with Sasha and his father to pursue forgiveness. Sasha didn't read the books, he avoided family friends, and he never participated in family therapy.

After months of individual trauma therapy, Sasha decided to reconnect with his family. To promote his safety, he established a firm boundary with his aunt.

"I'm glad forgiveness helped you, but it's not what I need," Sasha wrote in an email to her. "Please don't discuss forgiveness with me again. It's not helpful."

His aunt respected his boundary. As a result, she was able to support him in other ways, such as planning family gatherings without his father present so that Sasha could attend and asking family friends to retreat so that Sasha would feel safe to reengage with them. Years later, Sasha reported that his aunt became one of his most supportive and valued family relationships.

Self-reflection for Advocates

Those who have benefited from forgiveness and wish to recommend it to trauma survivors can ask themselves the following:

- If I have benefited from forgiveness, am I assuming that the survivor's experience and outcome will be the same as mine? What if it isn't?
- Can I ask the survivor for their consent before discussing forgiveness?
- Can I share my personal experiences with forgiveness without recommending it?
- Am I aware of how my biases (e.g., culture, religion, personal experiences) impact my perception of forgiveness? Have I communicated my biases to the survivor?

Responses for Survivors

Survivors who encounter advocates who believe that since forgiveness benefited them, it will benefit the survivor, can consider using these responses:

- Thank you for your insights. I'll consider it.
- I'm glad that forgiveness has helped you. It's just not what I need at this time in my recovery.
- It sounds like you've had good experiences with forgiving. My experiences have been different.
- In the future, please ask my permission before providing me with advice or feedback. I'll let you know when it's needed.

"IT WILL MAKE THINGS EASIER."

Those who encourage you to forgive may directly benefit from your forgiveness. They might be the actual offender, a family member who wishes to maintain dysfunctional family dynamics, or they have something to gain if you forgive or something to lose if you don't. Lawyers refer to this dilemma as *having a conflict of interest.*

Those who promote forgiveness must be aware of any conflicts of interest that they hold. Otherwise, they can be misleading in communicating their intentions. "If the person counseling forgiveness has an emotional, financial, or sympathetic connection with the one who injured you, then there is good reason to hesitate before trusting this counsel," writes attorney David Bedrick. "This could be one parent suggesting you forgive the other, a religious institution suggesting you forgive the clergy, a politician who would like to 'move on,' a friend who fails to make real amends or redress, or simply a person who can relate more to the injurer than to you. Essentially, where conflicts of interest are present, beware and slow down before trying to forgive."[2] In short, you should hesitate to take recommendations from those with a conflict of interest.

Abby was sexually assaulted in the workplace by a coworker. She reported the incident to the human resources department, and they conducted an investigation. Her offender claimed that it was a misunderstanding and profusely apologized.

"You know, if you forgive, it will make things easier," said Abby's supervisor.

"For who?" Abby asked, shocked.

"Everyone," the supervisor replied. "If we have to take action, it will be stressful for everyone, including your coworkers. You should consider the impact this will have."

Abby's forgiveness might have made things easier for her supervisor, her offender, her coworkers, and the company, but it would not have benefited Abby. Her supervisor even used her relationships with coworkers to coerce her into forgiveness, a common tactic. Instead of focusing on forgiveness, Abby left her job and pursued legal action against the company, and she won her case. Her offender was offered a promotion in another department, where he likely became someone else's problem—a pattern we often see in companies, educational settings, and religious institutions.

Offenders know that seeking justice will be difficult for you, and some rely on this to avoid accountability. Offenders are also aware that many people will act as bystanders. "All the perpetrator asks is that the bystander do nothing," writes Judith Herman. "He appeals to the universal desire to see, hear, and speak no evil. The victim, on the contrary, asks the bystander to share the burden of pain. The victim demands action, engagement, and remembering."[3] Loved ones of trauma survivors and bystanders alike can have many conflicts of interest, which would make them biased when recommending forgiveness.

Self-reflection for Advocates

Those who seek to promote forgiveness due to the belief that it will make things easier for the survivor can ask themselves the following:

- Are my conflicts of interest impacting my decision to promote forgiveness? What do I have to gain if they forgive? What do I have to lose if they do not forgive?
- Can I be honest with the survivor regarding my conflicts of interest?
- Am I aware that forgiveness is different from reconciliation and justice?
- Am I aware that forgiveness is not a pardon, as the offender(s) can be forgiven and experience consequences?

Responses for Survivors

Survivors who encounter advocates with the intention that forgiveness will make things easier for them can consider using these responses:

- Do you have any conflicts of interest that I should be aware of? What do you have to gain or lose if I forgive or do not forgive?
- It seems that you have a lot to gain from my forgiveness. Could this be influencing your recommendation for me to forgive?
- My forgiveness might make things easier for you or others, but it will not make things easier for me.
- You are unable to have an objective opinion in this situation. Therefore, I cannot take your advice.

"BE THE BETTER PERSON."

Forgiveness is often recommended because of its association with the moral high ground. How often have you heard the phrase *forgiveness is a virtue*? We are taught that good, moral, and loving people forgive. If I believe I am a good person or strive to be a good person, I may feel I need to forgive my offender(s) because that's what good people do. Abby's lack of forgiveness caused her to question her moral identity.

"I wonder if I'm just as wrong as he is," Abby said during her therapy session. "I have a friend who told me to forgive is to be 'the better person.' That stuck with me. Am I a bad person if I don't forgive him?"

Many advocate forgiveness as a method to validate and express one's identity. Mahatma Gandhi said, "The weak can never forgive. Forgiveness is the attribute of the strong."[4] Would Gandhi consider trauma survivors weak because they do not or cannot forgive their offenders? I hope not. Martin Luther King Jr. said, "He who is devoid of the power to forgive is devoid of the power to love."[5] Would King consider trauma survivors who do not or cannot forgive their offender(s) incapable of loving? Perhaps King and Gandhi were not considering trauma survivors when they made these statements. But they and many like them are often quoted by those who encourage you to forgive to align with a moral identity.

Forgiveness advocates may also promote forgiveness to encourage survivors to take their power back from their offenders. The goal is not to feel equal to the offender, but better than. This is not meant in a purely moral sense; instead, it is meant to instill a sense of superiority in the survivor, to make them feel that their offender is beneath them and thus beneath their concern.

"People would tell me, 'You're smarter, stronger, and more successful than him,'" said Abby. "It was like they were saying that I was not supposed to be impacted by his actions because he was lower than me. It's like they thought that if I believed I was better than him, I could forgive him because he had less value than me."

When forgiveness advocates claim that you are superior to your offender(s), they often hope you will experience increased self-worth and empowerment, which they believe will lead to forgiveness. However, this tactic is rarely successful. Feeling superior does not create or promote genuine self-worth, nor does it empower you. Moreover, for marginalized people, this "superiority" rings hollow. When an oppressed person is abused by a member of a privileged group, they know full well that they have no high ground of any kind. The privileged offender is treated as superior and will be supported by the power structures around them.

Self-reflection for Advocates

Those who believe that trauma survivors should forgive in order to validate a moral identity or claim their superiority can ask themselves the following:

- Is it possible that the survivor can be a moral person with or without forgiveness?
- What if the survivor is not unwilling to forgive but is simply unable? Are they weak or immoral?
- Do I feel more comfortable perceiving the survivor as superior to their offender? Will sharing this perception help the survivor to recover or meet my own needs?
- Is the survivor part of a marginalized population? If so, am I aware of how this status impacts their view of power structures in society?

Responses for Survivors

Survivors who encounter advocates who believe they should forgive in order to validate a moral identity or claim their superiority over their offender(s) can consider using these responses:

- I am a good, loving, and strong person regardless of my ability or willingness to forgive.
- It's not helpful when you compare my value to others. I don't need to see myself as having more or less value than offenders; I need to see myself as having value despite them.
- Do not equate my sense of empowerment with forgiveness. I can feel empowered with or without forgiveness.

"THEY'VE APOLOGIZED."

People may encourage survivors to forgive after their offender has apologized. There is a belief in many cultures that apologies must be followed by forgiveness. Children are taught to apologize when they offend and to quickly forgive when they are apologized to, regardless of whether they feel authentic remorse or forgiveness. This behavioral pattern can be reinforced in adulthood when others expect forgiveness after providing an apology.

Paul's wife physically abused him for five years. He left the family home, filed for divorce, and sought custody of his two young children. After he left, his wife profusely apologized. She sent him texts and emails, left voicemails, and created multiple public social media posts admitting her wrongdoing and apologizing. Yet Paul did not respond to her, and he continued with the legal proceedings.

"She's apologized, what more do you need?" texted Paul's friend. "Can't you just forgive her? What are you trying to prove?"

"She really wants to work this out. Can you give her a second chance?" asked his mother.

"Mommy's really sad. She needs to talk to you," said his seven-year-old daughter.

Paul's family and friends were confused by his resistance to communicating with his wife. They perceived her adamant apologies as a genuine effort on her part to change. No one questioned the physical abuse that Paul experienced, as his wife publicly admitted to it. Yet, instead of acknowledging how the abuse impacted Paul, they focused on his wife's apologies as evidence that she was now a safe person.

"I wonder if you would feel differently if it was I, a man, who abused her, a woman?" Paul asked his mother, who didn't respond. Yet, Paul had a point. Trauma survivors who are adult cismen are less likely to report crimes perpetrated against them by adult ciswomen offenders, especially in domestic settings.[6]At Paul's daughter's birthday party, which he attended with his wife and many others, his wife made a toast that included a public tearful apology and a guarantee that she had changed. After that, Paul's friends and family increasingly pressured him to engage with her, and he agreed to meet her in a public setting to see if they could reconnect and work toward an amicable divorce. The first meeting went well; Paul reported that she took accountability for the abuse, expressed empathy and compassion, and agreed to give him full custody of their children. A week later, Paul agreed to meet her at their house when the children were at school. This meeting started off well until she asked him to replace a lightbulb, which was his responsibility when they were together. He refused, stating that he felt this action was inappropriate as he no longer lived in the house. His wife started screaming and hitting him multiple times before Paul could run out the front door.

That night, her apologies flooded in through texts, emails, voicemail, and social media posts, just as before. Paul cut off contact with her, was granted a divorce, and received full custody of his children. For the next two years, his ex-wife would send group texts to Paul's family and friends profusely apologizing. She then remarried, and within a year, her new husband filed for divorce and a restraining order.

Apologies from offenders can be genuine and heartfelt or manipulative and harmful—sometimes they are both. At times, the offender is not even aware of their true intentions. To this day, Paul believes that his wife was sincere when she apologized, but this was not evidence that she was safe to be around or that she had the willingness or capability to change.

When we think of apologies, we usually consider the offender and the offended as peers or equals. What if they are not? "An apology offered by an offender who ultimately has power over the injured party, for example an incestuous father apologizing to his daughter, brings with it even more pressure for forgiveness," writes Lamb.[7] You might be pressured to forgive if your offender has power over you, because doing otherwise may threaten your safety. However, any forgiveness a person offers in order to stay safe is not authentic.

You may feel pressured to forgive when you receive an apology in private, but the pressure often increases when the apology is public. Image this scenario: A man proposes marriage to a woman before her family, friends, and community members. She says no. This scenario may cause the viewer to feel sad or embarrassed for the man or angry at the woman. This is why most couples have discussed marriage before any proposal, especially a public proposal, is made. In fact, many people will state, "I knew they were going to propose, I just didn't know when or how." What if marriage is not discussed? If a public rejection does not occur, some people will accept it at the moment and then communicate a rejection in private. This is also true for forgiveness. When offenders make a public apology, you may verbalize forgiveness at the moment without being sincere. This can also be true of private apologies, as you may feel unsafe denying forgiveness when you are alone with your offender.

Self-reflection for Advocates

Those who encourage trauma survivors to forgive their apologetic offenders simply because the offenders have apologized can ask themselves the following:

- Are you aware that an authentic apology does not mandate or require forgiveness?
- Have you considered that the apologizing offender might not be physically, emotionally, sexually, or financially safe?
- How much behavioral evidence do you have that indicates the offender is safe, has changed, or is actively working on changing?
- Have you taken on the role of a middle person in this dynamic? For example, are you acting as a communication liaison between the offender and survivor or rallying allies for the offender or survivor? If so, are your actions helping or harming the survivor?

Responses for Survivors

Survivors who encounter advocates who encourage their forgiveness due to the offender's apology can consider using these responses:

- They are not safe, and my safety is my top priority.
- Their actions do not match their words. I need to see a change in their actions.

- I have received their apology, which does not mandate a response of forgiveness.
- I need you to stop getting involved. Here's what I need from you: [list of behaviors that they need to cease, such as not passing messages back and forth, not sharing any information about you with the offender, and not trying to repair the relationship in any way). If you can't accept these boundaries, then I cannot involve you in my recovery going forward.

"THEY HAD A ROUGH LIFE."

Advocates may encourage trauma survivors to gain a better understanding of their offenders in the hopes that they will forgive. In fact, empathy for the offender(s) is a common experience that occurs before or in conjunction with forgiveness. Yet, this intention can be perceived by survivors as taking the offender's side or minimizing the survivor's experiences. Forgiveness advocates who encourage understanding and empathy for the offender(s) must be aware that they can easily come across as taking sides. This will cause survivors to feel unsafe, and they will take steps to protect themselves. Remember, safety always precedes forgiveness. Survivors must reestablish a sense of safety in their emotions, bodies, communities, and world before they are capable of understanding, empathizing, and feeling compassion for their offender(s).

When you are ready and have expressed consent, learning your offender's story can be beneficial. I've witnessed many survivors experience decreased anger, shame, fear, and grief when they learn about their offender(s) and begin to view them as vulnerable human beings instead of impenetrable monsters. When this transformation occurs, it's usually in the middle or near the end of trauma recovery, not at the beginning. Six years after I began my recovery, I asked my aunt to tell me my mother's story.

"Your mom was so sick for so long," my aunt said. "We were constantly told that she wouldn't live. Of course, she survived, but the damage had been done."

My mother suffered a significant heart-related illness as a small child and spent hours bedridden. When she was well enough to leave her bed, her family treated her like she would die at any moment. She was treated very differently from her siblings, who were physically abused by their father. He never touched my mother, not because he loved her more, but because he believed she was fragile. Her siblings were not allowed to distress her in any way, and they had to be careful of how they played with her. The entire family enabled her, and she became codependent, believing she was weak and helpless.

When I discovered my mother's childhood trauma, all the messages I received as a child made sense.

"You need to be nice to your mother. She needs you," said my grandmother.

"Promise me that you will look out for your mom," my aunt implored.

"You need to behave so your mother doesn't get too stressed," my uncle insisted.

"Don't upset your mother; you'll kill her," my father warned.

My mother lost valuable opportunities that she needed as a child to later thrive as a mother. As a result, she became an adult with a restricted identity, low self-worth, and an inability to promote her safety, which left her vulnerable to abuse by my father. She experienced years of spousal abuse, which caused her to work long hours (to finance her husband's spending and secret child), experience multiple physical illnesses, and become detached from her children. Then, she became an offender in her own right as she emotionally and physically neglected her children. This explains why, when I was nine years old, my mother disappeared, yet her physical body remained, and I was left alone.

"Your mother had a rough life," said a well-intended family member. "Hurt people hurt people. If you truly understand why she did the things she did, why haven't you forgiven her?"

"Because understanding and forgiving are not the same, and one does not always lead to the other," I replied.

Some trauma survivors achieve an understanding of their offender(s) and begin to view them as flawed human beings, which causes a change in their emotions or actions, which may bring about forgiveness. Others achieve an understanding without a change in their emotions or actions. Once I understood my mother's trauma, I noticed a significant shift in my recovery, as it helped me to see that I was not to blame. My mother's incapabilities never had anything to do with me, and there was nothing that I could have done to help her. When my shame dissipated, I no longer viewed my mother as the villain in my story. In fact, I can now see that sickly, lonely little girl who was left alone in her room while her family held their breath, hoping that she would survive but preparing for her death. This change in my perception of my mother was helpful, but it was not automatically followed by forgiveness.

Self-reflection for Advocates

Advocates who believe that survivors should forgive once they have a different perception of their offender(s) can ask themselves the following:

- Am I broaching this topic too soon in the survivor's recovery? Do they need and/or are they capable of learning about their offender(s) at this moment in their recovery?
- Can I provide the survivor with information about their offender(s) without having an agenda of forgiveness?
- How will I benefit if the survivor changes their perception of the offender(s)? What do I have to lose if their perception is unchanged?
- Is this topic more appropriate for a mental health professional to address with the survivor?

Responses for Survivors

Survivors who encounter advocates that promote forgiveness due to their change in perception of their offender(s) can consider using these responses:

- Thank you for this information. I will consider it in my recovery process.
- I do not feel safe enough to hear or consider my offender's story. I need to focus on safety first.
- I can understand and accept their story and not forgive them. The two can occur together, but not always.
- At this moment in my recovery, I don't find focusing on my offender's story helpful. Would you like to know what would be more helpful?

"THEY'RE FAMILY."

Blood is thicker than water, or so the proverb goes. This belief has been used to manipulate and shame many trauma survivors, but its actual meaning might be distorted. Some scholars argue that this proverb does not refer to the strength of connections with genetic family members but rather to the power of the bonds we forge with those with no genetic relation. The proverb originates from the saying "The blood of the covenant is thicker than the water of the womb," meaning that those who go to battle and shed their blood together ("the blood of the covenant") have stronger bonds than those between genetic family members ("the water of the womb").[8] This interpretation is debatable, but it prompts us to consider how popular sayings can easily become distorted to meet the needs of society, culture, and religion.

"They're family" is a phrase many survivors hear when they are encouraged to forgive an offender who is a genetic relation. There is a popular misconception in many societies that offenders who are genetically related to you are entitled to forgiveness. This makes little sense. If it were true, then genetic family members would be allowed to treat their relations however they wish with no consequences. Commonly, family members advocate forgiveness in order to maintain dysfunctional family dynamics. Philosopher Georgina H. Mills writes, "Often family members do not value forgiveness itself, rather they want the victim to set aside their anger or not speak about the abuse in order to promote harmony within the family."[9]

Dynamics are ingrained in families and have often been in place for generations. Families trapped in dysfunctional dynamics are constantly trying to maintain the status quo, and members who attempt to disrupt it are encouraged to get back in line and forgive. Yet, forgiveness is not the actual goal. The goal is often to preserve the dysfunctional family dynamic.

When I refused to participate in my family's dysfunctional dynamics, I not only lost my mother (who was already gone), but I lost most of my aunts, uncles, and cousins. They could not tolerate this shift in their belief system that their sister or aunt was and is, in fact, not more valuable than her three children. My two brothers and I have little to no contact with my mother as adults, and we are perceived as black sheep, a common term for those who break the cycle of family trauma. My family wants me to forgive my mother because they assume that if I do, the dysfunctional dynamics will resume and everyone can return to a system that they embrace and understand.

"I want to be a part of this family, but not like this," I informed my aunt, my mother's only sibling who has decided to be a part of my life. "I need my family to see me as a valuable person whose value is not connected to my mother in any way. I need my family to value me not because of what I can do for my mother but because I am a person. If I never forgive her, I have value. If I never speak to her again, I have value. Forgiveness isn't going to make things go back to the way they were. Does that make sense?"

My aunt didn't respond; she didn't have to. Her shocked and saddened expression told me everything that I needed to know. My mother's family would be unable to see me as a person of value. I was one person battling years of intergenerational trauma in a family system that didn't want to budge. To this day, my mother's family, excluding my aunt, have chosen not to be a part of my life or my brothers'. It's easy to feel like my family chose my mother over me, but that's too simple of an explanation. They chose their established family dynamic, a system they feel more comfortable living in. Sadly, my story is not unique, as there are many families who have chosen to continue their cycle of trauma, which has caused many survivors to become estranged from their families or labeled as black sheep.

Self-reflection for Advocates

Those encouraging trauma survivors to forgive because their offender is a genetic relation can ask themselves the following:

- Am I aware that forgiveness is not guaranteed, required, entitled, or obligated simply because the offender is a genetic relation or is considered a family member?
- Am I aware that forgiveness may not sustain the survivor's family dynamics or prevent estrangement?
- Instead of encouraging them to forgive, can I ask the survivor how their family dynamics have impacted them and their relationship with the offender?
- If I am a family member, am I willing to take steps to challenge and change my family's dysfunctional dynamics in order to help the survivor's recovery?

Responses for Survivors

Survivors who encounter advocates who ask them to forgive because their offender is a genetic relation can consider using these responses:

- Forgiveness is not guaranteed, required, entitled, or obligated simply because [the offender] is my genetic relation or is considered my family member.
- I accept your opinion regarding forgiving family, and I ask that you accept mine.
- This discussion is not helpful. Instead, would you like to discuss how dysfunctional family dynamics have contributed to my trauma?
- Let's discuss ways in which you can help me to change these dysfunctional family dynamics.

"THEY'RE DYING."

Forgiveness advocates often encourage survivors to forgive their offenders when they are dying. These advocates often seek to spare you any guilt or regret they may experience if you do not forgive your offender before their death.

"I need to talk to you. It's about mom," my brother texted.

"Is she dead?" I texted back immediately.

As I waited for his reply, I felt lighter, as if I had thrown off a weight that was crushing my heart. I imagined what it would be like if she was dead. My brother and I had discussed this often, and we'd decided we wouldn't attend the funeral. Instead, we would go away together to reconnect and process any grief that we felt. I quickly began creating a plan to protect myself from her family. I could feel the judgmental glances of my aunts, uncles, and cousins, still trapped in the intergenerational trauma perpetuating the belief that my mother, even in death, is more valuable than her children.

"No, she's fine. She's just sending weird emails again," my brother replied. My new sense of lightness quickly faded, and I returned to what I was doing. This was a practice run, and it gave me an idea of how I might feel when my mother dies. I would feel lighter, with a clear focus on my needs. I would plan for my safety and take steps to connect with my brother. There was no guilt or regret.

Advocates may be surprised to learn that my reaction is not uncommon. Many survivors anxiously wait for their offender(s) to die and aren't bothered by their death when it occurs, or they feel relieved when their offender(s) are finally gone. I've worked with many survivors who reported feeling safe, freed, calm, empowered, happy, and at peace after their offender died. Interestingly, these are also common emotions that people report after experiencing forgiveness.

Those who encourage forgiveness because of an offender's impending death might support the offender's needs, especially if the offender requests forgiveness. Advocates may pressure you to forgive so that your offender can die in peace. Sadly, when you do not or cannot forgive your dying offender, you are often villainized, as society tends to whitewash the legacies of the dead and dying.

How often do we see the deceased presented in an overly optimistic light, in defiance of factual accuracy? History is rife with figures whose negative impact on the world around them is ignored after death: Queen Elizabeth II was the longest-serving British monarch in history, and she supported colonialism, which resulted in slavery, violence, suppression, and genocide.[10] Mahatma Gandhi is considered to be the father of India, and he was also a misogynist and suspected of sexual abuse.[11]

"Why do we romanticize the dead?" asked survivor Jennette McCurdy. "Why can't we be honest about them? Especially moms. They're the most romanticized of anyone."[12] I have no doubt that my mother will be romanticized by her family and friends after she dies, and I will be the villain. The stigma about how we perceive or speak of the dead harms trauma survivors, who are villainized if they share their stories of dead offenders or if they deny their dying offender forgiveness.

Self-reflection for Advocates

Those who encourage trauma survivors to forgive because their offender is dying can ask themselves the following:

- If the offender was not dying, would I encourage the survivor to forgive them? Why or why not?
- Can I acknowledge how my guilt, regret, shame, and grief impact my need to encourage the survivor to forgive?
- Am I aware of my cultural, religious, and personal biases in regard to denying forgiveness to those who are dying?

- Am I a safe person for the survivor to speak ill of the dead or dying if these experiences aid their recovery? If not, can I admit this to myself and the survivor?

Responses for Survivors

Survivors who encounter advocates that encourage them to forgive their offender(s) because they are dying can consider using these responses:

- I am not ready or in a position to forgive. This process cannot be rushed or forced because [the offender] is dying.
- This isn't about me or what I need. It sounds like you are focused on [the offender] and their needs.
- Instead of forgiving or grieving their death, I need to focus on grieving everything I've lost due to [the offender's] actions or inactions.
- It feels like this is more about your needs than mine.

"YOU'LL MAKE PROGRESS IN YOUR RECOVERY."

Many survivors are told that they need to forgive their offenders in order to progress in their recovery. I hope that, at this point, you have learned that forgiveness does not dictate treatment success for all survivors and is not a mandatory component of trauma recovery. As we covered in chapter 3, suppositions to the contrary are poorly supported by empirical research, and the few studies that have been conducted are significantly flawed.

A forgiveness promotor who wants you to progress in recovery often has good intentions, yet their insistence on forgiveness as a method to assist in your recovery is inaccurate and can cause you harm. "When [forgiveness] is offered due to being guilted into believing that it is a condition of one's own emotional healing and personal growth, it becomes a tool of manipulation and harm, regardless of the good intentions of the one pursuing forgiveness as the price of emotional health and inherent goodness," writes author Umm Zakiyyah.[13]

Advocates of forgiveness may harbor conscious or subconscious criticisms of survivors who do not or cannot forgive. Myisha Cherry writes, "The mere fact that a person withholds forgiveness does not mean they are not interested in repair or relief. It does not mean they are resistant to a better future. Nor does it mean that they would rather wallow in misery for the rest of their lives. When we criticize withholders on the basis that they lack certain desires or motivations, we are engaging in an erroneous way of thinking. Our criticism doesn't hold up."[14]

Self-reflection for Advocates

Those who believe that a survivor must forgive in order to make progress in recovery can ask themselves the following:

- What sources (e.g., social media influencers, scientific studies, internet blogs, books) have I reviewed that report that forgiveness is a necessary component in trauma recovery? Are these reputable sources? Do these sources consider the unique needs of trauma survivors or are they addressing a more general population?
- If I cite peer-reviewed studies, have I reviewed the reports and identified the research limitations? Am I communicating these limitations to the survivor during discussions of forgiveness?
- Am I capable of supporting survivors who progress in recovery without experiencing forgiveness?
- If I'm a clinician, am I practicing forgiveness in therapy or forgiveness therapy? Have I communicated this distinction to trauma survivors who are under my care?

Responses for Survivors

Survivors who encounter advocates who believe that they will make progress in recovery only when they forgive can consider using these responses:

- Thank you for the information. What are your sources? Can you send them to me?
- Are you aware that studies/books/posts/podcasts/opinions often do not consider the specific needs of trauma survivors?
- Can you tell me the research limitations of the studies you have cited?

- I've read a book about how forgiveness is not required to make progress in recovery. Would you consider reading it?

AUTHORITY FIGURES WHO PROMOTE FORGIVENESS

Those in positions of perceived power or authority tend to have a greater influence on you when they recommend forgiveness. These authority figures can include family members, friends, experts, authors, celebrities, employers, religious and spiritual leaders, and community leaders. Being in a position of authority does not automatically make someone's recommendations valid or useful, but you may not realize this. There is currently a psychologist and social media influencer who has thousands of followers and two successful books that claim that trauma can be healed solely by positive thinking and self-empowerment. This might work for some survivors, but not all. Yet, the limitations of the psychologist's recommendations are not always clearly communicated, and it can appear as if they have the one right answer for all trauma survivors.

Mental health clinicians are often perceived as authority figures and can carry great influence. This can be misleading, as not all clinicians have the same training and experience. I have sixteen years of training as a trauma therapist and one year of training as a couples therapist. Therefore, I am much more equipped to provide recommendations to clients in trauma therapy than to clients in couples therapy. In fact, I could cause harm if I causally make recommendations for those in couples therapy. It's important to remember that not all clinicians are trained to treat trauma or know how to practice in a trauma-informed way. In fact, some clinicians conduct trauma research, give keynote speeches, and write best-selling books without ever working directly with survivors.

Self-reflection for Advocates

Those who are authority figures or can be perceived as authority figures by survivors can ask themselves the following:

- Am I aware that my position as an authority figure has a significant impact on trauma survivors when I make recommendations for their recovery?

- Is it my place to promote, encourage, or suggest anything that will impact a trauma survivor's recovery?
- Am I aware of biases (culture, religion, personal experiences, theoretical orientation) that impact my perception of forgiveness? Have I communicated my biases to the survivor?
- If I'm a clinician, does this survivor need to be referred to a clinician with more experience in trauma recovery? Am I primarily a researcher/presenter/author or a clinician, and am I communicating this important distinction to survivors who seek my counsel?

Responses for Survivors

Survivors who encounter authority figures or those whom they perceive as authority figures who promote forgiveness can consider using these responses:

- Thank you for your insight. I will take it into consideration.
- What are your biases associated with forgiveness and trauma?
- What is your background in regard to the relationship between trauma recovery and forgiveness?
- I would feel more comfortable speaking to an experienced clinician about these topics.

RESPONDING TO FORGIVENESS ADVOCATES

In the end, there is no right or wrong way for you to respond to forgiveness advocates, as your response is determined by your sense of safety, trauma responses, type of relationship with the advocate, and many other factors. Not all forgiveness advocates will be receptive to every or any type of response. In fact, many will hold on to their all-or-nothing beliefs regarding forgiveness no matter how well you respond to their attempts. However, there are some advocates who are receptive, especially those who are well-intended.

Here are a few additional scripts for survivors to consider when responding to those who promote forgiveness:

- I am not at the point in my recovery to consider forgiveness.
- I will not discuss the possibility of forgiveness, and I need you to respect that.

- Please do not mention forgiveness again. If you do, I will not engage in the conversation.
- I choose if I forgive or not, not you.
- I do not feel safe, and I cannot discuss or consider forgiveness at this time in my recovery.
- You are not helping me to forgive. In fact, you're making it more difficult for me to consider the possibility of forgiving.
- Instead of encouraging me to forgive, I need you too. . .
- Say nothing. Silence can serve as a response and a clear boundary.

CHAPTER TEN

Embracing Elective Forgiveness

Trauma recovery on your terms occurs when you can acknowledge and accept that only one person can decide if forgiveness will be a part of your recovery. That person is not a psychologist who specializes in forgiveness research. It's not a social media influencer with a large following. It isn't a friend or family member who cites a flawed research study they discovered. It's not your therapist or psychiatrist. It's not me, a trauma psychotherapist writing a book about the topic. It's *you*. You decide. No one else has the authority to make these decisions for you—not your clinicians, family, friends, religious leaders, community members, or anyone seeking to support your recovery. They must accept your decisions regarding what role forgiveness will or will not have in your recovery

To explore recovery on your terms, embrace elective forgiveness. Elective forgiveness is an alternative to approaches that maintain that forgiveness is a necessary part of the trauma recovery process. Elective forgiveness meets you where you are at in every stage of recovery and can help you experience the following:

- authentic forgiveness that is mostly consistent and occurs on your terms in your own time;
- various levels of authentic forgiveness that lie on a continuum;
- and organic forgiveness, which occurs without making a conscious intention or choice to forgive.

Alternatively, by embracing elective forgiveness, you may find that forgiveness does not come. This doesn't mean that you've failed, far from it. It just means you're not in a place to forgive right now; perhaps you never will be or may not need to forgive at all. Instead, you might:

- be incapable of forgiving, even when you decide to do so;
- withhold, resist, forgo, avoid, or oppose forgiveness;
- or not focus on forgiveness at all.

Elective forgiveness is an experiential process, not a compulsory goal. It takes forgiveness off your recovery table unless you need or want it to be there, but it also leaves space should forgiveness naturally manifest. It is not antiforgiveness; it gives you the agency to seek, discover, and embrace all forms of forgiveness if that is what you want or need. If you decide to embrace elective forgiveness, know that, like all types of forgiveness, it is not a panacea. It does not make trauma disappear, nor does it heal all emotional wounds. It's simply an experience that may or may not support your recovery.

Here are some methods that can help you embrace elective forgiveness:

WELCOMING UNFORGIVENESS

Have you ever tried to force yourself to do something only to realize that the pressure you placed on yourself made it harder to accomplish? If you couldn't do it despite all that pressure, did you then judge yourself? This has often happened to me when reading books. I've forced myself to read certain books because experts said I should read them. Some of these books were valuable to me, but others were not, and reading them felt like a chore. I put pressure on myself to finish them, and when I didn't, I felt like I was lazy and a failure.

Pressuring myself to read did not change my behavior. On the contrary, it caused me to read less often and triggered my shame. So, I decided to welcome an anticompletionist style of reading by accepting that there are some highly recommended books that I will never finish or even start. My new approach was much more lenient: I committed to reading seventy-five pages of each book, and if the book did not seem valuable, I put it away and moved on to another. My shameful thoughts and feelings decreased, and I began to read more often. This kindness I showed myself took the pressure off, leaving me free to decide how to spend my time. I even picked up books I had discarded months or years ago and finally finished them, something I never would have done if I had strictly policed my reading habits.

Pressuring yourself to forgive when you are unable or unwilling to do so could trigger shame and may sabotage your ability to forgive. Instead, consider welcoming unforgiveness, if that is what you are experiencing, to help you embrace elective forgiveness. For our purposes, *unforgiveness* is that state in which you have not forgiven your offender, as opposed to an inaction or character flaw, as some may define the term. When you experience unforgiveness, you can be unable, unwilling, or uninterested in forgiving, or perhaps all of the above. Embracing unforgiveness can actually help you to forgive if that's what you need. It might sound contradictory, but just like with reading, forgiveness is more likely to happen naturally if you don't brute force it. We often forget that unforgiveness is a valuable part of the forgiveness process and can be the first step toward elective forgiveness. Seeing it this way is far more valuable than writing it off as a destructive experience that we must overcome quickly.

"I start with unforgiveness and move to forgiveness, not the other way around," says psychologist Rosenna Bakari. "Once you have the space to move deeper into healing and you're able to understand and experience your pain, you may forgive, or you may not. You'll find out once you get there."[1] What if, instead of forcing yourself to forgive your offender(s), you start by welcoming the experience of unforgiveness and see what unfolds from there? You might be surprised by what occurs in your recovery.

Unforgiveness can be a starting point, an ending point, or a stop along the way; forgiving is a time-consuming process. You will likely spend most of your recovery in a state of unforgiveness. If forgiveness occurs, it usually happens in the later stages. Therefore, it doesn't make sense to devote time and energy to force forgiveness in recovery's initial or middle stages. It's more realistic to welcome unforgiveness for as long as it needs to be a part of your process. "How ironic that it was the act of not forgiving that finally freed me to forgive," writes Nancy Richards, who forgave her mother near the end of her recovery journey.[2]

Embracing unforgiveness promotes elective forgiveness, as it allows you to focus on where you are in your recovery while remaining open to experiencing forgiveness if it's what you need. To explore welcoming unforgiveness, ask yourself these questions:

- If I am experiencing unforgiveness, am I open to forgiveness occurring or not occurring in the future? If not, can I open myself up to these possibilities?
- Can I welcome unforgiveness without putting any pressure on myself to forgive?
- Am I experiencing shame? (See chapter six.) If so, could shame be sabotaging my ability to welcome unforgiveness? If it is, can I address my shame *before* considering any type of forgiveness?

ENGAGING IN EMOTIONAL PROCESSING

One of the most common reasons you might resist elective forgiveness is to avoid processing your emotions. You may have tried to forgive so you could let go of uncomfortable anger, debilitating fear, or devastating grief. However, you cannot truly relinquish your emotions without first experiencing them. Forgiveness has often been used as a Band-Aid in trauma recovery that can provide temporary relief. Yet, if you forgive without engaging in as much emotional processing as you need, those emotions will return, and you'll wonder if you ever truly forgave. The experience of emotional processing cannot be avoided. It's a necessary part of trauma recovery, and no amount of forgiveness—required or elective—can save you from it. Therefore, instead of seeking forgiveness to avoid emotional processing, it's more productive to engage in emotional processing as a method to embrace elective forgiveness.

Psychologist Jack Rachman describes emotional processing as "a process whereby emotional disturbances are absorbed and declined to the extent that other experiences and behavior can proceed without disruption."[3] When you engage in emotional processing, you experience emotional disturbances (fear, anger, confusion, sadness, grief) which were created by traumatic experiences with the goal of integrating these emotions so that they no longer impact you (or impact you less) in the present day. Integration can feel like a decrease in emotional disturbances, meaning that you are less disturbed when you remember the past or when you experience a trigger that reminds you of the past. Integration can also manifest as your distressing emotions (e.g., fear) becoming other emotions (e.g., confidence, empowerment) that serve you better in the present.

Here are a few examples of emotional processing:

- You feel enraged and allow yourself to sit with this rage in a safe environment. You may write a rage-filled letter to your offender, yell obscenities as if they were in front of you, or simply feel the sensations of anger in your body. Suddenly, you start to cry. You now feel more betrayed than angry. Over time, you notice that your anger hasn't evaporated, but it feels different; it's more frustration than rage, and your feelings of betrayal are now calling for your attention. You then allow yourself to feel betrayed in a safe environment, and the process continues.

- You feel fearful, and you express and share this emotion with safe and capable people. Those people accept and validate your fear and ask how they can help support your feelings of safety. You tell them, and they meet these needs. Slowly, you start to feel safer. You then notice that you rarely feel fearful. Instead, you might feel more generalized anxiety, certainly unpleasant but less debilitating than your previous fearfulness.

- You feel ashamed about how you were treated. You share your emotions with safe and capable people and notice their reactions of empathy, compassion, and acceptance. You start to question your feelings of shame and look at yourself as they see you. Eventually, you notice increased self-worth and less shame, which now feels more like insecurity—something people deal with whether they've suffered trauma or not.

Notice how none of these scenarios end in complete and total perfection. Emotional processing, like any trauma recovery interventions (including forgiveness), do not produce a perfect positive result. Although it can lead to emotional integration, your emotional slate is unlikely to be completely wiped clean. Your emotional experiences are a part of you. They do not need to define you or negatively impact your life, but they cannot be undone as if they never were.

Judith Herman reminds us that the goal of trauma recovery is "integration, not exorcism."[4] Integration occurs when your emotions have been transformed, not erased. Your feelings may decrease, become other emotions, or have little impact on your present-day feelings, thoughts, physical sensations, and behaviors. "Health comes not from exorcising painful events from our minds but from bearing witness to our pain, acknowledging its impact, commiserating with ourselves, mourning our loses, and new meaning and creating new connection with people," writes Janis Abrahms Spring.[5] Emotional processing may not be perfect, but it's an excellent method to embrace elective forgiveness, as the more your emotions are integrated, the closer you are to determining whether you need to forgive.

How do you engage in emotional processing? It's not a one-size-fits-all process, so it's essential to discover what works for you. When considering interventions, ask yourself: What would help me *feel*, not *think*? The intention of emotional processing is to *feel* your emotions, not to gain insight or awareness. Of course, you may arrive at a new insight as a result, but that's not the intention. Some clinicians avoid interventions that are intended to engage their clients in emotional processing because it's difficult for their clients and possibly for themselves. Usually, we feel more comfortable seeking insight and conducting sterile, intellectual interventions instead of truly feeling our emotions, so these methods might feel more challenging.

When you are deciding which emotional processing methods you will try, ask yourself: Which approaches do I already use, even if not for trauma-based emotional processing, that are already successful or have been successful in the past? You are looking for methods that have helped you to *feel* your emotions. Try to acknowledge interventions that already work for you and see if you can devote more time and effort to these established methods. We do not always need to reinvent the wheel.

When choosing which interventions to try, you can combine previously successful methods with new ones. For example, I realized that I needed to involve my body more in my recovery, but I was struggling to participate in body-focused methods. They felt odd and, at times, intimidating. Writing has always been a successful method for my emotional processing. I began engaging in gentle stretches in order to connect with the emotions that were causing my severe muscle tension, and then I immediately journaled about my experiences. I went back and forth, stretching and journaling, and this combination of methods helped me to experience and process some of the fear that is stuck in my body.

Here are a few methods that may help you engage in emotional processing:

- Share your trauma story with safe and capable people, or tell your story aloud with no one present.

- Write your trauma story and share it with safe and capable people, or keep it private.
- Write letters to your offender(s) without sending them.
- Listen to music, watch movies and TV shows, or look at pictures that allow you to connect with and experience emotions associated with the past.
- Create art that expresses your emotions associated with the past.
- Explore revenge fantasies to embrace and experience your anger (see chapter 5).
- Try guided meditations focused on your body's sensations or emotional acceptance.
- Move your body through trauma-informed yoga, exercise, dance, posturing, self-defensive movements, shaking, self-tapping, and any other movement that creates physical sensations in which emotions can be fully experienced.
- Engage in safe touch (e.g., being held/hugged, holding hands, brushing your hair, sex) provided by yourself or another safe and capable person.
- Participate in trauma-focused therapy and engage in one or more of the twenty trauma recovery methods described in chapter eleven.

One small practice that can help you better process your emotions is asking yourself which methods will allow you to notice, feel, and embrace physical sensations. Sensations in your body are the language of your emotions. It's how they communicate with you and how you can notice and connect with your feelings in turn. When in doubt, ask your body.

Survivors may not be able to engage in emotional processing if they do not feel safe enough. Remember, forgiveness may not be required to recover from trauma, but safety is. You must feel physically, sexually, emotionally, financially, spiritually, and relationally safe enough to be able to experience your emotions. Perfect safety is unobtainable, but feeling *safe enough* is possible.

It's important to keep in mind that feelings of safety are inconsistent—they often come and go; you may feel safe enough to engage in emotional processing one day, but not the next. You may need to take a break and then resume processing your emotions once you feel safer. It's common and encouraged to pause and shift your focus to reestablishing safety (see suggestions in chapter 4) before you reengage in emotional processing.

SEEKING ACCEPTANCE

Acceptance occurs when we acknowledge the reality of a situation, state, or process without resistance. Acceptance is not agreement or endorsement. One can accept the death of a loved one and not agree that they needed to die, should have died, or that one is happy that they died. One simply accepts the fact of this loved one's death.

Acceptance is a powerful experience in trauma recovery. When my clients experience acceptance, I often witness a decrease in emotional disturbances and trauma-related symptoms. When I experienced acceptance in my recovery, I felt less shame and increased self-worth.

Acceptance occurs in the present, not in the past or future. We can accept past events, as they cannot be changed, and this acceptance of the past occurs in the present. We can also accept how we think, feel, and act in the present because it is our current reality. But we cannot accept what hasn't yet occurred. Although many of us like to think that we have an idea of what will happen in the future, we really don't, so there is nothing to accept. For example, I accept that I experienced severe physical and emotional neglect in childhood, which has impacted my emotional, physical, and cognitive responses in the past. I accept that at this moment in my recovery, my trauma responses have significantly decreased, but I am still struggling to feel safe in my body. I cannot accept that I will or won't feel safe in my body in the future, as I don't know what the future holds. Acceptance is an experience that occurs in the here and now.

Acceptance is not complacency or giving up. You can accept that you are a trauma survivor while taking active steps to engage in recovery. Just because you are living with trauma now doesn't mean that it will hold sway over you for the rest of your life. My acceptance that I do not feel safe in my body has helped motivate me to take steps to address this issue so that I can continue to recover and improve my quality of life.

Acceptance or Forgiveness?

Acceptance and forgiveness have much in common. They both require a certain level of receptiveness or a decision to open oneself up to the possibility. They can occur organically or by making a conscious choice. They both lie on a continuum and fluctuate rather than existing in an all-or-nothing state, and they rarely happen instantaneously. Instead, they are processes that take time. Acceptance and forgiveness are electives in trauma recovery, as neither is required to recover.

Despite these similarities, they are two different experiences. Acceptance is a method to embrace elective forgiveness. Forgiveness can coexist with acceptance or can occur independently. "Forgiveness is a form of acceptance, but not all forms of acceptance constitute forgiveness," write Enright and Fitzgibbons. "If a client accepts what happened but does not accept the offender as a human being worthy of respect, he or she is not forgiving. Some people make peace with the past but not with the people of the past."[6] Acceptance might pave the way to forgiveness, but you can also accept without forgiving your offender(s).

You may find that acceptance better aligns with your needs than forgiveness, as the former may provide you with certain benefits that the latter does not. First, acceptance might feel safer than unconditional forgiveness, which does not require any changes to be made by your offender(s). This is helpful because you might need your offender to make changes before you can feel safe enough to forgive them, even if you don't intend to reconcile. "Acceptance is a gutsy, life-affirming response to a violation when the person who hurt you is unavailable or unrepentant," writes Spring. "It asks nothing of anyone but you."[7] When your offender is not able, available, or willing to make the necessary changes needed for you to experience conditional forgiveness, acceptance may feel like the safer option.

Acceptance can also be more obtainable than forgiveness, as it doesn't require changing your thoughts, emotions, or behaviors toward your offender. Our working definition of forgiveness is "a reduction in negative emotions, thoughts, and behavioral dispositions toward the offender(s) and an increase in positive thoughts, emotions, and behavioral dispositions toward the offender(s), all of which lie on a continuum." This might not be obtainable for everyone. Acceptance, on the other hand, only requires that you acknowledge the reality of a situation, state, or process without resistance. You do not need to change how you feel about your offender(s). "It is a process you enter into primarily to free yourself from the trauma of an injury," writes Spring. "Your goal is not necessarily to feel sorry for him, to feel compassion or pity for him, to excuse him, to develop positive feelings for him, to wish him well."[8] The focus of acceptance is entirely on you, not your offender(s).

Seeking acceptance often overlaps with engaging in emotional processing, so you might feel as if you are focusing on both at the same time.

To explore seeking acceptance, ask yourself these questions:

- What occurred in the past (e.g., events, experiences, circumstances,) that you are struggling to accept?
- Can these things be changed in the present day? Can you go back to the past and change them?
- How does it feel knowing that you cannot change them? Can you allow yourself to feel these emotions?
- What caused these past experiences that you are struggling to accept to occur in the first place? Remember, these are not excuses or justifications for the actions or inactions of your offender(s); they are simply factors that drive their behaviors.
  - Examples: your offender's trauma or life experiences, your offender(s) medical and mental health issues, dysfunctional family dynamics, systemic issues in society, coincidences, or the unknown.
- Can you imagine that you have accepted it? If so, how do you feel when you imagine this? Can you sit with those emotions and allow yourself to feel?
- How would you behave if you accepted the past? Can you try engaging in one of those behaviors and see how that feels?

EMBRACING ELECTIVE SELF-FORGIVENESS

We can't explore forgiveness in trauma recovery without acknowledging the benefits and harms of self-forgiveness. Enright defines self-forgiveness as "a willingness to abandon self–resentment in the face of one's own acknowledged objective wrong, while fostering compassion, generosity, and love toward oneself."[9] Self-forgiveness occurs when you are the offender, as your actions or inactions have harmed someone or yourself. In the process of forgiving yourself, you may notice decreased guilt and increased self-compassion, as well as fewer actions of self-sabotage and increased actions of self-care. Self-forgiveness is not letting go of shame, which is a perception that you are a flawed person that is not based upon your actual actions or inactions. It is also not a method to let go of self-blame for actions or inactions that were

not your fault. For example, I cannot forgive myself for my mother's incapabilities as a parent. I might believe that I am an offender and attempt to
engage in self-forgiveness, but this would not be genuine self-forgiveness as,
in this scenario, I am not an offender. Self-forgiveness requires "one's own
acknowledged objective wrong," and if our perception of the wrong is biased
or based on shame, we cannot practice self-forgiveness.[10]

Self-forgiveness is more widely accepted as a requirement in trauma
recovery than forgiving offenders, but it shouldn't be. It would be best if you
weren't forced, pressured, recommended, or encouraged to forgive anyone,
including yourself. Self-forgiveness must also be elective, as it is an experience
you might or might not have in recovery that may or may not benefit you.
When seeking to forgive yourself for harming another or yourself, remove
any pressure you place upon yourself and embrace this type of forgiveness
as an elective.

When embracing self-forgiveness, you need to consider who you'd like to
be involved in this process. You may choose to involve the person you harmed
or not. This is like the process of forgiving an offender, as the one who was
harmed gets to decide if the offender is involved in their forgiving process.
The participation of the offender is not required to forgive them, especially
considering that forgiveness is not reconciliation or an intention to have any
relationship with the offender.

Similarly, the participation of the one we harmed is not required for us
to experience self-forgiveness. We can choose whether to invite them to
participate. Let's say that you invite the one you harmed into your process
of self-forgiveness. When making this decision, it's essential to consider the
safety of all participants. You (the offender), the person you harmed, and
anyone who may have played both roles (those who take some but not all
responsibility) must be safe and capable enough to engage in this process. If
one person is unsafe or incapable, they shouldn't be involved. You may not
know if all parties are safe and capable at the start, and it's appropriate to
disinvite participants at any time in the process to support everyone's safety.

As the offender or someone who takes partial responsibility for the
offense, you can invite the person you harmed to participate in your process
of self-forgiveness—but they must be allowed to decide whether to participate. You must respect the agency of others and let them determine if they
wish to be involved in your process of self-forgiveness and how they wish to
be involved. You can create a safe environment by asking them what they

need from you to feel safe in this process and respect whatever boundaries or expectations they communicate. If you cannot do this for any reason, it's best not to involve them in your experience of self-forgiveness.

Seeking self-forgiveness and seeking forgiveness from others can overlap, as you might engage in actions that bring about both experiences. It's essential to identify your honest intentions. Are you seeking to forgive yourself, seeking forgiveness from others, or perhaps both? Acknowledging this distinction is crucial as it helps you to be more focused in your approach. You might use different methods depending on whether you intend to forgive yourself or seek the forgiveness of another.

If you seek forgiveness from someone you harmed, you must remember that you cannot control if or when they forgive you. Earning their forgiveness can be a long and painful process that you cannot control, and no matter what you do they may never forgive you. Some offenders report that they cannot forgive themselves unless those they've wronged forgive them, while others report that they can forgive themselves without the forgiveness of people they've hurt. You need to decide whether you seek self-forgiveness, forgiveness from those you harmed, or both. You can reassess your intentions at any point in your recovery; this will help you identify which methods are appropriate at present.

Psychologist Lydia Woodyatt and her colleagues researched self-forgiveness, defining this experience as involving three elements: (1) an appraisal of responsibility, (2) a release of negative emotions directed at oneself, and (3) fostering positive emotions directed toward oneself.[11] We will explore these components of self-forgiveness in three phases, along with methods to engage in these experiences.

Appraisal of Responsibility

Before you can determine if you need to forgive yourself, you should identify if there is anything to forgive. People rationalize trauma differently, and you might take all, none, or some of the blame for your traumatic experiences. Sometimes, taking all or some blame is justified; other times, it is not. We ascribe our current capabilities—including our knowledge, skills, insights, experiences, resources, relationships, and feelings of safety—to our past selves. This leads to an inaccurate self-appraisal as we appear far more capable and powerful in our recollections than we really were. Owen, the survivor of physical abuse and neglect in chapter 6, believed that he, as a three-year-old, was responsible for his abuse because he, at sixteen years old, now had more bodily strength, social support, and safety. During his appraisal of responsibility, he discovered that he had had none of these qualities or resources as a three-year-old and was, therefore, not responsible for preventing or stopping the abuse and had no need for self-forgiveness. Before even considering self-forgiveness, then, you need to be sure you have an unbiased understanding of what you were capable of in the past.

Here are a few questions that may help your appraisal of responsibility:

- What actions or inactions are you specifically taking responsibility for?
- How much responsibility lies with you, and how much lies with others? What evidence do you have that you are responsible?
- If you believe you are the sole offender, what evidence do you have to support this?
- What were you realistically capable of when the trauma occurred? What were you incapable of at that time?
- If you are taking some or all responsibility, are you experiencing guilt or shame?

When appraising your responsibility, be mindful of any feelings of shame. As we've learned, this is different from guilt, which results from how you feel and what you believe about *your actions*—or lack thereof—and how they impact others. Feeling guilty can lead you to take some or all responsibility for your actions or inactions. In contrast, shame results from how you feel and what you believe about *yourself*. Shame does not lead to an accurate self-appraisal because it has nothing to do with your actions. Seeking self-forgiveness will not challenge shame because it is focused on your actions or inactions, not you as a person. If you need help determining whether shame is hindering your self-appraisal, consider reviewing chapter 6. If you are experiencing shame rather than guilt, I suggest you focus your recovery on addressing your shame first, as shame tends to obstruct forgiveness of others and yourself.

If the result of your self-appraisal is that you accept no responsibility, then self-forgiveness is unnecessary. Instead, you might want to focus on accepting that you were not responsible, and it's possible that you will need to process any emotions associated with this experience. If your appraisal results in accepting some or all responsibility (in other words, if you determine that you are an offender), you may consider progressing to the next step.

A Release of Negative Emotions Directed at Oneself

Discovering that you are an offender can cause significant "negative" emotions such as anger, sadness, guilt, fear, grief, and disappointment. If you feel safe enough, you must experience these emotions, as you feel them for a reason. They might be present to remind you never to behave the way you did in the past, to feel empathy for those you harmed, or that your past actions or inactions do not align with your morals, values, or identity. Consider engaging in emotional processing methods (see above) to help connect with, experience, and allow these emotions to integrate as needed. You might also wish to engage in additional interventions specifically for offenders that involve or do not involve those you harmed.

Here are a few methods to release negative emotions directed at oneself:

- Express your emotions to your past self.
  - Imagine your past self (the offender) and express your current emotions (speaking in your head or out loud, or writing a letter) directly to them. For example, some offenders will speak to an empty chair and imagine that their past self is sitting there. It's important to imagine your past self as a part of you, not as a villain or enemy.
- Align your past self with your present self.
  - Tell your past self everything that has changed. Are you more capable now? Do you feel safer in the present when compared to the past? Do you have more resources and a better support system? Have you changed as a person? What does your past self need to know about the present that will prove to them that you will not harm others or yourself in the future?
  - Imagine that your past self can be a part of your current self. It does not need to disappear or be cast out. Ask your past self: What do you need to feel safe to live with me in the present? What value, skills, roles, and insights do you bring to me that will help me in the present?

- When possible, repair your relationship with the one you harmed.
  - Ask the person or people you harmed what they need from you to repair. Do they have specific needs that will help build safety and trust in the relationship? Do they have boundaries or expectations that they need you to follow? If they inform you that the relationship is not reparable, then you need to focus on accepting their decision.
  - Apologize to them. You can communicate with them in your head, out loud, or in writing; you can write a letter, email, or text apologizing to them and either send it to them or not. Allow yourself to communicate anything that you need to say to them. You can do these interventions with the person you harmed present or not. Just remember that you cannot expect anyone to accept or even want your apology.
  - Take actions aimed at making amends. These actions show you and others that you have genuinely changed. Some examples are replacing or repairing items that were damaged, paying for someone's medical treatment, trauma therapy, or legal services, taking on more of the emotional labor or effort in the relationship to earn trust, informing others of your mistakes (especially if they did not believe the person or people you harmed), and following the expectations and boundaries set by those you've hurt.

Fostering Positive Emotions Directed Toward Oneself

Some people may think that it's easy to foster positive emotions (e.g., patience, understanding, empathy, gratitude, and self-compassion) directed at yourself. After all, why wouldn't you want to feel good about yourself? But the truth is that this can be the most challenging part of the self-forgiveness process. It can seem counterintuitive to feel good about yourself knowing that you have harmed another. However, challenging doesn't mean impossible. You don't have to live in constant self-loathing, and in fact, you shouldn't. When we harm others, we also harm ourselves, and the less we hurt ourselves, the less likely we are to harm others in the future.

Here are a few methods to foster positive emotions directed at oneself:

- Embrace your present self.
  - Acknowledge all the changes you have made since you offended. Identify your present-day capabilities, resources, insights, skills, social support system, feelings of safety, efforts to change, and self-worth. Notice any emotions you experience as you acknowledge these changes and allow yourself to fully experience these emotions to fully embrace who you are now.
- Repair your relationship with yourself.
  - Consider what you need to repair your relationship with yourself. Do you need actions, reassurance, or self-imposed boundaries? Try to meet these needs to support this process of relationship repair.
  - Apologize to yourself and allow yourself to experience any emotions that arise during and after the apology.
  - Make amends to yourself. What realistic actions do you need to see from yourself to prove you have genuinely changed? For example, if you avoided mental health treatment and your unmet mental health needs contributed to you harming another, you might participate in treatment to build trust in your relationship with yourself.
- Repair your relationship with your community.
  - You might not be able to take actions to make amends to the person or people you harmed, or your actions may not be sufficient for you to feel like you've made amends. If this is the case, giving back to your community is an alternative form of reparations. For example, if you engaged in domestic violence, you may donate money to a domestic violence shelter. If you were a neglectful parent, you may volunteer to support and guide children in your community.
  - If your community (e.g., family, social groups, company, congregation) has ostracized or judged someone you harmed due to your actions, you can set the record straight by informing the community of the harm you caused them. This can help the one you harmed to feel seen, heard, and believed and to possibly reconnect with their support system. You cannot force others to reconnect with the person or people you harmed; you can

only tell the truth and take responsibility for what you've done or failed to do.

- Practice self-compassion.
  - What would a loved one say to you regarding your past mistakes? This might be what you need to say to yourself. Often, we feel more compassion for our loved ones than we do for ourselves. When we talk to ourselves like we'd talk to a loved one, we are practicing self-compassion.

This exploration of self-forgiveness is not a step-by-step process, and you do not need to incorporate all three phases. Some survivors might complete a self-appraisal and determine they are not responsible; therefore, there is nothing for them to forgive. Others might know for certain that they are responsible. They will bypass the appraisal, focus on releasing negative emotions, and then experience self-forgiveness without a need to foster positive emotions, as this change occurs naturally for them. You might even find that none of these phases support your process of self-forgiveness. Be aware that you may experience constant negative thoughts when engaging in self-forgiveness, which can be a trauma response. This painful rumination can feel like a broken record. If this occurs, consider taking a break to reestablish safety and possibly focus on decreasing shame.

TRUSTING THE PROCESS

Trauma therapists commonly use the phrase *trust the process*. Although I am a therapist myself, I find it quite annoying at times; I'd much rather trust the outcome. I'd rather know the outcome of my recovery and all my clients' recoveries. I want verification that it will work. Unfortunately, it's impossible to know the outcome of trauma recovery and the outcome of elective forgiveness. The goal of elective forgiveness is to assist in recovery, whatever that may be, not predict it. When you embrace elective forgiveness, you accept that you do not know how it will end. You may experience acceptance, forgive your offender(s), forgive yourself, or forgive no one at all. Embracing elective forgiveness helps us to *trust the process* of recovery. When you trust the process, you embrace and accept whatever comes your way, and typically, these experiences are precisely what you need.

CHAPTER ELEVEN

Twenty Trauma Recovery Methods

If trauma survivors cannot or do not wish to forgive their offender, how can they recover? There are many recovery methods in which forgiveness is not a requirement. I have compiled a list of various recovery methods that embrace elective forgiveness. But first, a few things to consider.

This is not an all-exclusive list.

These methods were chosen based on my own recovery experiences, the recovery successes of my clients, and the most frequent recommendations provided by clinicians specializing in trauma recovery. I've included both therapeutic approaches and holistic methods, as survivors who I've worked with often report having more success when they combine mental health therapy and alternative practices. I encourage you to try many methods to find what works for you. For example, my recovery consisted of the therapies eye movement desensitization and reprocessing (EMDR), internal family systems (IFS), somatic experiencing (SE), attachment-based therapy, and animal-assisted therapy (AAT), along with the holistic approaches of nature therapy, self-defense, and support groups. I didn't engage in all these methods at once, as I would participate in them as needed at different stages of my recovery. You might need one approach at a certain stage in your recovery and another approach at a different stage. As you recover, your capability, tolerance level, and needs can change drastically.

There is no "fix."

Forgiveness is not a panacea, and neither is any other trauma recovery approach. None of these therapies or methods have been proven to work for all trauma survivors. Clinicians who are loyal to their specific type of therapy can struggle with this truth and tend to believe their clients are at fault. "Unfortunately, therapists get so tied to their one method that when they don't see a person benefiting from it, they assume there must be something wrong with the client, like they're not serious enough about the work, or they've got secondary gains, when actually the method may not be the right fit, or the therapist isn't a good fit," says psychologist Babette Rothschild.[1] Bessel van der Kolk writes, "There is no one 'treatment of choice' for trauma, and any therapist who believes that his or her particular method is the only answer to your problems is suspect of being an ideologue rather than somebody who is interested in making sure that you get well."[2]

Survivors often engage in different recovery approaches, and they tend to combine methods. Remember, trauma isn't healed, it's integrated. Keep this in mind when engaging in your recovery so that your expectations are realistic and sound.

There is no one-size-fits-all approach.

One recovery method doesn't work the same way for every survivor. You may find that a specific approach works for you but in a different way. For example, EMDR therapists follow a standard protocol that works for some trauma survivors. Yet therapists will deviate from that protocol in order to assist survivors who have needs that the protocol cannot meet. Therefore, your EMDR experiences can be very different from another's experience.

Don't try to mimic someone else's recovery. Instead, find what works for you and how it works for you.

There is no quick method.

Often, the process of trauma recovery doesn't happen quickly or on a schedule. Some survivors may report that they experience a quick recovery. I worked with a client who witnessed the violent death of a woman in the street. After two months, we ended treatment, as his symptoms had significantly decreased and did not return. This quick result is an outlier however; this client had experienced only one traumatic event in his life, had had a solid support system since childhood, had self-worth, steady employment, and financial security, and had no health concerns or substance use struggles. As a white cisgender heterosexual male Protestant, he was a member of a privileged population. In short, the client's quick progress had little to do with the method that he chose or his commitment to treatment, as he already had many resources and lots of support. As a survivor of complex trauma (for whom treatment is often much longer than for single-event trauma survivors), my intense recovery took three years, and I am continuing to engage in multiple recovery methods to this day. I will likely need to do so for the rest of my life. You can expect that your recovery will take some time as well.

Safety trumps every method.

Forgiveness isn't required in trauma recovery, but safety is. If you don't feel safe, it doesn't matter what recovery method you choose. It likely won't succeed. When you don't feel safe, your mind and body constantly focus on self-protection, leaving little room for anything else. How can you promote your safety? Focus on your relationship with your providers (therapist, counselor, yoga instructor, doctor, group facilitator, etc.). These relationships can create feelings of safety, which make your recovery methods more effective. If you feel that changes need to be made in your relationship with your providers, tell them. You can also focus on your physical environment. Do you feel safe in that environment? Are there any changes that need to be made to your environment to promote your safety? For example, I worked with a teenager who requested to sit next to the door during their therapy sessions. When they did, they felt safer and they made more progress.

Not every approach is evidence-based, and that's fine.

The term *evidence-based practice (EBP)* is defined by the APA as "the integration of the best available research with clinical expertise in the context of patient characteristics, culture, and preferences."[3] Some survivors may believe that an EBP approach is automatically better than an approach that is not EBP. This is not accurate. "Evidence-based therapy has quickly become an empty phrase that slights the competition," writes psychiatrist Steven Reidbord. "The evidence is real, but its relevance often is not. This false narrative has misled insurers, government agencies, and many patients into believing certain approaches to psychotherapy are inherently superior when they are not."[4] There are many reasons why an approach may not be an EBP: the method is newer and the research has not yet been conducted or repeated; funding is limited as large-scale trials are expensive; or specific recovery methods are difficult to isolate in studies, as people often engage in multiple recovery methods at the same time. Don't be too quick to disregard a recovery method just because it isn't evidence-based.

You may experience forgiveness.

These methods don't require forgiveness, but they also don't prevent it from naturally occurring. When a recovery approach embraces elective forgiveness, it creates space for organic forgiveness without requiring it as a part of the process. In your recovery, you may forgive your offender, forgive yourself, experience acceptance, or some combination of the three. If forgiveness occurs, it might be precisely what you need.

ANIMAL-ASSISTED THERAPY (ATT)

Animal-assisted therapy (AAT) "is a goal-directed intervention in which an animal meeting specific criteria is an integral part of the treatment process," reports the American Veterinary Medical Association. "[AAT] is designed to promote improvement in human physical, social, emotional, or cognitive function."[5] There are many different types of working animals, and this creates confusion. AAT animals have a specific temperament and training that allow them to engage with people therapeutically and with their handlers to provide therapeutic services. They wear vests displaying the word *therapy*. Service animals, on the other hand, are trained to assist people with disabilities (physical, sensory, psychiatric, or intellectual). They have unrestricted access to public spaces and wear vests with the word *service* on them. As for emotional support animals, the Americans with Disabilities Act and the Fair Housing Act define them as "an animal of any species, the use of which is supported by a qualified physician, psychiatrist or other mental health professional based upon a disability-related need."[6] Emotional support animals are not always trained to perform a particular task, and they do not always provide animal-assisted therapy services. They do not have unrestricted access to public spaces and will sometimes wear vests displaying the words *emotional support, support,* or the acronym *ESA.* These animals live with the person they serve or a clinician who utilizes them in therapy. Others live in treatment facilities or with their trainers.[7]

How does AAT support trauma recovery? An AAT animal is brought into a physical environment where they can engage with you, such as a therapy office, hospital, prison, or residential center. You dictate the type of interactions that you have with the animal. Some survivors need the animal to simply be present, while others benefit from physical engagement. An AAT animal might respond to feedback (verbal or nonverbal) provided by you, and the animal's response to you can support recovery. For example, if the animal senses that you are anxious, they may physically place themselves next to you in order to provide co-regulation. I've observed AAT dogs travel across conference rooms to lay at the feet of a survivor who was silent and sitting still and having a panic attack. AAT animals can also mimic the emotions of humans, which can allow you to observe how you are feeling. For example, I observed a horse who spooked easily when a survivor attempted to pet them. This survivor, who desperately wanted to connect with this horse, was able to see how their anxiety impacted the horse. The survivor worked with the horse and learned to regulate their emotions in order to match the horse's calming presence. Animal-assisted therapy can help you build self-worth, improve your relationships with humans, and increase your ability to regulate your emotions.

For information about ATT, consider these resources:

- Animal Assisted Intervention International (AII), www.aai-int.org and the International Association of Human-Animal Interaction Organizations (IAHAIO), www.iahaio.org
- For survivors: *Transforming Trauma: Resilience and Healing Through Our Connections with Animals* by Philip Tedeschi and Molly Anne Jenkins
- For clinicians: *Handbook on Animal-Assisted Therapy: Foundations and Guidelines for Animal-Assisted Interventions* by Aubrey H. Fine

ATTACHMENT-BASED THERAPY

"Traumatized human beings recover in the context of relationships," writes Van der Kolk. "The role of those relationships is to provide physical and emotional safety, including safety from feeling ashamed, admonished, or judged, and to bolster the courage to tolerate, face, and process the reality of what has happened."[8] It has become common knowledge that survivors heal within relationships, not in isolation. These relationships can include friends, family, animals, colleagues, clinicians, neighbors, and community members. There is a strong positive impact on recovery when you can create, maintain, embrace, and revise your social support system. Therapists will often assist you, if you lack a support system, in creating one, reconnecting with an established support system, and identifying and reassessing people who might not be safe or capable of providing a supportive relationship. Clinicians might even encourage you to participate in couples and family therapy to support your relationships.

Attachment-based therapy is a type of therapy based on the work of John Bowlby that entirely focuses on supportive relationships. The APA defines attachment-based therapy as "an approach to therapy that specifically targets those thoughts, feelings, communications, behaviors, and interpersonal exchanges that patients have learned either to suppress and avoid or to amplify and overemphasize because of early attachment experiences."[9] The two main processes in attachment-based therapy are the creation of a secure-based relationship (which can be with any safe capable person) and the reclaiming of lost capacities (such as the ability to feel safe in relationships and express vulnerability). Attachment therapist Shirley Crenshaw works with child survivors and spends much of her time with their caregivers. "I typically see parents of kids with early trauma (most often adopted children) and teach them to make sense of these children's defensive behaviors, as well as learning to empathize and validate the trauma that made those behaviors useful for survival."[10] This education helps caregivers cultivate supportive relationships for child survivors. Both adults and children can engage in attachment-based therapy, and it's not uncommon for adult survivors to welcome members of their support system into therapy so they can receive education or engage in therapy together.

For information about attachment-based therapy, consider these sources:

- ATTACh, www.attach.org
- For survivors: *Trauma and Attachment: Over 150 Attachment-Based Interventions to Heal Trauma* by Christian Reese
- For clinicians: *Facilitating Developmental Attachment: The Road to Emotional Recovery and Behavioral Change in Foster and Adopted Children* by Daniel A Hughes

BRAINSPOTTING

Brainspotting (BSP) is a technique in which you use your field of vision to access, locate, and process brainspots, which are stationary eye positions that create a connection to neutral networks that carry trauma. "To resolve trauma, BSP can get into the mammalian brain and bypass the thinking brain," reports psychologist Christine Ranck, one of the earliest BSP practitioners. "This means bypassing the neo-cortex and getting to the deeper, more emotional responses of the sub-cortex." Instead of using talking as a processing method, BSP providers focus on where you are looking when you experience trauma-related thoughts, emotions, and physical sensations. Dr. David Grand, the creator of BSP, sums up this technique in one sentence: "Where you look affects how you feel."[11]

Imagine that you are exploring a memory, physical sensation, thought, or emotion with your BSP provider, and they bring a pointer into your field of vision. It reminds you of a tool that an eye doctor uses to test your eye mobility. The provider is observing and responding to your verbal and nonverbal feedback. They locate a brainspot, and by using the pointer, they prompt you to continue gazing in that direction. "When a brainspot is stimulated, the deep brain appears to reflexively signal the therapist that the problem's source has been found," says Ranck. The practitioner then asks you to continue looking at the brainspot until they or you notice a difference. "With focus and precision—*like a laser beam*—the brainspot locates where the patient is holding the trauma and then allows the brain to process through the trauma in a way that talk therapy alone cannot."[12]

For information about Brainspotting, consider these resources:

- Brainspotting International, www.brainspotting.com
- For survivors: *Brainspotting: The Revolutionary New Therapy for Rapid and Effective Change* by David Grand
- For clinicians: *The Power of Brainspotting: An International Anthology* by Gerhard Wolfrum

COGNITIVE PROCESSING THERAPY (CPT)

Cognitive processing therapy (CPT) was developed by Patricia A. Resick and is "a specific type of cognitive behavioral therapy that helps patients learn how to modify and challenge unhelpful beliefs related to the trauma." The APA writes, "CPT is generally delivered over 12 sessions and helps patients learn how to challenge and modify unhelpful beliefs related to the trauma. In so doing, the patient creates a new understanding and conceptualization of the traumatic event so that it reduces its ongoing negative effects on current life."[13] If you want to change your thought patterns and beliefs, you might consider CPT. It can be conducted individually or in a therapy group setting, and it requires you to complete assignments outside of sessions.

"I didn't realize that blaming myself caused me so much pain," reports Bridgette, an incest survivor who participated in CPT. "I believed that I was to blame for what happened, like I tempted my father or caused it somehow. Eventually, I learned that I didn't have the evidence to support this belief, and I was able to move past it. Now, whenever I think that it was my fault, I remind myself that I was a child, and it was the adult's fault. It was *his* fault." CPT therapists will provide you with psychoeducation, help you to identify your unhelpful beliefs and thoughts, and teach you strategies to challenge and change these thoughts and beliefs.

For information about CPT, consider these resources:

- Cognitive processing therapy for PTSD, cptforptsd.com
- For survivors: *Getting Unstuck from PTSD: Using Cognitive Processing Therapy to Guide Your Recovery* by Patricia A. Resick, Shannon Wiltsey Stirman, and Stefanie T. LoSavio
- For clinicians: *Cognitive Processing Therapy for PTSD: A Comprehensive Therapist Manual* by Patricia A. Resick, Candice M. Monson, and Kathleen M. Chard

EYE MOVEMENT DESENSITIZATION
AND REPROCESSING (EMDR)

EMDR (Eye Movement Desensitization and Reprocessing) developed by Francine Shapiro "is a therapy that helps you safely process and heal from disturbing experiences that have caused trauma and emotional wounds," explains EMDR-certified therapist Maggie Reynolds. "The transformative part of EMDR occurs when various parts of your brain and body are communicating effectively, allowing you to arrive at new conclusions, insights, and emotions."[14] EMDR looks different from traditional psychotherapy, as the therapist utilizes bilateral stimulation to bring about changes in the brain and body. The therapist creates bilateral stimulation by moving the survivor's eyes from side to side, providing them with a tactile device (which causes a vibrating sensation that alternates from the right and left hand), an audio device (which causes sounds that alternate in the left and right ears), and physical tapping (which alternates on the left and right sides of the body). Imagine that you are focusing on a memory, physical sensation, thought, or emotion with your EMDR provider. They ask you to focus on this sensation as you receive bilateral stimulation and to report any changes that you experience. For example, a survivor may notice that they feel angry at the beginning of a session, then they feel sad, and then feel a sense of calm and acceptance.

Common goals of EMDR are decreasing the levels of emotional disturbance associated with past experiences and reprocessing physical sensations, thoughts, and beliefs that are negatively impacted by those past experiences. "The benefits of EMDR can sometimes become apparent during and immediately following a session, such as a shift or a reduction of pain and discomfort in the body or being able to call to mind a difficult memory without becoming emotionally overwhelmed," describes Reynolds. "However, sometimes the benefits show up weeks later when the client encounters a situation that would have triggered them before and are able to remain calm and handle it in a new and positive way."[15]

For information about EMDR, consider these resources:

- EMDR International Association (EMDRIA), www.emdria.org
- For survivors: *Getting Past Your Past: Take Control of Your Life with Self-Help Techniques from EMDR Therapy* by Francine Shapiro
- For clinicians: *Eye Movement Desensitization and Reprocessing (EMDR) Therapy: Basic Principles, Protocols, and Procedures* by Francine Shapiro

EMOTIONAL FREEDOM TECHNIQUE (EFT)

Emotional freedom technique (EFT) is "a practical self-help method that involves using the fingers to gently tap on the body's acupuncture points along the meridian lines of Chinese medicine," describes EFT International.[16] Some participants refer to this method as *tapping*. The tapping points are specific locations on your body such as the top center of your head, inside edge of one eyebrow, outside edge of one eye, the bone underneath one eye, nose, and upper lip, between the lower lip and chin, beneath one collarbone, and under one armpit. EFT is a simple intervention that is easy to learn. You can tap with a practitioner present or independently. However, *EFT practitioners advise trauma survivors not to engage in trauma processing using EFT on their own, as they can experience adverse emotional reactions.*

In trauma recovery, the focus of EFT is to change the energy meridians. These changes can have a positive impact on physical sensations. "The patient revisits the event(s) in question [traumatic experience], the energy meridians are thus redisturbed, and then the physical symptoms caused by that particular disturbance can be healed by correcting the meridians with EFT," explains EFT's creator Gary Craig.[17] EFT can also be used to change negative beliefs and thoughts. "There are two different ways to approach shifting subconscious beliefs," write authors Jack Canfield and Pamela Bruner. "One, you can bring the subconscious beliefs to the conscious mind by examining your emotions, and the thoughts behind them. Then you can tap on those thoughts that are now conscious rather than subconscious. Two, you can tap on the negative emotion even if you don't know the thought that's causing it."[18]

For information about EFT, consider these resources:

- EFT International, www.eftinternational.org
- For survivors: *Official EFT from A to Z: How to use both forms of Emotional Freedom Techniques for self-healing* by Gabriëlle Rutten and Gary Craig
- For clinicians: *EFT For PTSD* by Gary Craig

EXPRESSIVE ARTS THERAPY

Expressive arts therapy is "the purposeful application of art, music, dance/movement, dramatic enactment, creative writing, and imaginative play—[it] is largely a nonverbal way of self-expression of feelings and perceptions," writes expressive arts psychologist Cathy A. Malchiodi.[19] This type of therapy is highly experiential, meaning that it's focused on you having an *experience* as opposed to *talking* about an experience. For example, you might notice a change in your emotions and thoughts while you are in the process of writing. An expressive arts therapist may not need to discuss the content of your writing or the experience that you had because the change has already occurred. Malchiodi writes that expressive arts therapy is "action-oriented and tap implicit, embodied, experiences of trauma that can defy expression through verbal therapy or logic."[20] Therefore, this could be a beneficial approach if you may not need to or cannot talk about your trauma.

As a participant in expressive arts therapy, you may engage in such interventions as self-holding practices, bilateral drawings, body mapping, psychodrama, and mirroring. "People may think that expressive arts therapy is just for kids but in the last twenty-five years, I have used this dynamic modality with every age," explained expressive arts therapist Eve Brownstone. "With children, I've facilitated imagination games and art therapy. With teens, I have facilitated role-playing groups in which they process relationship issues and writing or journaling exercises to promote insight. With adults, I have used various interventions, including psychodrama. I have found that clients of all ages still love to play and create."[21]

For information about expressive arts therapy, consider these resources:

- International Expressive Arts Therapy Association (IEATA), www. ieata.org
- For survivors: *The Art Therapy Sourcebook* by Cathy A. Malchiodi
- For clinicians: *Trauma and Expressive Arts Therapy: Brain, Body, & Imagination in the Healing Process* by Cathy A. Malchiodi

INTERNAL FAMILY SYSTEMS (IFS)

Internal family systems (IFS) is "a transformative tool that conceives of every human being as a system of protective and wounded inner parts led by a core Self," reports the IFS Institute.[22] Some survivors and clinicians call this therapy *parts work*, as it is based on the belief that we all have subpersonalities, or parts. Imagine that you are a family unit and all your parts are important members of that family, with each having its own personality. These parts are called the managers, exile parts, firefighters, and the Self (you).[23] When you experience trauma, your parts change in order to support your survival—yet these changes can negatively impact your entire system. IFS supports all your parts, as no part is ever labeled as "bad." In fact, all the parts have good intentions, as they are trying to help you to survive, even if their contributions aren't always productive. The goal of IFS is not to eliminate any part of you but to help all of your parts work together to best support you.

A typical IFS session may consist of exploring your parts and how they are impacting your thoughts, emotions, actions, and physical sensations, as well as helping these parts to communicate and work together in order to support recovery. You may find that you are better able to identify, connect, and support their parts when they experience trauma responses. "At its core, IFS is a loving way of relating internally (to your parts) and externally (to the people in your life), so in that sense, IFS is a life practice, as well," writes IFS creator Richard C. Schwartz. "It's something you can do on a daily, moment-to-moment basis—at any time, by yourself or with others."[24]

For information about IFS, consider these resources:

- IFS Institute, www.ifs-institute.com
- For survivors: *No Bad Parts: Healing Trauma and Restoring Wholeness with the Internal Family Systems Model* by Richard C. Schwartz
- For clinicians: *Internal Family Systems Skills Training Manual: Trauma-Informed Treatment for Anxiety, Depression, PTSD and Substance Abuse* by Frank Anderson, Richard Schwartz, and Martha Sweezy

MDMA-ASSISTED PSYCHOTHERAPY

MDMA-assisted psychotherapy is a combination of drug therapy and psychotherapy. 3,4-Methylenedioxymethamphetamine (MDMA) is the active ingredient in illicit ecstasy. However, the MDMA that's used in MDMA-assisted psychotherapy is different; it is pharmaceutical-grade MDMA that's administered by a medical professional in a controlled environment. MDMA increases the chemicals of norepinephrine, serotonin, and dopamine in the brain. Common goals of MDMA-assisted psychotherapy are the regulation of emotions and behaviors, increased relational bonding, and decreased anxiety, all of which might allow survivors to access traumatic memories without feeling overwhelmed.[25]

A typical MDMA treatment plan might consist of fifteen sessions: three sessions of eight hours spent under the influence of MDMA, occurring three to five weeks apart, and twelve psychotherapy sessions with no MDMA.[26] Treatment providers will provide specific recommendations based on your needs. You are never left alone during an MDMA session, as a facilitator is present to provide you with support and guidance if needed. The therapy sessions without MDMA allow you to explore and process anything that came up during the MDMA sessions or after, such as new thoughts, emotions, memories, and bodily sensations. "One thing the MDMA facilitates is thinking about traumatic experiences in a neutral, safe manner," described an MDMA-assisted therapy clinical trial participant. "I could objectively think about them and talk about them. Then, it seems those memories are put back in their place in the brain in a different configuration—a configuration that does not cause as many problems, such as bad dreams, intrusive thoughts all the time or having horrible insomnia. This has continued to this day, a year and a half after the last MDMA session."[27]

For information about MDMA-assisted psychotherapy, consider these resources:

- Multidisciplinary Association for Psychedelic Studies, www.maps. org
- For survivors: *Psychedelic Psychotherapy: A User Friendly Guide to Psychedelic Drug-Assisted Psychotherapy* by R. Coleman
- For clinicians: *The Theradelic Approach: Psychedelic Therapy Perspective, Preparation, and Practice* by Sunny Strasburg and Richard Schwartz

MINDFULNESS MEDITATION

Mindfulness meditation is the process of "training your attention to achieve a mental state of calm concentration and positive emotions," writes the APA.[28] This type of meditation comprises two parts: attention and acceptance.

Attention is when you focus on what is occurring in the present, such as your breath, thoughts, emotions, or physical sensations. Acceptance involves observing what you notice without judgment. For example, when I meditate, I always notice that my breath is shallow. I'm tempted to judge my breath as "wrong," but instead, I try to embrace it. I simply notice my shallow breathing as it is. Sometimes, my breath deepens on its own and when it does, I try to notice that change without judgment.

It is important for you to seek out meditation practices that are trauma-sensitive. Imagine not feeling safe to close your eyes and being told by your meditation facilitator that you must close your eyes or you are "not doing it right." Interactions like this are typical in recovery interventions that are not trauma-sensitive, and meditation is no different. "For people who've experienced trauma, mindfulness meditation can exacerbate symptoms of traumatic stress," writes David A. Treleaven. "This can include flashbacks, heightened emotional arousal, and dissociation. . . . While meditation can appear to be a safe and innocuous practice, it can thrust trauma survivors directly into the heart of wounds that require more than mindful awareness to heal."[29]A trauma-sensitive approach to meditation may consist of invitations instead of commands, an emphasis on choice, and options related to posture (seated, standing, laying down) and techniques (eyes open or closed, moving or sitting still).

For information about mindfulness meditation, consider these resources:

- The Mindfulness Meditation Institute, www.mindfulnessmeditationinstitute.org
- For survivors: *Trauma-Sensitive Mindfulness: Practices for Safe and Transformative Healing* by David A. Treleaven
- For clinicians: *Mindfulness-Oriented Interventions for Trauma: Integrating Contemplative Practices* by Victoria M. Follette, John Briere, Deborah Rozelle, James W. Hopper, and David I. Rome

NEUROAFFECTIVE RELATIONAL MODEL (NARM)

The NeuroAffective relational model (NARM) is a method of psychotherapy that was created to treat complex trauma (e.g., developmental trauma, relational trauma, impacts of Adverse Childhood Experiences [ACEs], and disrupted attachment). "The practitioner and client work together in a shared relational field to heal the body-mind, helping clients with nervous system re-regulation as well as connection to self," describes NARM master practitioner Maureen Kebo. "The model is not organized around what is broken but rather works with a client's strengths and builds on this over time which assists in the re-regulation process allowing access to a self that was previously buried in trauma. This brings more connection to authentic self as well as connection to others."[30] This relational framework embraces a nonpathologizing approach to trauma and seeks to embrace and promote your agency.

"Unfortunately, we are often unaware of the internal roadblocks that keep us from experiencing the connection and aliveness we yearn for," writes NARM developer Laurence Heller. "These roadblocks develop in reaction to developmental and shock trauma and the related nervous system dysregulation, disruptions in attachment, and distortions of identity. The goal of the NeuroAffective Relational Model (NARM) is to work with these dysregulations, disruptions, and distortions while never losing sight of supporting the development of a healthy capacity for connection and aliveness."[31]

Here's an example of an outcome of a NARM session: "A session is always organized around what the client wants for themselves and what is in the way of what they want for themselves," explains Kebo. "As we explore what is in the way, clients typically have new insights into how their internal world is organized. Through this, clients tend to recognize the adaptations they made as a result of their trauma were very effective in order to survive; however, they no longer serve them."[32]

For information about NARM, consider these resources:

- NARM Training Institute, www.narmtraining.com
- For survivors: *Healing Developmental Trauma: How Early Trauma Affects Self-Regulation, Self-Image, and the Capacity for Relationship* by Laurence Heller and Aline LaPierre
- For clinicians: *The Practical Guide for Healing Developmental Trauma: Using the NeuroAffective Relational Model to Address Adverse Childhood Experiences and Resolve Complex Trauma* by Laurence Heller and Brad J. Kammer

NATURE THERAPY

The oldest recovery method on this list is nature therapy, as humans have utilized nature in trauma recovery since the beginning. "The mind is nature, and nature, the mind," wrote Robert Greenway, whose work led to the awareness of nature therapy, also called *ecopsychology*, a belief that the psychological wellness of human beings is connected to the natural world. There are many ways to embrace nature therapy. One example is horticultural therapy, the use of plant-based activity and plants in healing and rehabilitation.[33] Some of my clients reported that having plants in their environment helps to calm them. You might also embrace nature therapy by spending time in nature, enjoying activities such as gardening, bird watching, hiking in forests or parks, camping, swimming in a lake, river, or ocean, or interacting with animals. All these activities can create opportunities to benefit from nature therapy.

My clients have reported that simply being in nature has a positive impact on their recovery. "I can't really explain it, when I'm near a body of water, my mind opens up and I have all of these new realizations," reports Holly, a survivor of domestic violence. "When I'm completing therapy assignments, I make sure to be near water, even if it's just sitting in my bathtub." Kent, a survivor of combat trauma, prefers the woods. "I have to hike at least once a week, or else I'll go crazy. Walking on the trail, I sometimes think about my experiences in the war. I notice that I think or feel differently when I'm done hiking. I try not to think about those memories outside of the woods because if I do, it's too much."

For information about nature therapy, consider these resources:

- Center for Nature Informed Therapy, www.natureinformedtherapy.com
- For survivors: *The Nature Fix: Why Nature Makes Us Happier, Healthier, and More Creative* by Florence Williams
- For clinicians: *Nature-Based Therapy: A Practitioner's Guide to Working Outdoors with Children, Youth, and Families* by Nevin J. Harper, Kathryn Rose, and David Segal

NEUROFEEDBACK

"It's like yoga for your brain," says neurofeedback therapist and trainer Leanne Hershkowitz. "Neurofeedback uses learning principles and electroencephalogram biofeedback to help you change how the neurons in your brain fire, communicate with each other, and much more." Neurofeedback can support trauma recovery, as it focuses on changing the nervous system. "It helps increase stability and appropriate flexibility in the nervous system and does not require insight or lots of talking," reports Hershkowitz.[34] Neurofeedback, which was pioneered by the work of Barry Sterman, can be beneficial for adults, adolescents, and child trauma survivors.

What does a neurofeedback session look like? Imagine sitting in an office in front of a computer screen. Your neurofeedback provider places small sensors on your head to read your brain waves. Then, a computer game begins playing on the computer screen. You are in control of the game but you don't use a handheld controller; you use your brain. "As you adjust your brain waves based on the feedback you're getting (from the computer game), your brain and nervous system become more regulated, and targeted symptoms can reduce or go away completely," explains Hershkowitz. "A lot of the learning process is unconscious but by setting the intention of wanting the game to work and trying to relax while still staying focused, your brain will try different things until it gets the reward."[35]

For information about neurofeedback, consider these resources:

- The International Society for Neuroregulation & Research (ISNR), www.isnr.org
- For survivors: *Neurofeedback 101: Rewiring the Brain for ADHD, Anxiety, Depression and Beyond* by Michael P. Cohen
- For clinicians: *Beginning Neurofeedback in Your Practice: A Guide for Clinicians Using Neurofeedback From Intake to Discharge* by Robert Longo and Becky Bingham

PELVIC FLOOR PHYSICAL THERAPY

I had never heard of pelvic floor physical therapy as a recovery method for trauma until my clients informed me. They reported positive changes, such as decreased physical pain, improved sexual health, and an increased ability to physically relax after participating in this type of physical therapy. "Your pelvic floor is a muscular sheet at the base of your pelvis," explained pelvic floor physical therapist Amy Healy. "The muscles go from the pubic bone in the front, the sit bones on the sides, and the tailbone in the back. When the muscles are tight, the muscular sheet can be rigid and flat. When the muscles are at an optimal length, they look like a hammock." Trauma can impact your pelvic floor, which Healy calls "the natural guardian." "Think of it as the first line of defense—against trauma in your body. When your pelvic floor reflexively tightens up during trauma, you might ultimately feel that tightening impact all sorts of functionality and day-to-day activities, including (but definitely not limited to) painful sex."[36]

The goals of pelvic floor physical therapy include improving core stability, increasing control over urination and bowel movements, and improving sexual function. This is done by strengthening and/or relaxing the muscles of the pelvic floor with physical interventions such as Kegels, manual therapy, biofeedback, electrical stimulation, and dilators. This type of physical therapy isn't just for women. Men have also benefited, and in fact, it was my cisgender male clients who brought this recovery method to my attention. How do you know if your physical symptoms are pelvic-related? Healy recommends that all clients complete a medical evaluation with their primary care doctor before considering pelvic floor therapy in order to rule out medical causes. She also recommends completing the Cozean Pelvic Dysfunction Screening Protocol, which is a brief assessment that can be found online for free.[37]

For information about pelvic floor therapy, consider these resources:

- The Academy of Pelvic Health Physical Therapy, www.apta pelvichealth.org
- For survivors: *Your Pelvic Floor Sucks: But It Doesn't Have To: A Whole Body Guide to a Better Pelvic Floor* by Lindsay S. Mumma
- For clinicians: *Evidence-Based Physical Therapy for the Pelvic Floor: Bridging Science and Clinical Practice* by Kari Bø, Bary Berghmans, Siv Mørkved, and Marijke Van Kampen

SENSORIMOTOR PSYCHOTHERAPY

Sensorimotor psychotherapy (SP) was created by Pat Ogden as a body-based talk therapy specifically for trauma and attachment recovery. "SP welcomes the body as an integral source of information which can guide resourcing and the accessing and processing of challenging, traumatic, and developmental experience," explains the Sensorimotor Psychotherapy Institute.[38]

SP is influenced by somatic, attachment, and cognitive theories, the Hakomi method, and neuroscience. In regard to trauma, "Sensorimotor psychotherapy emphasizes helping clients develop resources within themselves to be able to self-regulate affect, or to move out of the fight/flight/freeze response, and into a higher-functioning mode where they can think clearly and feel appropriately," writes sensorimotor psychotherapist Julie Westlin-Naigus. "Clients can become less reactive and more proactive in their relationships, work, and families."[39]

What does a typical SP session look like? Imagine discussing a traumatic experience, and your therapist asks you to remember a few moments before the event. They ask that you be mindful of the sensations that you notice in your body. Your therapist will work with you to discover if there is a physical movement that you would have liked to have made before, during, or after the event but couldn't. Then, the therapist will encourage the survivor to engage in the movement safely. For example, a survivor discusses a memory in which their father physically abused them. They focus on the moments before the abuse and notice a tightening in their chest and arms and a surge of energy. They feel the need to block their father's fists and push him away. The therapist helps the survivor to complete the physical movement (using their body to block him and push him away). The survivor might block and push away a pillow that is being held by their therapist, or they might push against a wall. The goal is to allow the survivor to move as they need to, leaving them with an experience of triumph that can change their nervous system.

For information about SP, consider these resources:

- Sensorimotor Psychotherapy Institute, www.sensorimotorpsycho-therapy.org
- For survivors: *Sensorimotor Practices for Awareness, Regulation, and Expansion Card Deck* by Pat Ogden
- For clinicians: *Sensorimotor Psychotherapy: Interventions for Trauma and Attachment* by Pat Ogden and Janina Fisher

SELF-DEFENSE

Self-defense classes, trainings, and courses are recommended for trauma survivors because of their focus on creating and restoring an ability to verbally and nonverbally protect oneself. You could benefit from self-defense skills training, which may help you to manage your fight, flight, freeze, and fawn responses when you feel unsafe. Judith Herman writes, "The survivor places herself in a position to experience the 'fight or flight' response to danger, knowing that she will elect to fight. In so doing, she establishes a degree of control over her own bodily and emotional responses that reaffirm a sense of power."[40] The ability to control responses to danger increases the likelihood that you will be able to protect yourself and supports feelings of empowerment.

"I signed up for the Chicago Impact self-defense course for myself and to better understand how self-defense courses could be a potential resource for my clients who are predominantly trauma survivors," writes psychotherapist Bianka Hardin. "I had no idea how profoundly empowering and life-changing the course would be for myself in my own healing. The experience provided a profound opportunity for deep personal, collective, and intergenerational healing. While taking the course, I learned how to face my fears from a place of strength, and I learned how strong I really am. After the course, I noticed an increased sense of control, power, self-efficacy, and well as a greater sense of safety within myself and within the world."[41]

For information about self-defense, consider these resources:

- IMPACT Violence Prevention, www.impactselfdefense.org
- For survivors: Resolve blog, www.resolvenm.org/blog/; Prepare blog, www.prepareinc.com/category/blog/
- For clinicians: *Transforming Trauma with Jiu-Jitsu: A Guide for Survivors, Therapists, and Jiu-Jitsu Practitioners to Facilitate Embodied Recovery* by Jamie Marich and Anna Pirkl

SOMATIC EXPERIENCING

Somatic experiencing (SE) is "a body-focused trauma healing modality that utilizes the wisdom of the body in the healing process," reports SE psychotherapist Bianka Hardin. "SE is different than traditional talk therapy in that it is focused on the client's biology (their nervous system) instead of the client's biography (their trauma story)."[42] Imagine a deer being stalked by a wolf. This deer might attack the wolf (fight), run away (flee), or remain still (freeze). If the deer survives, their brain will automatically send a signal throughout their body that they are safe and that their fight, flight, or freeze response is no longer needed. The deer will then automatically react in a way that helps their body to transition out of their survival response as opposed to becoming stuck in that response. "The bodies of traumatized people portray 'snapshots' of their unsuccessful attempts to defend themselves in the face of threat and injury," writes SE creator Peter A. Levine. "Trauma is a highly activated incomplete biological response to threat, frozen in time."[43]

What does SE therapy look like? "This healing method is respectful, consensual, and gentle," reports Hardin. "I teach my clients about trauma and its impact on the mind and body. Clients learn experientially in session how to increase their body awareness, support increased regulation and sense of calm within themselves, and work through incomplete fight and/or protective responses. When working with clients, we trust that each client has the inherent ability to heal given the right circumstances."[44]

For information about SE, consider these sources:

- Somatic Experiencing International, www.traumahealing.org
- For survivors: *Healing Trauma: A Pioneering Program for Restoring the Wisdom of Your Body* by Peter A. Levine
- For clinicians: *Trauma and Memory: Brain and Body in a Search for the Living Past: A Practical Guide for Understanding and Working with Traumatic Memory* by Peter A. Levine and Bessel van der Kolk

SUPPORT AND THERAPY GROUPS

Therapy and support groups can benefit trauma survivors by providing validation, empathy, acceptance, community, information, coping methods, and mentorship. Therapy groups are facilitated by a mental health professional, often require a fee, and tend to focus on specific populations, recovery methods, or recovery needs. A few examples of therapy groups are dialectical behavior therapy (DBT) skills groups, process groups for male domestic violence survivors, and trauma-focused art therapy groups for children. Support groups, on the other hand, are usually facilitated by volunteers or peers, are often free, and tend to be more generalized in their focus. A few support groups that have benefited my clients are Adult Survivors of Child Abuse (ASCA), Adult Children of Alcoholics/Dysfunctional Families (ACA), and National Alliance on Mental Illness (NAMI). No two groups are the same, and they can look very different from each other. One group may be highly structured with a specific topic discussed each week, and another may be more process-based, with topics determined by its members.

Groups, like any other recovery method, can benefit and harm survivors. There are groups that romanticize, glorify, or embrace a victim identity, which can encourage you to remain stuck, as opposed to a group environment that encourages growth. There are groups that are not focused on trauma recovery and are not trauma-informed or trauma-sensitive. In addition, some group facilitators and participants create and maintain a safe environment for recovery, while others do not. In both therapy and support groups, safety must be present for survivors to benefit. Before joining a group, consider connecting with the group's leader(s) to see if the goals, culture, structure, and community of the group are a right fit for you. If you join a group and it feels unsafe or doesn't feel like the right fit, you can end your engagement and either try a different recovery method of seek out another group that better meets your needs.

For information about groups, consider these sources:

- For survivors: Adult Survivors of Child Abuse (ASCA), www. ascasupport.org; Adult Children of Alcoholics/Dysfunctional Families (ACA), www.adultchildren.org; and National Alliance on Mental Illness (NAMI) www.nami.org
- For clinicians: *Group Trauma Treatment in Early Recovery: Promoting Safety and Self-Care* by Judith Lewis Herman, Diya Kallivayalil, and Members of the Victims of Violence Program
- For clinicians: *The Trauma Recovery Group: A Guide for Practitioners* by Michaela Mendelsohn, Judith Lewis Herman, Emily Schatzow, Melissa Coco, Diya Kallivayalil, and Jocelyn Levitan.

TRAUMA CENTER TRAUMA-SENSITIVE YOGA (TCTSY)

Trauma center trauma-sensitive yoga (TCTSY) was developed by Dave Emerson and his colleagues and is "the first yoga-based empirically validated clinical intervention for complex trauma or chronic, treatment-resistant post-traumatic stress disorder (PTSD)," according to the Center for Trauma and

Embodiment. For decades, trauma survivors have embraced yoga in their recovery due to its focus on physical connection and processing. TCTSY is influenced by trauma theory, attachment theory, neuroscience, and hatha yoga. Common goals of TCTSY are to create and cultivate a positive relationship with one's body and to maximize experiences of empowerment.[45]

What's the difference between TCTSY and more traditional yoga? First, TCTSY doesn't focus on perfection. Often, yoga practices insist that you focus on your posture and/or sequential movements while receiving corrections from a facilitator. In contrast, "TCTSY encourages you to focus on their internal physical experience in order to dictate decision-making," reports the Center for Trauma and Embodiment. "Although TCTSY employs physical forms and movements, the emphasis is not on the external expression or appearance (i.e., doing it 'right') or receiving the approval of an external authority. Rather, the focus is on the internal experience of the participant. This shift in orientation, from the external to the internal, is a key attribute of TCTSY as a treatment for complex trauma and PTSD. With our approach, the power resides within the individual, not the TCTSY facilitator (TCTSY-F)."[46] Second, TCTSY facilitators do not physically touch participants, which would violate a boundary that some trauma survivors need to maintain in order to feel safe. Instead, facilitators provide participants with feedback based on their observations.

For information about TCTSY, consider these resources:

- The Center for Trauma and Embodiment, www.traumasensitiveyoga. com.
- For survivors: *Overcoming Trauma through Yoga Reclaiming Your Body* by David Emerson and Elizabeth Hopper
- For clinicians: *Trauma-Sensitive Yoga in Therapy: Bringing the Body Into Treatment* by David Emerson

TRAUMA-FOCUSED COGNITIVE BEHAVIORAL THERAPY (TF-CBT)

Trauma-focused cognitive behavioral therapy (TF-CBT) was developed by Anthony Mannarino, Judith Cohen and Esther Deblinger. It is "an evidence-based treatment for children and adolescents impacted by trauma and their parents or caregivers," reports the National Child Traumatic Stress Network. "It is a components-based treatment model that incorporates trauma-sensitive interventions with cognitive behavioral, family, and humanistic principles and techniques. TF-CBT has proved successful with children and adolescents (ages three to eighteen) who have significant emotional problems (e.g., symptoms of PTSD, fear, anxiety, or depression) related to traumatic life events."[47] A diagnosis of PTSD is not required for a survivor to participate, as many child survivors do not meet the criteria for PTSD despite having experienced trauma.

"That's me, my mom, my grandma, Pastor Greene, and my dog Luna," said eight-year-old Keisha, a sexual abuse survivor, as she showed me a drawing she'd created in a TF-CBT session. Her assignment was called "Your Circle of Safety," and it asked her to draw herself with a circle of safety around her. Inside that circle, she was asked to draw all the people who keep her safe. "They can't get me now because I'm in the circle," Keisha said, smiling. This assignment helped Keisha to feel safe, knowing that she had a social support system that would promote her safety. TF-CBT is a skill-based approach that provides skills and tools for survivors like Keisha and their caregivers. Participants may receive a variety of interventions, such as psychoeducation, relaxation, affective modulation, cognitive coping, trauma narrative and emotional processing, in vivo desensitization, and conjoint sessions.

For information about TF-CBT, consider these resources:

- Trauma-Focused Cognitive Behavioral Therapy, www.tfcbt.org
- For survivors: *Your Very Own TF-CBT Workbook* by Alison Hendricks, Judith A. Cohen, Anthony P. Mannarino, and Esther Deblinger
- For clinicians: *Trauma-Focused CBT for Children and Adolescents: Treatment Applications* by Judith A. Cohen, Anthony P. Mannarino, and Esther Deblinger

CHOOSING YOUR METHODS

Take some time to reflect on which of these methods you might be willing to try. Feel free to try as many as you wish, as it's likely that you'll need and will benefit from multiple interventions in recovery. Remember, there is no one method that works for every survivor, and trauma recovery is not a one-size-fits-all experience. The trick is to find the combination of recovery methods that work for you, and this combination may change over time. It's common to utilize a successful intervention for a period of time and then abandon it if it no longer meets your needs. You might return to it later or not at all. You may find that one method is not beneficial at the beginning of your recovery, only to discover that is more helpful later on. Just as you decide if forgiveness will be a part of your recovery, you decide what methods are a part of it as well.

Will you forgive? It's possible that while engaging in these or other trauma recovery methods, you may forgive your offender(s), forgive yourself, experience acceptance, or none of the above—and make progress in recovery. Psychotherapist Hannah Alderete writes, "For now, let this be your mantra: I don't have to forgive to be okay."[48] We can be and feel okay again, or for the first time in our lives. We can recover from trauma, with or without forgiveness.

Conclusion

"Time is running out. Time to reconnect," wrote my mother in a social media direct message, the only method she had left to communicate with me. "Time to make peace with the past."

"I'm willing to participate in a dialogue in family therapy," I wrote back. "Is this something you are willing to do?"

"Yes, I would welcome the opportunity to reconnect in family therapy," she responded.

When I finished writing this book, I began participating in family therapy with my seventy-three-year-old mother. It was the first time I had seen or spoken to her in seven years. The goal of family therapy was not forgiveness; it was to see if we could safely have any relationship in the future. I was worried that my mother might attempt to restore our established dysfunctional family dynamic, which casts her as the helpless, codependent, valuable mother and me as the strong, self-sacrificing, "good daughter" whose value is determined by her contributions to her mother. Some offenders will participate in family or couples therapy to placate survivors, as they have no intention or capability of doing the work on themselves that is required to improve or sustain the relationship. After a few family therapy sessions, it was clear that my mother was capable, as she had been working with her individual therapist for years.

My mother was patient, understanding, and accepting of my need to promote my safety. She agreed to no communication outside therapy sessions, and we worked together to decide what topics were discussed and which would be avoided until safety was reestablished. We agreed to discuss the impact of her childhood and marriage on her parenting, as well as my experiences of physical and emotional neglect perpetrated by her and my father. As she shared her trauma narrative, she exposed her family's secrets, and I didn't realize how much I needed to hear them.

TRAUMA THRIVES IN SECRECY

"We're a family of secrets," said my mother during a session.

Trauma thrives in secrecy. Survivors have attempted to protect others (especially children) from their trauma by not disclosing it. There once was a universally accepted belief that if people don't know about your trauma, it wouldn't impact them. We've discovered that this is not true, as trauma responses do not occur in a vacuum but within relationships. Family members, friends, romantic partners, and even children are not protected from our trauma when we keep them in the dark. They are impacted; they don't know why or how, but they are affected. Children especially can sense and absorb the trauma of their attachment figures even when their sensations are never explained or validated. I didn't know my parents' family secrets when I was a child, yet their trauma had a significant negative impact on my life and still does to this day. In family therapy, my mother and father's trauma was finally exposed, and the great silence was broken.

My maternal great-grandfather lived with chronic kidney pain and a gambling addiction. One day, he called his daughter, my grandmother, after he had lost a lot of money gambling.

"I just can't take it anymore," he cried into the phone, begging. He was frightened of facing his wife with the news of his monetary loss yet again.

"I'm tired of hearing it. Why don't you go do it?" my grandmother responded.

He hung up the phone and moments later died by suicide.

I suspect that my maternal grandmother carried the guilt with her for the rest of her life. She likely believed she had killed her father or, at the very least, regretted how she spoke to him before he died. When she received that call, she was pregnant with my mother. The prenatal environment impacts a child's development, and it's possible that the stress, guilt, and grief negatively impacted my mother's development in the womb. This may explain why my mother has an undeveloped emotional maturity.

My mother's father was a World War II B-29 bomber co-pilot in the Pacific. He completed three tours, and during the last one, his plane crashed, killing his best friend. The Air Force's investigation concluded that a pilot's error caused the accident. After that day, my grandfather despised himself, as he was convinced that he had killed his friend. The shame consumed him. My great-grandmother, who knew him before and after the war, said it best: "He came back from the war a different man." My grandfather returned home with PTSD, which was never diagnosed or treated. He abused alcohol for decades, physically abused his children, and had a secret family, fathering two sons.

Two traumatized parents raised my mother, who had a severe heart-related illness as a child. Her role in her family was that of the sick child who was destined to die. When she survived, she became the family's fragile child or "DLD" (Daddy's Little Darling), as her siblings resentfully called her, as they were physically abused by their father and she was not. As a preadolescent, she became her father's bartender and her mother's emotional support system. As an adult, she learned from her parents that it doesn't matter how badly you are abused in your marriage, you don't leave. As a result, she stayed with her husband, my father, who was a horrific abuser.

My father's family had secrets as well. My paternal grandfather was a kind, shy man who was also completely emotionally detached. So, my father, like myself, never honestly had a father. How would he know how to be someone's father? My father's family was and is plagued with mental illness to this day, with few members ever seeking treatment. Most of my aunts and uncles have debilitating anxiety, depression, personality disorders, or schizophrenia. Like my father, most of his family could not be safe and supportive attachment figures in my life.

Many people kept these family secrets from me. They were trying to protect me, themselves, or perhaps both, but their efforts had the opposite effect. Silence doesn't protect us from trauma. Silence allows trauma to thrive. The silence in my family made me vulnerable to repeating the intergenerational trauma cycle, which I did. I married a man who, like my father, was financially and emotionally abusive and, like both my parents, was incapable of secure attachment. In my first marriage, I became like my mother: dissociated, controlled, and lacking in identity and self-worth. Learning my family's secrets did not inflate or add to my trauma. Instead, it gave me a greater understanding of my trauma and aided in my recovery.

HAVE I FORGIVEN?

After writing this book and embracing elective forgiveness in my trauma recovery, have I forgiven my parents?

I have not forgiven my father. I rarely think of him, and when I do, I don't feel much of anything. I do not feel angry or resentful. I don't feel sympathy or empathy for him. I don't feel much of anything toward him. How is this possible? It makes sense if you consider that, from my emotional perspective, the man never existed. I never really knew him, was not attached to him, and did not love him. It's as if there were a stranger who just happened to live in the same home as I did when I was a child. A stranger who might have rented out a room but was not a part of my life. This is why I didn't need to grieve when he died suddenly. The truth is that I wish he would have died sooner, as his death was the best thing to happen to my family. It freed me, my mother, and my brothers from his control and abuse, and it allowed us the opportunity to transition from surviving to thriving, which would have never occurred if he had been alive.

Apathy is not forgiveness. Our working definition of forgiveness is "an emotional process that results in a reduction in negative emotions, thoughts, and behavioral dispositions toward the offender(s) and an increase in positive thoughts, emotions, and behavioral dispositions toward the offender(s), all of which lie on a continuum." I do not have negative emotions, thoughts, and behaviors associated with my father. Still, the absence of positive thoughts, emotions, and behaviors implies that I have not forgiven him. Do I need to forgive him? No. My unforgiveness has not negatively impacted my life or my recovery. If anything, it's helped me to accept that I never had a father and to embrace my grief—not grieving the loss of him per se, but the loss of a father in general.

What about my mother? Have I forgiven her? That's much more compli-cated. My mother physically and emotionally detached from me when I was nine years old. Before then, she was emotionally present in my life. I knew her, was attached to her, and I loved her. I don't feel angry or resentful toward her. I no longer view her as the villain in my story. Instead, I see her as the sickly, lonely little girl who was left alone in her room as her family held their breath, hoping she wouldn't die. I see her as that young girl who served her father drinks until he passed out or beat her siblings. My mother did not have the opportunities that she needed as a child to thrive as a mother. She entered into a marriage without an identity, self-worth, or capability. As a result, she was vulnerable to my father's abuse and unable to protect herself or her children. I feel empathy for her. But have I forgiven her?

I can say that I meet the first criteria of forgiveness in that I've experienced a reduction in "negative" emotions, thoughts, and behaviors. I do not feel anger or resentment toward her, and I do not in any way wish her harm. But I'm not sure if I've met the second criterion. I empathize with her and wish her well, which are "positive" emotions and thoughts. Perhaps this means I have forgiven her even if these emotions are on the continuum's lower end. At this moment, I do not like my mother, and I do not love her. I do not wish to support her in any way in the future or to be a part of her life, although I am reminded that reconciliation is not forgiveness and vice versa. Am I describing unforgiveness? I'm not sure. I, a trauma therapist who's written a book on forgiveness in trauma recovery, am not sure if I have forgiven my offender. You might also be unsure if you've forgiven your offender(s), and that's okay. Based on my reports, some will say I've forgiven my mother, and others will say I have not. Yet, the more important question is not *Have I forgiven?* but *Do I need to forgive?*

Forgiveness is not a part of my trauma recovery, and it may never be. I might never forgive my father. On the other hand, I could wake up one day and find that I have forgiven him. I could also feel more confident in my state of forgiveness or unforgiveness toward my mother. Regardless, I simply don't need to focus on forgiveness. I haven't focused on forgiveness thus far, and I've made significant progress in recovery. But I'm not finished.

When are we done with trauma recovery? We are never fully finished. We may notice progress in one area of our lives and move on to another area that needs our attention. We may engage in one trauma recovery method, soaking up all it has to offer, and discard it when it no longer meets our needs, moving onto another to absorb from it before we move on again. We will have days in which we will thrive and days when we must focus on surviving, only to thrive again once we feel safer. Trauma is not healed; it's transformed and integrated. Recovery is a lifelong process.

And we can recover with or without forgiveness.

Acknowledgments

Like trauma recovery, *You Don't Need to Forgive* was a process that involved years of researching, writing, editing, and promoting; it was a journey that I could not have taken alone. This book would not exist without the brilliant philosopher, masterful proofreader, and my loving partner, J.D. Singer, PhD. One day, J.D. told me "This could be a book" after proofreading a blog I'd written for *Psychology Today* about the harmful impacts of forced forgiveness upon trauma survivors. Since then, J.D. has been my strongest supporter by encouraging me to forge ahead when I was stuck and to take breaks when I pushed myself too hard. Always the social justice advocate, J.D. championed inclusivity in this book and reminded me never to lose sight of the marginalized survivors who have been and continue to be harmed by society's unapologetic acceptance of forgiveness as a universal cure. While researching this book, I was disappointed by the restricted ideas and practices in the field of psychology. Thankfully, the field of philosophy emerged to fill in the gaps and pick up the pieces, as it has done since psychology's inception. Philosophers have been historically underpaid and unappreciated in our society, a mistake that I fear has delayed progress and will continue to delay it.

I want to offer copious appreciation to my parents-in-law, Stewart and Ellin Singer, whose generosity allowed me the opportunity to complete this book. Their unwavering, unconditional love for their child is a testament to the many parents who provide and maintain secure attachments with their children. Parents like Stewart and Ellin Singer will and have made the most significant positive changes in our society by sending their healthy, nurtured children into the world. I hope I have and will continue contributing to their legacy.

I would also like to thank senior acquisitions editor Lil Copan of Broadleaf Books, who followed my writing online and asked me if I wanted to write a book. Lil wasted no time presenting and promoting *You Don't Need to Forgive* to her colleagues. Two months later, she presented me with a contract. Can you get a book deal without an agent? You can when you are recruited by editors like Lil Copan, who are on the prowl looking for fresh ideas and perspectives.

I'm grateful for my editor, Lisa Kloskin, who insisted that *You Don't Need to Forgive* be written for and accessible to trauma survivors. Without Lisa, this book could have become a boring, tedious, dry clinical textbook. Lisa's understanding, patience, and flexibility were evident as she navigated the obstacles of working with a full-time therapist who was often only accessible three days out of the week and who never figured out how to use tracking in Microsoft Word.

To my brothers, Kenneth and T.J., thank you for providing respite retreats of beaches, shelling, and sibling shenanigans. They would prefer that I wrote Floridian murder mystery novels, but they were willing to concede that perhaps this book would be more useful. Thank you to my colleagues and friends who assured me this book needed to be written and never failed to ask me the ultimate question of author accountability, "How's the book coming?" These persistent souls include but are not limited to Christy Campbell, Michele Day, Alex Fliess, Cory Neusche, Colleen Reilly, Maggie Reynolds, Katie Rodenkirch, Kalpana Sabapathy, and Eryn Smith-Moeller. Lastly, I have an undying appreciation for Mr. BoJangles, my sassy black cat, who was vital to my trauma recovery, as he has served as my secure attachment figure for the past seven years. Bo often laid on my lap while I was writing this book, occasionally providing his own comments and critiques, which were all considered.

Notes

INTRODUCTION

1 Edward Tronick, footage from "Still Face Experiment," Zero to Three, 2007, posted by UMass Boston, "Developmental Sciences at UMass Boston," 2010, video, 1:03, https://www.youtube.com/watch?v=vmE3NfB_HhE.

2 Jeffrie G Murphy, *Getting Even: Forgiveness and Its Limits* (Oxford: Oxford University Press, 2005), VIII.

CHAPTER ONE: TRAUMA

1 Bessel van der Kolk, *The Body Keeps the Score: Brain, Mind, and Body in the Healing of Trauma* (London: Penguin, 2014), 18.

2 Gabor Maté and Daniel Maté, *The Myth of Normal: Trauma, Illness and Healing in a Toxic Culture* (Toronto: Penguin, 2023), 19.

3 SAMHSA's Trauma and Justice Strategic Initiative, *SAMHSA's Concept of Trauma and Guidance for a Trauma-Informed Approach*, accessed February 20, 2024, https://ncsacw.acf.hhs.gov/userfiles/files/SAMHSA_Trauma.pdf.

4 Peter A. Levine, *Healing Trauma: Study Guide* (Boulder, CO: Sounds True, 1999), 3.

5 Lexi Pandell, "How Trauma Became the Word of the Decade," Vox, updated January 25, 2022, https://www.vox.com/the-highlight/22876522/trauma-covid-word-origin-mental-health.

6 American Psychological Association, s.v. "trauma (*n.*)," updated April 19, 2018, https://dictionary.apa.org/trauma.

7 Peter A. Levine, *Healing Trauma: Study Guide* (Boulder, CO: Sounds True, 1999), 4.

8 Kaytlyn Gillis, *Breaking the Cycle: The Six Stages of Healing from Childhood Family Trauma* (self-pub., 2023), 24.

9 Lisa Amaya-Jackson, Lauren Absher, Ellen Gerrity, Christopher M. Layne, and Jane Halladay Goldman, "Beyond the ACE Score: Perspectives from the NCTSN on Child Trauma and Adversity Screening and Impact," (Durham, NC: National Center for Child Traumatic Stress, 2021), 1–2.

10 Gabor Maté and Daniel Maté, *The Myth of Normal: Trauma, Illness and Healing in a Toxic Culture* (Toronto: Penguin, 2023), 23.

11 Bruce D. Perry and Oprah Winfrey, *What Happened to You? Conversations on Trauma, Resilience, and Healing* (New York: Flatiron Books, 2021), 103.

12 SAMHSA's Trauma and Justice Strategic Initiative, *SAMHSA's Concept of Trauma and Guidance for a Trauma-Informed Approach,* published July 2014, https://store.samhsa.gov/sites/default/files/sma14-4884.pdf.

13 American Psychiatric Association, *Diagnostic and Statistical Manual of Mental Disorders, Fifth Edition, Text Revised* (Washington DC: American Psychiatric Association Publishing, 2022).

14 Viktor E. Frankl, *Man's Search for Meaning* (Boston: Beacon Press, 1946), 38.

15 Rachel Zimmerman, "How Does Trauma Spill from One Generation to the Next?" *Washington Post,* published June 12, 2023, https://www.washingtonpost.com/wellness/2023/06/12/generational-trauma-passed-healing/.

16 Scott Barry Kaufman, "Post-Traumatic Growth: Finding Meaning and Creativity in Adversity," *Scientific American,* published April 20, 2020, https://blogs.scientificamerican.com/beautiful-minds/post-traumatic-growth-finding-meaning-and-creativity-in-adversity/.

17 Resmaa Menakem, "White Supremacy as a Trauma Response," published April 14, 2018, https://www.resmaa.com/somatic-learnings/white-supremacy-as-a-trauma-response.

18 Judith Herman, *Trauma and Recovery: The Aftermath of Violence—from Domestic Abuse to Political Terror* (New York: Basic Books, 1992), 181.

CHAPTER TWO: FORGIVENESS

1 Sharon Lamb and Jeffrie G. Murphy, *Before Forgiving: Cautionary Views of Forgiveness in Psychotherapy* (Oxford: Oxford University Press, 2002), 90.

2 T. Edward Damer, *Attacking Faulty Reasoning: A Practical Guide to Fallacy-free Arguments,* 6th ed. (Belmont, CA: Wadsworth Cengage Learning, 2009), 95.

3 Jeffrie G. Murphy, *Getting Even: Forgiveness and Its Limits* (Oxford: Oxford University Press, 2003), 13.

4 Nourtan Salahieh, Taylor Romine, and Holly Yan, "The White Homeowner Accused of Shooting a Black Teen Who Rang His Doorbell Turns Himself In and Is Released on Bail," CNN, updated April 19, 2023, https://www.cnn.com/2023/04/18/us/kansas-city-ralph-yarl-shooting-tuesday/index.html.

5 Robert D. Enright, "Interview with Robert D. Enright about *The Forgiving Life,*" transcript from the 2011 APA Convention in Washington, DC, September 10–13, 2011, American Psychological Association, published 2011, https://www.apa.org/pubs/books/interviews/4441016-enright.

6 Janis Abrahms Spring, *How Can I Forgive You?: The Courage to Forgive, the Freedom Not To* (New York: HarperCollins, 2004), 15.

7 Oprah Winfrey, "Oprah's Favorite Definition of Forgiveness," Oprah Winfrey Network, video, 1:06, published 2018, https://www.oprah.com/own-digitaloriginals/oprahs-favorite-definition-of-forgiveness-video.

8 Robert D. Enright and Richard P. Fitzgibbons, *Helping Clients Forgive: An Empirical Guide for Resolving Anger and Restoring Hope* (Washington, DC: American Psychological Association, 2000), 50.

9 Martha Minow, *When Should Law Forgive?* (New York: W. W. Norton, 2019), 2.

10 Everett L. Worthington Jr., "The Science of Forgiveness," John Temple Foundation, published April 2020, https://www.templeton.org/wp-content/uploads/2020/06/Forgiveness_final.pdf.

11 Robert D. Enright and Joanna North, *Exploring Forgiveness* (Madison: University of Wisconsin Press, 1998), 46–47.

12 Thomas W. Baskin and Robert D. Enright, "Intervention Studies on Forgiveness: A Meta-Analysis," *Journal of Counseling & Development* 82 (Winter 2004): 82, https://doi.org/10.1002/j.1556-6678.2004.tb00288.x.

13 Everett L. Worthington Jr., "Hope-Focused Marriage: Recommendations for Researchers, Clinicians, and Church Workers," *Journal of Psychology and Theology* 31, no. 3 (September 2003): 4.

14 Frank Fincham, "The Kiss of the Porcupines: From Attributing Responsibility to Forgiving," *Personal Relationships* 7, no. 1 (May 2005): 9.

15 Everett L. Worthington Jr., "Hope-Focused Marriage: Recommendations for Researchers, Clinicians, and Church Workers," *Journal of Psychology and Theology* 31, no. 3 (September 2003): 4. https://doi.org/10.1177/009164710303100308.

16 Sharon Lamb (psychologist), in discussion with the author, December 2022.

17 Nancy Richards, *Mother, I Don't Forgive You: A Necessary Alternative for Healing* (Nevada City: Blue Dolphin, 2017), 112.

18 Margaret Stroebe, Henk Schut, and Kathrin Boerner, "Cautioning Health-Care Professionals: Bereaved Persons are Misguided Through the Stages of Grief," *OMEGA—Journal of Death and Dying* 74, no. 4 (February 2017): 455.

19 Robert D. Enright and Richard P. Fitzgibbons, *Helping Clients Forgive: An Empirical Guide for Resolving Anger and Restoring Hope* (Washington, DC: American Psychological Association, 2000), 32.

20 Janis Abrahms Spring, *How Can I Forgive You?: The Courage to Forgive, the Freedom Not To* (New York: HarperCollins, 2004), 123.

21 Everett L. Worthington Jr., "Hope-Focused Marriage: Recommendations for Researchers, Clinicians, and Church Workers," *Journal of Psychology and Theology* 31, no. 3 (September 2003): 7.

22 Judith Herman, *Truth, and Repair: How Trauma Survivors Envision Justice* (New York: Basic Books, 2023), 98.

23 Robert D. Enright and Richard P. Fitzgibbons, *Helping Clients Forgive: An Empirical Guide for Resolving Anger and Restoring Hope* (Washington, DC: American Psychological Association, 2000), 29.

24 Robert D. Enright and Richard P. Fitzgibbons, *Helping Clients Forgive: An Empirical Guide for Resolving Anger and Restoring Hope* (Washington, DC: American Psychological Association, 2000), 30.

25 Everett L. Worthington Jr., "Hope-Focused Marriage: Recommendations for Researchers, Clinicians, and Church Workers," *Journal of Psychology and Theology* 31, no. 3 (September 2003): 8.

26 Robert D. Enright and Richard P. Fitzgibbons, *Helping Clients Forgive: An Empirical Guide for Resolving Anger and Restoring Hope* (Washington, DC: American Psychological Association, 2000), 29.

27 Robert D. Enright and Richard P. Fitzgibbons, *Helping Clients Forgive: An Empirical Guide for Resolving Anger and Restoring Hope* (Washington, DC: American Psychological Association, 2000), 30.

28 Sharon Lamb and Jeffrie G. Murphy, *Before Forgiving: Cautionary Views of Forgiveness in Psychotherapy* (Oxford: Oxford University Press, 2002), 74.

29 Suzanne Freedman (psychologist), in discussion with the author, December 2022.

30 Janis Abrahms Spring, *How Can I Forgive You?: The Courage to Forgive, the Freedom Not To* (New York: HarperCollins, 2004), 180.

CHAPTER THREE: THE LIMITATIONS OF FORGIVENESS RESEARCH AND FORGIVENESS THERAPY

1 Suzanne Freedman (psychologist), in discussion with the author, December 2022.
2 Loren L. Toussaint et al., "Effects of Lifetime Stress Exposure on Mental and Physical Health in Young Adulthood: How Stress Degrades and Forgiveness Protects Health," *Journal of Health Psychology* 21, no. 6 (June 2016): 1004–14.
3 Katelyn N. G. Long et al., "Forgiveness of Others and Subsequent Health and Well-being in Mid-life: A Longitudinal Study on Female Nurses," *BMC Psychology* 8, no. 104 (2020), https://doi.org/10.1186/s40359-020-00470-w.
4 Yu-Rim Lee and Robert D. Enright, "A Meta-analysis of the Association between Forgiveness of Others and Physical Health," *Psychology and Health* 34, no. 5 (January 2019): 1–18.
5 Martina A. Walkman et al., "The Effects of a Forgiveness Intervention on Patients with Coronary Artery Disease," *Psychology and Health* 24, no. 1 (January 2009): 11–27.
6 Loren L. Toussaint et al., "Forgiveness and Physical Health", *Handbook of Forgiveness: Second Edition,* edited by Everett L. Worthington Jr. and Nathaniel G. Wade, 2020, pp. 178–187.
7 Yu-Rim Lee and Robert D. Enright, "A Meta-analysis of the Association between Forgiveness of Others and Physical Health," *Psychology and Health* 34, no. 5 (January 2019): 1–18.
8 Yu-Rim Lee and Robert D. Enright, "A Meta-analysis of the Association between Forgiveness of Others and Physical Health," *Psychology and Health* 34, no. 5 (January 2019): 1–18.
9 Yu-Rim Lee and Robert D. Enright, "A Meta-analysis of the Association between Forgiveness of Others and Physical Health," *Psychology and Health* 34, no. 5 (January 2019): 1–18.
10 Loren L. Toussaint et al., "Forgiveness and Physical Health," in *Handbook of Forgiveness*, 2nd ed., ed. Everett L. Worthington Jr. and Nathaniel G. Wade (London: Routledge, 2020), 184.
11 Robert D. Enright and Richard P. Fitzgibbons, *Helping Clients Forgive: An Empirical Guide for Resolving Anger and Restoring Hope* (Washington, DC: American Psychological Association, 2000), 6.
12 Everett L. Worthington, Jr., *Your Path to REACH Forgiveness Become a More Forgiving Person in Less Than Two Hours Self-Directed Learning Exercises to Build Forgiveness* (self-pub., 2016), 1–56.
13 Roger Baker, et al., *Emotional Processing Scale Manual* (Oxford: Hogrefe, 2015).
14 Everett L. Worthington, Jr., *The Path to Forgiveness: Six Practical Sections for Becoming a More Forgiving Person. Self-Directed Learning Workbook* (self-pub., 2016), 4.
15 Nathaniel G. Wade et al., "Efficacy of Psychotherapeutic Interventions to Promote Forgiveness: A Meta-Analysis," *Journal of Consulting and Clinical Psychology* 82, no. 1 (December, 2013), 13.
16 Robert D. Enright and Richard P. Fitzgibbons, *Helping Clients Forgive: An Empirical Guide for Resolving Anger and Restoring Hope* (Washington, DC: American Psychological Association, 2000), 18–19.

17   Sharon Lamb and Jeffrie G. Murphy, *Before Forgiving: Cautionary Views of Forgiveness in Psychotherapy* (Oxford: Oxford University Press, 2002), 78.

18   Suzanne Freedman and Robert D. Enright, "Forgiveness as an Intervention Goal with Incest Survivors," *Journal of Consulting and Clinical Psychology* 64, no. 5 (November 1996): 983–992.

19   Gayle L. Reed and Robert D. Enright, "The Effects of Forgiveness Therapy on Depression, Anxiety, and Posttraumatic Stress for Women after Spousal Emotional Abuse," *Journal of Consulting and Clinical Psychology* 75, no. 5 (2006): 920–929.

20   Yu-Rim Lee and Robert D. Enright, "A Forgiveness Intervention for Women With Fibromyalgia Who Were Abused in Childhood: A Pilot Study," *Spirituality in Clinical Practice* 1, no. 2 (2014): 203–217.

21   Robert D. Enright and Richard P. Fitzgibbons, *Helping Clients Forgive: An Empirical Guide for Resolving Anger and Restoring Hope* (Washington, DC: American Psychological Association, 2000), 124.

22   Nathaniel G. Wade et al., "Efficacy of Psychotherapeutic Interventions to Promote Forgiveness: A Meta-Analysis," *Journal of Consulting and Clinical Psychology* 82, no. 1 (December, 2013): 12.

23   Sharon Lamb and Jeffrie G. Murphy, *Before Forgiving: Cautionary Views of Forgiveness in Psychotherapy* (Oxford: Oxford University Press, 2002), 9.

CHAPTER FOUR: SAFETY PRECEDES FORGIVENESS

1   Judith Herman, *Trauma and Recovery: The Aftermath of Violence—From Domestic Abuse to Political Terror* (New York: Basic Books, 1992), 159.

2   Simon Wiesenthal, *The Sunflower: On the Possibilities and Limits of Forgiveness* (New York: Schocken Books, 1997), 54.

3   Battered Women's Support Services, "Eighteen Months after Leaving Domestic Violence is Still the Most Dangerous Time," BWSS, June 11, 2020, https://www.bwss.org/eighteen-months-after-leaving-domestic-violence-is-still-the-most-dangerous-time/.

4   Sharon Lamb and Jeffrie G. Murphy, *Before Forgiving: Cautionary Views of Forgiveness in Psychotherapy* (Oxford: Oxford University Press, 2002), 89.

5   Sharon Lamb and Jeffrie G. Murphy, *Before Forgiving: Cautionary Views of Forgiveness in Psychotherapy* (Oxford: Oxford University Press, 2002), 46.

6   Robert D. Enright and Richard P. Fitzgibbons, *Helping Clients Forgive: An Empirical Guide for Resolving Anger and Restoring Hope* (Washington, DC: American Psychological Association, 2000), 274.

7   Robert D. Enright and Richard P. Fitzgibbons, *Helping Clients Forgive: An Empirical Guide for Resolving Anger and Restoring Hope* (Washington, DC: American Psychological Association, 2000), 271.

8   James K. McNulty, "The Dark Side of Forgiveness: The Tendency to Forgive Predicts Continued Psychological and Physical Aggression in Marriage," *Personality and Social Psychology Bulletin* 37, no. 6 (June 2011): 1.

9   Joseph Spinazzola, et al., "Unseen Wounds: The Contribution of Psychological Maltreatment to Child and Adolescent Mental Health and Risk Outcomes," *Psychological Trauma: Theory, Research, Practice, and Policy* 6, no. S1 (2014): S18–S28.

10 James W. Moore, "What Is the Sense of Agency and Why Does it Matter?" *Frontiers in Psychology* 29, no. 7 (August 2016): 1272.

11 Judith Herman, *Trauma and Recovery: The Aftermath of Violence—From Domestic Abuse to Political Terror* (New York: Basic Books, 1992), 133.

12 Robert D. Enright and Richard P. Fitzgibbons, *Helping Clients Forgive: An Empirical Guide for Resolving Anger and Restoring Hope* (Washington, DC: American Psychological Association, 2000), 25.

13 Sharon Lamb (psychologist), in discussion with the author, December 2022.

14 Robert D. Enright and Richard P. Fitzgibbons, *Helping Clients Forgive: An Empirical Guide for Resolving Anger and Restoring Hope* (Washington, DC: American Psychological Association, 2000), 118.

15 Judith Herman, *Trauma and Recovery: The Aftermath of Violence—From Domestic Abuse to Political Terror* (New York: Basic Books, 1992), 8.

16 Cheryl Richardson, "Week 41—A Letter I Wish I Could Send to Every 'Checked Out' Healthcare Provider," published October 5, 2014, https://cherylrichardson.com/newsletters/week-41-letter-wish-send-every-checked-healthcare-provider/.

17 Allison Creech, "The Healing Power of Relationship: Relational Neuroscience and the Power of Presence," Naturopathic Doctor News and Review, published June 2, 2021, https://ndnr.com/mindbody/the-healing-power-of-relationship-relational-neuroscience-the-power-of-presence/.

18 Lysa TerKeurst, *Forgiving What You Can't Forget: Discover How to Move On, Make Peace with Painful Memories, and Create a Life That's Beautiful Again* (Thomas Nelson: 2020), 127.

CHAPTER FIVE: DESTIGMATIZING AND EMBRACING ANGER

1 Judith Herman, *Truth and Repair: How Trauma Survivors Envision Justice* (New York: Basic Books, 2023), 110.

2 Nadine El-Bawab, "Highland Park Shooting Victims File Lawsuits Against Gun-Maker Over Advertising Practices," ABC News, published September 28, 2022, https://abcnews.go.com/US/highland-park-shooting-victims-file-lawsuits-gun-maker/story?id=90630705.

3 American Psychiatric Association, *Desk Reference to the Diagnostic Criteria from DSM-5* (Arlington, TX: American Psychiatric Association Publishing, 2022).

4 Christina Caron, "Don't Shut Down Your Anger. Channel It," *The New York Times*, published November 2, 2023, https://www.nytimes.com/2023/11/02/well/mind/anger-benefit-motivation-goals.html.

5 *APA Dictionary of Psychology*, s.v. "anger (n.)," updated April 19, 2018, https://dictionary.apa.org/anger.

6 Peter Allen, "The Protective Side of Anger," Counseling Today, published April 26, 2023, https://ctarchive.counseling.org/2023/04/the-protective-side-of-anger/.

7 Martha C. Nussbaum, *Anger and Forgiveness: Resentment, Generosity, Justice* (Oxford: Oxford University Press, 2016), 211.

8 X, Malcom. "Introduction of Fannie Lou Hamer," Speech at Harlem's Williams Institutional CME Church, Harlem, NY, December 20, 1964.

9 Peter Allen, "The Protective Side of Anger," Counseling Today, published April 26, 2023, https://ctarchive.counseling.org/2023/04/the-protective-side-of-anger/.

10 Audre Lorde, "The Uses of Anger," *Women's Studies Quarterly* 9, no. 3 (Fall 1981): 1, https://academicworks.cuny.edu/cgi/viewcontent.cgi?article=1654&context=wsq.

11 Sharon Lamb and Jeffrie G. Murphy, *Before Forgiving: Cautionary Views of Forgiveness in Psychotherapy* (Oxford: Oxford University Press, 2002), 22.

12 Stephanie Foo, *What My Bones Know: A Memoir of Healing from Complex Trauma* (New York: Penguin Random House, 2022), 30.

13 Robert D. Enright and Richard P. Fitzgibbons, *Helping Clients Forgive: An Empirical Guide for Resolving Anger and Restoring Hope* (Washington, DC: American Psychological Association, 2000), 120–121.

14 Georgina H. Mills, "Swallowing Traumatic Anger: Family Abuse and the Pressure to Forgive," *Public Philosophy Journal* 2, no. 2 (2019): 6.

15 Robert D. Enright and Richard P. Fitzgibbons, *Helping Clients Forgive: An Empirical Guide for Resolving Anger and Restoring Hope* (Washington, DC: American Psychological Association, 2000), 118.

16 Sharon Lamb (psychologist), in discussion with the author, December 2022.

17 Bonnie Burstow, *Radical Feminist Therapy: Working in the Context of Violence* (Thousand Oaks, CA: SAGE, 1992), 140.

18 Robert D. Enright and Richard P. Fitzgibbons, *Helping Clients Forgive: An Empirical Guide for Resolving Anger and Restoring Hope* (Washington, DC: American Psychological Association, 2000), 120.

19 Robert D. Enright and Richard P. Fitzgibbons, *Helping Clients Forgive: An Empirical Guide for Resolving Anger and Restoring Hope* (Washington, DC: American Psychological Association, 2000), 120.

20 Peter Allen, "The Protective Side of Anger," Counseling Today, published April 26, 2023, https://ctarchive.counseling.org/2023/04/the-protective-side-of-anger/.

21 Michael E. McCullough, *Beyond Revenge: The Evolution of the Forgiveness Instinct* (San Franciso: Jossey-Bass, 2008), 5.

22 Judith Herman, *Truth and Repair: How Trauma Survivors Envision Justice* (New York: Basic Books, 2023), 189.

23 George Orwell, "Revenge Is Sour," published 1945, accessed February 24, 2024, https://www.orwell.ru/library/articles/revenge/english/e_revso.

24 Sharon Lamb and Jeffrie G. Murphy, *Before Forgiving: Cautionary Views of Forgiveness in Psychotherapy* (Oxford: Oxford University Press, 2002), 94.

25 Nancy Richards, *Mother, I Don't Forgive You: A Necessary Alternative for Healing* (self-pub., 2017), 120.

26 Michelle P. Maidenberg, "The Intrigue of Revenge Fantasies," *Psychology Today*, published April 6, 2021, https://www.psychologytoday.com/us/blog/being-your-best-self/202104/the-intrigue-revenge-fantasies.

CHAPTER SIX: SHAME OBSTRUCTS FORGIVENESS

1 Brené Brown, "Shame vs. Guilt," Brené Brown (blog), January 15, 2013, https://brenebrown.com/articles/2013/01/15/shame-v-guilt/.

2 J. Daw Holloway, "Guilt Can Do Good," *Monitor on Psychology* 36, no. 10 (Nov 2005): 22, https://www.apa.org/monitor/nov05/guilt.

3 Brené Brown, "Shame vs. Guilt," Brené Brown (blog), January 15, 2013, https://brenebrown.com/articles/2013/01/15/shame-v-guilt/.

4 Linda M. Hartling, "Shame and Humiliation: From Isolation to Relational Transformation," in *The Complexity of Connection: Writings from the Stone Center's Jean Baker Miller Training Institute*, ed. Judith V. Jordan et al. (New York: The Guilford Press, 2004), 3.

5 Judith Herman, *Trauma and Recovery: The Aftermath of Violence—from Domestic Abuse to Political Terror* (New York: Basic Books, 1992), 101.

6 Sharon Lamb and Jeffrie G. Murphy, *Before Forgiving: Cautionary Views of Forgiveness in Psychotherapy* (Oxford: Oxford University Press, 2002), 25.

7 Sharon Lamb and Jeffrie G. Murphy, *Before Forgiving: Cautionary Views of Forgiveness in Psychotherapy* (Oxford: Oxford University Press, 2002), 30.

8 Janis Abrahms Spring, *How Can I Forgive You?: The Courage to Forgive, the Freedom Not To* (New York: HarperCollins, 2004), 68.

9 Sharon Lamb, *The Trouble with Blame: Victims, Perpetrators, and Responsibility* (Cambridge, MA: Harvard University Press, 1999), 22.

10 Sharon Lamb and Jeffrie G. Murphy, *Before Forgiving: Cautionary Views of Forgiveness in Psychotherapy* (Oxford: Oxford University Press, 2002), 81.

11 Judith Herman, *Trauma and Recovery: The Aftermath of Violence—from Domestic Abuse to Political Terror* (New York: Basic Books, 1992), 54.

12 Judith Herman, *Trauma and Recovery: The Aftermath of Violence—from Domestic Abuse to Political Terror* (New York: Basic Books, 1992), 199.

13 Sharon Lamb and Jeffrie G. Murphy, *Before Forgiving: Cautionary Views of Forgiveness in Psychotherapy* (Oxford: Oxford University Press, 2002), 82.

14 Nathaniel G. Wade et al., "Helping Clients Heal: Does Forgiveness Make a Difference?" *Professional Psychology: Research and Practice* 36, no. 6 (December 2005): 634.

15 Suzanne Freedman and Tiffany Clark-Zarifkar, "The Psychology of Interpersonal Forgiveness and Guidelines for Forgiveness Therapy: What Therapists Need to Know to Help Their Clients Forgive," *Spirituality in Clinical Practice* 3, no. 1 (2016): 51.

16 Varda Konstam et al., "Toward Forgiveness: The Role of Shame, Guilt Anger, and Empathy," *Counseling and Values* 46, no. 1 (2011): 26–39.

17 Laura B. Luchies et al., "The Doormat Effect: When Forgiving Erodes Self-respect and Self-concept Clarity," *Journal of Personality and Social Psychology,* 98, no. 5 (2010): 745.

18 Laura B. Luchies et al., "The Doormat Effect: When Forgiving Erodes Self-respect and Self-concept Clarity," *Journal of Personality and Social Psychology,* 98, no. 5 (2010): 745.

19 Sharon Lamb and Jeffrie G. Murphy, *Before Forgiving: Cautionary Views of Forgiveness in Psychotherapy* (Oxford: Oxford University Press, 2002), 45.

20 David Bedrick, "6 Reasons Not to Forgive, Not Yet," *Psychology Today*, September 25, 2014, https://www.psychologytoday.com/us/blog/is-psychology-making-us-sick/201409/6-reasons-not-forgive-not-yet.

21 Nancy Richards, *Mother, I Don't Forgive You: A Necessary Alternative for Healing* (self-pub., 2017), 70.

22 Nancy Richards, *Mother, I Don't Forgive You: A Necessary Alternative for Healing* (self-pub., 2017), xii.

CHAPTER SEVEN: RECOGNIZING RELIGIOUS INFLUENCES

1 Darren M. Slade et al., "Percentage of U.S. Adults Suffering From Religious Trauma: A Sociological Study," *Socio-Historical Examination of Religion and Ministry* 5, no. 1 (2023): 1–28.
2 Paula Arai (professor of women and Buddhist studies at the Institute of Buddhist Studies, Berkeley, CA), in discussion with the author, October 2023.
3 Paula Arai (professor of women and Buddhist studies at the Institute of Buddhist Studies, Berkeley, CA), in discussion with the author, October 2023.
4 Eli Brown (dharma teacher at Midwest Buddhist Temple, Chicago, IL), in discussion with the author, October 2023.
5 Paula Arai (professor of women and Buddhist studies at the Institute of Buddhist Studies, Berkeley, CA), in discussion with the author, October 2023.
6 Eli Brown (dharma teacher at Midwest Buddhist Temple, Chicago, IL), in discussion with the author, October 2023.
7 Paula Arai (professor of women and Buddhist studies at the Institute of Buddhist Studies, Berkeley, CA), in discussion with the author, October 2023.
8 Eli Brown (dharma teacher at Midwest Buddhist Temple, Chicago, IL), in discussion with the author, October 2023.
9 Judith Herman, *Truth and Repair: How Trauma Survivors Envision Justice* (New York: Basic Books, 2023), 100.
10 John Blackwell (retired United Methodist pastor and dean), in discussion with the author, October 2023.
11 Kenna Hollingshead (chaplain), in discussion with the author, October 2023.
12 John Blackwell (retired United Methodist pastor and dean), in discussion with the author, October 2023.
13 Leslie Vernick, "Forgiving Doesn't Erase Consequences," Leslie Vernick (blog), January 2022, https://leslievernick.com/blog/forgiving-doesnt-erase-consequences/.
14 Kenna Hollingshead (chaplain), in discussion with the author, October 2023.
15 Kenna Hollingshead (chaplain), in discussion with the author, October 2023.
16 John Blackwell (retired United Methodist pastor and dean), in discussion with the author, October 2023.
17 Maisha Z. Johnson, "Don't Believe in Christian Privilege? These 15 Examples Will Leave No Doubt," *Everyday Feminism*, January 12, 2016, https://everydayfeminism.com/2016/01/believing-christian-privilege/.
18 Aaron Finkelstein (rabbi at Anshe Sholom B'nai Israel Congregation, Chicago, IL), in discussion with the author, October 2023.
19 Rishe Groner (rabbi at Congregation Beth Ohr, Bellmore, NY), in discussion with the author, October 2023.
20 Aaron Finkelstein (rabbi at Anshe Sholom B'nai Israel Congregation, Chicago, IL), in discussion with the author, October 2023.
21 Rishe Groner (rabbi at Congregation Beth Ohr, Bellmore, NY), in discussion with the author, October 2023.

22 Aaron Finkelstein (rabbi at Anshe Sholom B'nai Israel Congregation, Chicago, IL), in discussion with the author, October 2023.

23 Rishe Groner (rabbi at Congregation Beth Ohr, Bellmore, NY), in discussion with the author, October 2023.

24 Rishe Groner (rabbi at Congregation Beth Ohr, Bellmore, NY), in discussion with the author, October 2023.

25 Nicole Chavez and Nicquel Terry Ellis, "2022 Saw the Highest Rate of Recorded Antisemitic Incidents in the US. American Jews Fear the Israel-Hamas Conflict Could Make Things Worse," *CNN*, October 12, 2023, https://www.cnn.com/2023/10/13/us/us-jewish-community-fear-rise-antisemitism-reaj/index.html.

26 Rishe Groner (rabbi at Congregation Beth Ohr, Bellmore, NY), in discussion with the author, October 2023.

27 Rami Sivan, "The Concept of Forgiveness in Sanatan Dharma Differs Vastly from That of Abrahamic Monotheistic #Religions," *The Hindu Portal*, July 12, 2019, https://www.thehinduportal.com/2019/07/the-concept-of-forgiveness-in-sanatan.html.

28 Olusegun Obasanjo, "The Universality of Forgiveness: Perspectives from Religion and Culture," *E-Journal of Religious and Theological Studies* 5, no. 2 (June 2019): 54, https://doi.org/10.32051/06241906.

29 Rami Sivan, "The Concept of Forgiveness in Sanatan Dharma Differs Vastly from That of Abrahamic Monotheistic #Religions," *The Hindu Portal*, July 12, 2019, https://www.thehinduportal.com/2019/07/the-concept-of-forgiveness-in-sanatan.html.

30 Abhishek Ghosh (scholar of Hinduism), in discussion with the author, October 2023.

31 Abhishek Ghosh (scholar of Hinduism), in discussion with the author, October 2023.

32 Abhishek Ghosh (scholar of Hinduism), in discussion with the author, October 2023.

33 Narmi Thillaninathan, "Rogers to Reincarnation: Counseling People of the Hindu Faith," Breakthrough Psychology Practice (blog), September 8, 2021, https://www.btpsychology.com.au/post/rogers-to-reincarnation-counselling-people-of-the-hindu-faith.

34 Abhishek Ghosh (scholar of Hinduism), in discussion with the author, October 2023.

35 Narmi Thillaninathan, "Rogers to Reincarnation: Counseling People of the Hindu Faith," Breakthrough Psychology Practice (blog), September 8, 2021, https://www.btpsychology.com.au/post/rogers-to-reincarnation-counselling-people-of-the-hindu-faith.

36 Murtada Muhammad Gusau, "The Importance of Forgiveness in Islam," *Premium Times*, February 2021, https://www.premiumtimesng.com/opinion/442363-the-importance-of-forgiveness-in-islam-by-murtadha-gusau.html?tztc=1.

37 Omer Mozaffar (chaplain and theologian at Loyola University, Chicago, IL), in discussion with the author, October 2023.

38 Umm Zakiyyah (author), in discussion with the author, October 2023.

39 Umm Zakiyyah (author), in discussion with the author, October 2023.

40 The Pew Research Center, "Pew I: Diversity in Islam," Wilson Center, January 2013, https://www.wilsoncenter.org/article/pew-i-diversity-islam.

41 ADL Education, "Myths and Facts about Muslim People and Islam," Anti-Defamation League, May 30, 2017, https://www.adl.org/resources/tools-and-strategies/myths-and-facts-about-muslim-people-and-islam.

42 Georgetown University, "What Is Islamophobia?" Bridge Initiative, Accessed February 25, 2024, https://bridge.georgetown.edu/about-us/what-is-islamophobia.

43 Umm Zakiyyah (author), in discussion with the author, October 2023.

44 Umm Zakiyyah (author), in discussion with the author, October 2023.

45 Brian E. Eck, "An Exploration of the Therapeutic Use of Spiritual Disciplines in Clinical Practice," *Journal of Psychology and Christianity* 21, no. 3 (2002): 266–280.

CHAPTER EIGHT: FORGIVENESS AND SOCIAL JUSTICE

1 Sharon Lamb and Jeffrie G. Murphy, *Before Forgiving: Cautionary Views of Forgiveness in Psychotherapy* (Oxford: Oxford University Press, 2002), 10.

2 Myisha Cherry, *Failures of Forgiveness: What We Get Wrong and How to Do Better* (Princeton: Princeton University Press, 2003), 182.

3 Judith Herman, "Justice From the Victim's Perspective," *Violence Against Women* 11, no. 5 (June 2005): 574, https://doi.org/10.1177/1077801205274450.

4 Judith Herman, *Truth and Repair: How Trauma Survivors Envision Justice* (New York: Basic Books, 2023), 45.

5 Jerusalem Demsas, "The Promise—and Problem—of Restorative Justice," *Vox*, March 2022, https://www.vox.com/22979070/restorative-justice-forgiveness-limits-promise.

6 Bureau of Justice Assistance, "Repairing Harm through Community Dialogue," *Justice Matters Newsletter*, November 2023, https://bja.ojp.gov/news/feature-stories/repairing-harm-through-community-dialogue.

7 Yotam Shem-Tov et al., "The Impacts of the Make-It-Right Program on Recidivism," *California Policy Lab*, August 2021, https://www.capolicylab.org/impacts-of-make-it-right-program-on-recidivism/.

8 Robert Goldman, "Restorative Justice as a Trauma-Informed Approach," *Psychology Today*, January 17, 2023, https://www.psychologytoday.com/us/blog/building-resilient-minds/202301/the-use-of-restorative-justice-as-a-trauma-informed-approach.

9 Pavithra Rajesh et al., "Expanding the Circle: The Reality of Implementing Restorative Justice across the Country," *Boston Globe*, September 19, 2023, https://www.bostonglobe.com/2023/08/23/opinion/expanding-circle-reality-implementing-restorative-justice-across-country/.

10 Jerusalem Demsas, "The Promise—and Problem—of Restorative Justice," *Vox*, March 2022, https://www.vox.com/22979070/restorative-justice-forgiveness-limits-promise.

11 Nathalie M. Dumornay, "Racial Disparities in Adversity During Childhood and the False Appearance of Race-Related Difference in Brain Structure," *The American Journal of Psychiatry* 108, no. 2 (2023): 127–138.

12 Jude Mary Cénat, "Complex Racial Trauma: Evidence, Theory, Assessment, and Treatment," *Perspectives in Psychological Science* 18, no. 3 (2023): 675.

13 Jude Mary Cénat, "Complex Racial Trauma: Evidence, Theory, Assessment, and Treatment," *Perspectives in Psychological Science* 18, no. 3 (2023): 675.

14 Umm Zakiyyah, *The Abuse of Forgiveness: Manipulation and Harm in the Name of Emotional Healing* (Baltimore, MD: Al-Walaa Publications, 2017): 33.

15 Umm Zakiyyah, *The Abuse of Forgiveness: Manipulation and Harm in the Name of Emotional Healing* (Baltimore, MD: Al-Walaa Publications, 2017): 32.

16 Chauncey DeVega, "Black America Owes No Forgiveness: How Christianity Hinder Racial Justice," *Salon*, August 2015, https://www.salon.com/2015/08/23/the_hypocrisy_of_Black_forgiveness_partner.

17 Chauncey DeVega, "Black America Owes No Forgiveness: How Christianity Hinder Racial Justice," Salon, August 2015, https://www.salon.com/2015/08/23/the_hypocrisy_of_Black_forgiveness_partner.

18 Myisha Cherry, *Failures of Forgiveness: What We Get Wrong and How to Do Better* (Princeton: Princeton University Press, 2023), 83.

19 Myisha Cherry, *Failures of Forgiveness: What We Get Wrong and How to Do Better* (Princeton: Princeton University Press, 2023), 91–92.

20 Jerusalem Demsas, "The Promise—and Problem—of Restorative Justice," *Vox*, March 2022, https://www.vox.com/22979070/restorative-justice-forgiveness-limits-promise.

21 Judith Herman, *Trauma and Recovery: The Aftermath of Violence—From Domestic Abuse to Political Terror* (New York: Basic Books, 1992), 33.

22 PlanStreet, "Quick Facts about Sexual Assault in America—2023," PlanStreet (blog), May 25, 2022, https://www.planstreetinc.com/quick-facts-about-sexual-assault-in-america/.

23 "What Is Patriarchy? What Does it Mean and Why is Everyone Talking about it?" CNN, accessed January 18, 2024, https://www.cnn.com/2023/08/03/world/what-is-patriarchy-explainer-as-equals-intl-cmd/index.html.

24 Rakesh Kochhar, "The Enduring Grip of the Gender Pay Gap," *Pew Research Center*, March 1, 2023, Accessed March 1, 2024, https://www.pewresearch.org/social-trends/2023/03/01/the-enduring-grip-of-the-gender-pay-gap/.

25 "Women Still Handle Main Household Tasks in U.S.," Gallup, accessed January 18, 2024, Accessed March 1, 2024, https://news.gallup.com/poll/283979/women-handle-main-household-tasks.aspx.

26 Rabbi Susan Schnur, "Beyond Forgiveness: Women, Can We Emancipate Ourselves from a Model Meant for Men?" *Lilith*, September 17, 2001, Accessed March 1, 2024, https://lilith.org/articles/beyond-forgiveness/.

27 Sharon Lamb and Jeffrie G. Murphy, *Before Forgiving: Cautionary Views of Forgiveness in Psychotherapy* (Oxford: Oxford University Press, 2002), 164.

28 Sharon Lamb and Jeffrie G. Murphy, *Before Forgiving: Cautionary Views of Forgiveness in Psychotherapy* (Oxford: Oxford University Press, 2002), 165.

29 Audre Lorde, *Your Silence Will Not Protect You* (London: Silver Press, 2017), 115.

30 IMPACT Chicago, "What Are the Benefits of Self-Defense Training?" *IMPACT*, accessed March 1, 2024, https://www.impactchicago.org/frequently-asked-questions.html.

31 IMPACT Chicago, "What Are the Benefits of Self-Defense Training?" *IMPACT*, accessed March 1, 2024, https://www.impactchicago.org/frequently-asked-questions.html.

32 Sharon Lamb and Jeffrie G. Murphy, *Before Forgiving: Cautionary Views of Forgiveness in Psychotherapy* (Oxford: Oxford University Press, 2002), 164.

33 Sharon Lamb and Jeffrie G. Murphy, *Before Forgiving: Cautionary Views of Forgiveness in Psychotherapy* (Oxford: Oxford University Press, 2002), 165.

34 Sharon Lamb and Jeffrie G. Murphy, *Before Forgiving: Cautionary Views of Forgiveness in Psychotherapy* (Oxford: Oxford University Press, 2002), 166.

35 Sharon Lamb and Jeffrie G. Murphy, *Before Forgiving: Cautionary Views of Forgiveness in Psychotherapy* (Oxford: Oxford University Press, 2002), 45.

36 Loyd D. Easton and Kurt H. Guddat, *Writings of the Young Marx on Philosophy and Society* (New York: Anchor Books, 1967), 250.

37 Umm Zakiyyah, *The Abuse of Forgiveness: Manipulation and Harm in the Name of Emotional Healing* (Baltimore, MD: Al-Walaa Publications, 2017), 1–108.

38 Luke Brunning and Per-Erik Milam, "Oppression, Forgiveness, and Ceasing to Blame," *Journal of Ethics and Social Philosophy* 14, no. 2 (December 2018): 173.

CHAPTER NINE: RESPONDING TO FORGIVENESS ADVOCATES

1 Rosenna Bakari (psychologist), in discussion with the author, June 2022.

2 David Bedrick, "6 Reasons Not to Forgive, Not Yet," *Psychology Today*, September 25, 2014, https://www.psychologytoday.com/us/blog/is-psychology-making-us-sick/201409/6-reasons-not-forgive-not-yet.

3 Judith Herman, *Trauma and Recovery: The Aftermath of Violence—from Domestic Abuse to Political Terror* (New York: Basic Books, 1992), 7.

4 Zafar Ibrahim, "Embracing Forgiveness," *The Times of India*, September 10, 2020, https://timesofindia.indiatimes.com/readersblog/zafarreads/embracing-forgiveness-25820/.

5 Birmingham Times, "Dr. Martin Luther King Jr.'s Quotes on Life, Love and Leadership," *Birmingham Times*, January 16, 2020, https://www.birminghamtimes.com/2020/01/dr-martin-luther-king-jr-s-quotes-on-life-love-and-leadership/.

6 Julie C. Taylor, et al., "Barries to Men's Help Seeking for Intimate Partner Violence," *Journal of Interpersonal Violence* 37 (October 2022): 19–20.

7 Sharon Lamb and Jeffrie G. Murphy, *Before Forgiving: Cautionary Views of Forgiveness in Psychotherapy* (Oxford: Oxford University Press, 2002), 165.

8 Santana McDriguez, "Misunderstood Saying. . .and Books the Prove the Counterparts True," *Anythink*, March 1, 2021, https://www.anythinklibraries.org/blog/misunderstood-sayings.

9 Georgina H. Mills, "Swallowing Traumatic Anger: Family Abuse and the Pressure to Forgive," *Public Philosophy Journal* 2, no. 2 (2019): 2.

10 Anisha Kohli, "Queen Elizabeth II's Death Is a Chance to Examine the Present-Day Effects of Britain's Colonial Past," *Time*, September 13, 2022, https://time.com/6212772/queen-elizabeth-ii-colonialism-legacy/.

11 Michael Connellan, "Women Suffer from Gandhi's Legacy," *The Guardian*, January 27, 2010, https://www.theguardian.com/commentisfree/2010/jan/27/mohandas-gandhi-women-india.

12 Jennette McCurdy, *I'm Glad My Mom Died* (New York: Simon and Schuster, 2022), 303.

13 Umm Zakiyyah, *The Abuse of Forgiveness: Manipulation and Harm in the Name of Emotional Healing* (Baltimore, MD: Al-Walaa Publications, 2017), 5.

14 Myisha Cherry, *Failures of Forgiveness: What We Get Wrong and How to Do Better* (Princeton: Princeton University Press, 2023), 43.

CHAPTER TEN: EMBRACING ELECTIVE FORGIVENESS

1 Rosenna Bakari (psychologist), in discussion with the author, June 2022.

2 Nancy Richards, *Mother, I Don't Forgive You: A Necessary Alternative for Healing* (elf-pub., 2017), 124.

3 "Definitions," *Emotional Processing*, accessed January 27, 2023, https://emotionalprocessing.org/definitions/.

4 Judith Herman, *Trauma and Recovery: The Aftermath of Violence—From Domestic Abuse to Political Terror* (New York: Basic Books, 1992), 181.

5 Janis Abrahms Spring, *How Can I Forgive You?: The Courage to Forgive, the Freedom Not To* (New York: HarperCollins, 2004), 58.

6 Robert D. Enright and Richard P. Fitzgibbons, *Helping Clients Forgive: An Empirical Guide for Resolving Anger and Restoring Hope* (Washington, DC: American Psychological Association, 2000), 50.

7 Janis Abrahms Spring, *How Can I Forgive You?: The Courage to Forgive, the Freedom Not To* (New York: HarperCollins, 2004), 53.

8 Janis Abrahms Spring, *How Can I Forgive You?: The Courage to Forgive, the Freedom Not To* (New York: HarperCollins, 2004), 70.

9 Robert D. Enright, "Counseling within the Forgiveness Triad: On Forgiving, Receiving Forgiveness, and Self–forgiveness," *Counseling & Values* 40, no. 2 (1996): 115.

10 Robert D. Enright, "Counseling within the Forgiveness Triad: On Forgiving, Receiving Forgiveness, and Self–forgiveness," *Counseling & Values* 40, no. 2 (1996): 115.

11 Lydia Woodyatt et al., *Handbook of the Psychology of Self-forgiveness* (New York, NY: Springer, 2017), 7–10.

CHAPTER ELEVEN: TWENTY TRAUMA RECOVERY METHODS

1 Ryan Howes and Babette Rothschild, "Babette Rothschild on What's Missing in Trauma Work," *Psychotherapy Networker*, November/December 2023, https://www.psychotherapynetworker.org/article/babette-rothschild-on-whats-missing-in-trauma-work/.

2 Bessel van der Kolk, *The Body Keeps the Score: Brain, Mind, and Body in the Healing of Trauma* (London: Penguin Books, 2014), 214.

3 American Psychological Association, "Evidence-Based Practice in Psychology," APA, 2008, https://www.apa.org/practice/resources/evidence.

4 Steven Reidord, "Evidence-Based Psychotherapy," *Psychology Today*, June 22, 2019, https://www.psychologytoday.com/us/blog/sacramento-street-psychiatry/201906/evidence-based-psychotherapy.

5 American Veterinary Medical Association, "Animal-assisted Interventions: Definitions," Accessed February 25, 2024, https://www.avma.org/resources-tools/avma-policies/animal-assisted-interventions-definitions.

6 Saginaw Vally State University, "Emotional Support Animal Policy and Procedures," *Saginaw Vally State University*, accessed February 25, 2024, https://www.svsu.edu/ac/cess/policies/emotionalsupportanimals.

7 Amanda Ann Gregory, "Defining Service, Therapy, and Emotional Support Animals," accessed February 25, 2024, https://www.amandaanngregory.com/service-therapy-and-emotional-support-animals-whats-the-difference.

8 Bessel van der Kolk, *The Body Keeps the Score: Brain, Mind, and Body in the Healing of Trauma* (London: Penguin Books, 2014), 212.

9 American Psychological Association, "Attachment-Based Psychotherapy in Practice," APA, August 2014, https://www.apa.org/pubs/videos/4310926?tab=2.

10 Shirley Crenshaw (attachment therapist), in discussion with the author, August 2023.

11 Anita Vasudeva, "Brainspotting: An Interview with Dr. Christine Ranck," accessed February 25, 2024, https://brainspotting-training.com/brainspotting-an-interview-with-dr-christine-ranck/.

12 Anita Vasudeva, "Brainspotting: An Interview with Dr. Christine Ranck," accessed February 25, 2024, https://brainspotting-training.com/brainspotting-an-interview-with-dr-christine-ranck/.

13 American Psychological Association, "Cognitive Processing Therapy (CPT)" APA, July 31, 2017, https://www.apa.org/ptsd-guideline/treatments/cognitive-processing-therapy.

14 Maggie Reynolds (certified EMDR therapist), in discussion with the author, August 2023.

15 Maggie Reynolds (certified EMDR therapist), in discussion with the author, August 2023.

16 EFT International, "What is EFT Tapping?" accessed February 25, 2024, https://eftinternational.org/discover-eft-tapping/what-is-eft-tapping/.

17 Newport Institute, "What Is Emotional Freedom Technique?" accessed February 25, 2024, https://www.newportinstitute.com/our-clinical-model/modalities/emotional-freedom-technique/.

18 Christa Smith, "Inspiring Quotes from Tapping into Ultimate Success," accessed February 25, 2024, https://christa-smith.com/inspiring-quotes-from-tapping-into-ultimate-success/.

19 Cathy A. Malchiodi, *Trauma and Expressive Arts Therapy: Brain, Body, and Imagination in the Healing Process* (New York: The Guilford Press, 2020), 1.

20 Cathy A. Malchiodi, *Trauma and Expressive Arts Therapy: Brain, Body, and Imagination in the Healing Process* (New York: The Guilford Press, 2020), 1.

21 Evan Brownstone (expressive arts therapist), in discussion with the author, August 2023.

22 IFS Institute, "What Is Internal Family Systems?" accessed February 25, 2025, https://ifs-institute.com.

23 IFS Institute, "The Internal Family Systems Model Outline," accessed February 25, 2025, https://ifs-institute.com/resources/articles/internal-family-systems-model-outline.

24 Richard C. Schwartz, *No Bad Parts: Healing Trauma and Restoring Wholeness with the Internal Family Systems Model* (Boulder, CO: Sounds True, 2021), 4.

25 Beth Sissons, "What Is MDMA Therapy Used For?" *Medical News Today*, September 30, 2022, https://www.medicalnewstoday.com/articles/mdma-therapy.

26 Beth Sissons, "What Is MDMA Therapy Used For?" *Medical News Today*, September 30, 2022, https://www.medicalnewstoday.com/articles/mdma-therapy.

27 Allison A. Feduccia and Michael C. Mithoefer, "MDMA-assisted Psychotherapy for PTSD: Are Memory Reconsolidation and Fear Extinction Underlying Mechanisms?" *Progress in Neuro-Psychopharmacology and Biological Psychiatry* 84, Pt A (June 2018): 221–228, https://doi.org/10.1016/j.pnpbp.2018.03.003.

28 J. David Creswell et al., "Mindfulness Meditation: A Research-proven Way to Reduce Stress," APA, October 30, 2019, https://www.apa.org/topics/mindfulness/meditation.

29 David A. Treleaven, *Trauma-Sensitive Mindfulness: Practices for Safe and Transformative Healing* (New York: W. W. Norton, 2018), 2.

30 Maureen Kebo (NARM master practitioner), in discussion with the author, August 2023.
31 Laurence Heller and Aline LaPierre, *Healing Developmental Trauma: How Early Trauma Affects Self-Regulation, Self-Image, and the Capacity for Relationship* (Berkeley, CA: North Atlantic Books, 2012), 1.
32 Maureen Kebo (NARM master practitioner), in discussion with the author, August 2023.
33 INTEGRIS Health, "Can Nature Help Heal Trauma?" August 22, 2022, https://integrishealth.org/resources/on-your-health/2022/august/can-nature-help-heal-trauma.
34 Leanne Hershkowitz (neurofeedback therapist and trainer), in discussion with the author, August 2023.
35 Leanne Hershkowitz (neurofeedback therapist and trainer), in discussion with the author, August 2023.
36 Kelley Boymer, "How Pelvic Floor Therapy Helped Heal My Trauma," Jess Ann Kirby (blog), June 23, 2022, https://www.jessannkirby.com/how-pelvic-floor-therapy-helped-heal-my-trauma/.
37 Kelley Boymer, "How Pelvic Floor Therapy Helped Heal My Trauma," Jess Ann Kirby (blog), June 23, 2022, https://www.jessannkirby.com/how-pelvic-floor-therapy-helped-heal-my-trauma/.
38 Sensorimotor Psychotherapy Institute, "What Is Sensorimotor Psychotherapy?" accessed February 25, 2024, https://sensorimotorpsychotherapy.org/about/.
39 Julie Westlin-Naigus, "What Is Sensorimotor Psychotherapy?" accessed February 26, 2024, https://www.juliewestlin-naigus.com/new-page.
40 Judith Herman, *Trauma and Recovery: The Aftermath of Violence—from Domestic Abuse to Political Terror* (New York: Basic Books, 1992), 199.
41 Bianka Hardin (psychotherapist), in discussion with the author, August 2023.
42 Bianka Hardin (psychotherapist), in discussion with the author, August 2023.
43 Peter A. Levine, *Waking the Tiger: Healing Trauma* (Berkeley, CA, North Atlantic Books, 1997).
44 Bianka Hardin (psychotherapist), in discussion with the author, August 2023.
45 Center for Trauma and Embodiment, "TCTSY Is the Original Yoga for Trauma," accessed February 25, 2024, https://www.traumasensitiveyoga.com/about.
46 Center for Trauma and Embodiment, "TCTSY Is the Original Yoga for Trauma," accessed February 25, 2024, https://www.traumasensitiveyoga.com/about.
47 National Child Traumatic Stress Network, "TF-CBT," accessed February 24, 2024, www.nctsn.org/interventions/trauma-focused-cognitive-behavioral-therapy.
48 Hannah Alderete, "When Forgiveness Is Bullshit," *Medium*, February 10, 2020, https://medium.com/@hannahalderete/when-forgiveness-is-bullshit-e86f8e966b37.